Conflict and Change
in the Catholic Church

Conflict and Change in the Catholic Church

John Seidler and Katherine Meyer

 *Rutgers University Press*
New Brunswick and London

Library of Congress Cataloging-in-Publication Data
Seidler, John, 1933–1985.
Conflict and change in the Catholic Church / John Seidler
and Katherine Meyer.
p.   cm.
Bibliography: p.
Includes index.
ISBN 0-8135-1384-7 (cloth)   ISBN 0-8135-1385-5 (pbk.)
1. Catholic Church—History—1965–   2. Catholic Church—United
States—History—1965–   3. United States—Church history—20th
century.   I. Meyer, Katherine, 1943–   II. Title.
BX1390.S38 1989
282'.73—dc19   88-21758

British Cataloging-in-Publication information available

To Anne Meyer Seidler
and Elizabeth Meyer Seidler

our celebration of life

Contents

Figures and Tables

Figures

Tables

Preface

This book examines the conflict and struggle accompanying the changes which the Roman Catholic Church underwent after the Second Vatican Council, convened in the early 1960s. It sets the background for change with Vatican I and then focuses on conflict in the American Church through the 1960s, 1970s, and 1980s. Data from three research projects and time periods are brought together into a general conflict perspective on a major transitional period in Catholicism.

Our book is addressed to several audiences. For sociologists, the Catholic Church is a normative organization which has changed and continues to feel the pressures of innovation both internally and externally. We examined the nature and substance of conflict within the hierarchy and between the Church and the rest of the world. We drew insights from theory and research on organizations, social movements, social change, and religions. We adapted those insights and produced new ones which were integrated into a modified conflict perspective. Catholicism exemplifies a deviant case of organizational change, a late-blooming adaptation to contemporary society. In part, it portrays the resistance of certain normative organizations to fit the typical adjustment processes of industrial organizations that must compete in the marketplace with updated technologies, satisfying salaries, and other rational processes. But Catholicism is not another case of delayed or resistant adaptation. A myriad of religious, educational, even paramilitary, associations exist today as if the democratic and industrial revolutions had never occurred. Their authority structures are autocratic and traditional. Their aim is to resist adjustment to contemporary society, whether seen as secular, democratic, or socialist. Reaction to change in Catholicism has followed a different course.

For scholars of religion, we presented highlights of the structure and setting of American Catholicism from Vatican I to Vatican II. Then, our major focus on the decades of the 1960s through 1980s viewed the upheaval occurring as a special kind of social movement for change. The struggle of the Church to modernize typifies in large measure the common problem of living in organizational society, i.e., trying to make structures correspond to ideal patterns of communications, decision making, social networks, and efficiency. The attempt to rapidly change structures within the network of clergy was but one example of these problems. New structures of decision making demanded new attitudes toward authority, new thought patterns, new kinds of communication and accompanying organizational and personal struggle.

For diocesan clergy who gave so generously of their time in surveys and interviews, we aimed to clarify both the turbulence and the transition of priestly life in the United States. Seidler, in particular, devoted years of scholarly work to the historical development of American Catholicism and the excitement and anguish of changes in Church theology and social structures, especially in American dioceses. Wherever he went, he found priests eager to speak about the direction of their dioceses. As front-line professionals, their concerns and struggles are important to the Church. Many remain eager to see the Catholic episode of Vatican II narrated in a way that helps to make sense of their experiences and of the council.

For Catholics and others interested in contemporary religion in the United States, we placed Church events of the 1960s through 1980s in the larger context of modernization. The changes activated by Vatican II created a great deal of interest and of positive and negative emotion in Catholicism. We think that examining the specifics of struggle within the hierarchy and of the Church with the larger society helps the interested reader make better sense of this period. The Church was, to a large extent, reinterpreted, demystified, and made more responsible to laity. Bishops and priests were brought into a different kind of interaction. American dioceses struggled to reach professional goals and to deal with other similar thrusts coming from the impetus to update.

John Seidler died shortly after the first draft of this manuscript was completed. Its fine scholarship, accurate attention to the precise detail or the telling event, careful handling and processing of data, and insightful interpretations are hallmarks of John's work in the sociology of religion, the sociology of organizations, conflict theory, and the sociology of social movements. As a student of theology as well as of sociology, Seidler brought empathy and rigor to the enormous task of putting Vatican II in perspective in the United States diocesan context. Seidler and I shared professional concerns with social movements and organizational conflict and change, which added fertile common ground to our individual intellectual interests in the many stages of this project. My task of bringing the manuscript to its completion has been a joy and a privilege. The dynamics of the American Catholic diocese, known to me from studies in Church history and theology, has been a rich source for challenging and deepening my sociological interests in political processes and behavior.

Columbus, Ohio   Katherine Meyer
September 1988

Acknowledgments

Many individuals and organizations have contributed significantly to this book. Over the years the work has been supported and funded by the Society for the Scientific Study of Religion, by a National Science Foundation grant to the Department of Sociology, University of North Carolina at Chapel Hill, and by The Ohio State University. We are grateful to these agencies and especially to Lorraine D'Antonio, Business Manager, Society for the Scientific Study of Religion, for her encouragement and support. Several colleagues and friends provided helpful insights and editing along the way: Charles Albright, C.S.P., Karen Feinberg, Elizabeth Martin, and Robert Schmitz. Others gave encouragement and comments at various stages of the research: Gerhard E. Lenski, Hubert M. Blalock, Jr., Patrick McNamara, Richard L. Simpson, Russell R. Dynes, Robert Szafran, Madeline Adriance, Paul Besanceney, and Carroll Bourg. Anne Sykes, Mary Irene Moffitt, Judy Doty, Peter Veracka, Eleanor Byerly, John Corrigan, Corinne Mullen, and Barbara Werner gave clerical or research assistance. We are deeply indebted to them.

Some themes in this book were anticipated in essays published elsewhere: "Contested Accommodation: The Catholic Church as a Special Case of Social Change," *Social Forces* 64:4 (1986); "Priest Resignations in a Lazy Monopoly," *American Sociological Review* 44 (October); "On Using Informants: A Technique for Collecting Quantitative Data and Controlling Measurement Error in Organizational Analysis," *American Sociological Review* 39 (December);" "Priest-Protest in the Human Catholic Church," *National Catholic Reporter* 10 (May 3):7, 14, and "Priest Resignations, Relocations, Passivity," *National Catholic Reporter* 10 (May 10):7,14. The ideas presented in the following pages draw from and expand these earlier essays.

Finally, we appreciate the continued interest in this work of Marlie Wasserman, Jane McCaskey-Beatty, Clark Roof, Edward Arroyo, S.J., Colin Campbell, S.J., Laurel Richardson, Edward Langlois, and Harold Himmelfarb.

*Conflict and Change
in the Catholic Church*

Chapter One

The Changing
Catholic Church

Catholicism is a special kind of organization: a carryover organization whose current characteristics were adapted meaningfully to an earlier era, in this case the age of agrarian societies (Lenski and Lenski 1987). As such, it holds special interest for sociologists interested in social movements and organizational change.

At least in the Western world, pre–Vatican II Catholicism was well suited to a feudal society, in ideology and in structure (Berger 1967). In other parts of the world still under agrarian regimes or in early phases of industrialization, traditional Catholicism may remain well suited to the comtemporary social situation, where it may feel less pressure to adapt by incorporating broader participation and Western notions of personal autonomy.[1] The basic problem of this book will be to explain how and why such a carryover organization, which retained strong powers of self-maintenance, finally accommodated partially to modernization in the mid-twentieth century.

Many of these accommodations included constructive changes—new structures, actions, and beliefs that were in accord with the vision of the Second Vatican Council. The language of the Mass and other rituals was changed into the more readily understood vernacular. Higher percentages of Catholics received weekly communion as communicants jumped to over one-half of weekly churchgoers in 1973, from less than one-fifth in 1963 (Greeley 1977: 127). Preaching took on greater significance (Gallup and Poling 1980:69). Lay participation in liturgy increased substantially (ibid.: 68), and attempts were made to explain the meaning of liturgy. Massive numbers of Catholics accepted ecumenism and began to see the common ground between Protestants and Catholics (ibid.: 62–67). Priests' councils, diocesan pastoral councils, and other structures of shared governance came into existence (Sacred Congregation on Clergy 1970; Sacred Constitution on the Church 1965, in Abbott 1966).

Catholics basically were happy with the changes (Greeley 1977:130); indeed, they were proud of their church. In the late 1970s, despite all the turmoil of change, Catholics had "one of the highest levels of self-esteem and good feelings about being in the church among Christian bodies," as measured by the endorsement of the Church by 91 percent of Catholics (Gallup and Poling 1980:145). The accommodations did not come easily, however. A spate of dramatic conflicts signaled a church in transition during the late 1960s and early 1970s. The fact that religious confrontations coincided with the great wave of civil revolt, urban riots, and antiwar activities seems only minimally relevant. Political protest may have set the model for imitation, but the Catholic Church was undergoing a dramatic transformation of its own, with its own sources and processes.

Between 1963 and 1973 the percentage of Catholics who were certain that Jesus handed over the leadership of his church to Peter and the popes fell from a strong majority (70 percent) to a minority (42 percent) (Greeley 1977: 128). In the same decade, Catholics reporting weekly Mass attendance decreased from 71 percent to 50 percent, and those approving artificial contraception increased from 45 percent to 83 percent (ibid.: 127–129). Although basic loyalty to the Church remained high (ibid.: 128), a mighty current of change occurred, mostly indicating a transformation of certain traditional Catholic beliefs and actions.

How are we to understand these changes? Certainly, there is merit in Greeley's emphasis (ibid.: 130–145) on the influence of Pope Paul's encyclical letter (1968) maintaining the ban on artificial birth control. This letter appeared to have been the precipitating event (Smelser 1963) that occasioned the "partial alienation of Catholics" (Greeley 1977:143). Additional social processes were at work, however, even before the famous encyclical was issued. These included a dramatic increase in birth control practices among Catholics and a substantial switch in technique from rhythm to the pill (ibid.: 142–143). Yet even these trends derive from a microcosm of events. What larger social processes were occurring within the Catholic Church, and between the Church and its general social milieu, to help explain the whole complex set of events?

Most surprising and shocking to many Catholics was the sharp rise in resignations by priests. Resignation rates in the United States quadrupled from about .5 percent per year in the mid-1960s to about 2 percent per year by the late 1960s (National Opinion Research Center 1972:277; Schoenherr and Greeley 1974:408). Perhaps even more noteworthy than the actual rates was the public nature of many resignations. Often a well-known priest wrote a book or newspaper column explaining the reasons for his transition (e.g., Davis 1967). Related events included the tremendous drop in priest replacement potential, as the number of seminarians decreased by 50 percent between 1966 and 1972 (Schoenherr and Sorensen 1982). In addition, apostasy rates among Catholics doubled from 7 percent in the 1950s and mid-1960s to 14 percent by the early 1970s, becoming higher than the Protestant rate (Greeley 1977:143).

How are we to explain these changes in commitment to church and to priestly vocation? The desire to marry was a major factor (Schoenherr and

Greeley 1974). Just after the Second Vatican Council, according to Fichter (*National Catholic Reporter* 1966), 62 percent of priests favored freedom to marry at some point in their career. Alienation was another reason for priest resignations (Schallert and Kelley 1970). We can obtain a more complete understanding of these factors by studying the structural features in which they occurred. A look at a longer time period will enhance our interpretation.

We can come to understand the apparently functional changes, as well as the more disruptive ones. Certainly, the positive dynamic of the Second Vatican Council itself (Greeley 1977:138–139) made a strong contribution. But were there also local factors in the American Catholic Church that explain these changes? And what about larger social trends and forces?

We are left with questions, which are largely the work of this book: Can we understand more fully the historical swing that resulted in the Council and its aftermath? Can we understand more fully the process of change in the local church structures, namely, in the diocese and in the American Church?

Profiles of Change

A number of authors have depicted profiles of Church change. Writers have been theologians, social scientists, or both. They have tended to portray the differences in pre- and post-Vatican II Catholicism. They emphasized a variety of items, including the official meaning of the Vatican Council (Fesquet 1967; Rynne 1968; Schillebeeck 1967), the ideal Church implied by the Council (Greeley 1973; Murnion 1978; Osborne 1968; Wegmann 1969), *de facto* changes (Fichter 1968, 1974, 1977; Gallup and Poling 1980; Greeley 1977; NORC 1972; Schoenherr and Sorensen 1982), and predictions about the future Church (Greeley 1977:146–150; Schoenherr and Sorensen 1982). Some interpretations are hopeful (Brown 1969; Fichter 1977) and some are rather pessimistic (Hitchcock 1979; Kelley 1979).

Much of this literature interprets recent Catholicism as embracing the modern world (Gallup and Poling 1980), building on the American Church (O'Brien 1981–1982; Ellis 1979) and undergoing cultural change (Gleason 1972). For some, this modernization involves a crisis for the Church (Hitchcock 1979; Kelly 1979; Greeley 1979).

Researchers have examined Catholic changes in a long-range context by looking at a longer time period. Some have reported the historical trends in the United States that preceded the Second Vatican Council (Ahlstrom 1975; Ellis 1969; Hennesey 1981). Most of this writing is relatively descriptive; O'Dea's book (1969) is one example of social history by a sociologist.

Researchers have dealt with problems in the Church. Many have analyzed the problem of authority, outlining the proposed new models of leadership (Dulles 1974; Fichter 1977; McCormick 1970; McKenzie 1966), sketching the social sources of dissent or poor authority relations (Kelly and Campion 1970; Haughey 1971), or presenting strategies for viable authority structures (Dulles 1970; Jonsen 1970; Meissner 1970). Issues related to the authority problem include conflict between church leaders and their subjects (Houtart 1969; Schneider and Zurcher 1970), organizational work lives of priests (Fichter 1974; Hall and Schneider 1973), and priest professionalism (Struzzo 1970).

Writers have also grappled with the problem of commitment or loyalty to the Church. They have given much attention to priest resignations (NORC 1972; Schallert and Kelley 1970; Schoenherr and Greeley 1974) and have analyzed the basic loyalty to church given by many lay Catholics, who also reject aspects of institutional leadership or structure (Greeley 1977).

Many writers have noted the difficulties of massive cultural transformations, which produce normlessness and confusion (Greeley 1981), conflicts over norms and ideologies (Dulles 1977; McSweeney 1980), and the search for new paradigms (Greeley 1981; Haughton 1979). The problem is one of changing beliefs.

Structures changed, too. Analysts have detailed the difficulties of introducing new structures in such a traditional institution (Dulles 1974; Fichter 1974; McBrien 1973).

This overview is consciously limited; we have referred only to studies on Catholicism itself. Numerous writing on related topics occurs in sociological theory, social movement theory, sociology of organizations, and sociology of religion.

This research has many strengths, especially the analyses of cultural change: that is, changes in ideal Church orientations, in beliefs, and in the symbols representing these beliefs. Authors have extensively described changes in liturgical and religious practice, sacramental ritual, and religious beliefs. They have also depicted, from various viewpoints, the battles for dominance of belief structure, whether traditional or modern.

Other strengths include the depiction of structural changes, including conflicts over authority, additional problems of change, strategies for achieving the newly proposed ideals, and the history of Catholicism.

The research has the following limitation: it tends to be largely descriptive. The profiles of change, as well as many depictions of conflict, fit this category. So also does much of the history of Catholicism. Even Hennesey, whose history of American Catholicism (1981) is a work of solid scholarship, decries the lack of sociological history of American Catholicism (Hennesey 1982:22). Presumably, he would like to see an increase in the presentation of social facts and sociological explanations.

Studies of Catholic structures often focus on the individual in a social context (Fichter 1974; NORC 1972; Schoenherr and Greeley 1974), or on national tendencies in structure (Haughey 1971). Missing are studies of crucial inter-mediate structures, such as dioceses, and quantitative studies of diocesan structures.

This literature is weak on large theories to explain both change in general and specific aspects of change. Microlevel theories exist in abundance to explain and interpret specific authority conflicts, problems of role commitment, and so forth, but macrolevel and mesolevel theories are lacking. Needed are theories that show the relationship between Catholic organization and its social environment, that show the processes of change, and that satisfactorily explain the thrust for the achievement of modernization within Catholicism.

A Structural Approach to Change

This book concentrates on change understood in the larger social context. By looking at Catholicism before, during, and after the Second Vatican Council and at its interaction with the social environment, we hope to develop an explanatory theory that should aid our understanding of this and other organizations undergoing societal pressure to modernize.

Change has a problematic aspect. It causes disruptions, normlessness, and a variety of other problems. We depict problems as social facts and provide new, particularly structural, explanations. Here is a sacred organization, accustomed to keeping its inner problems private, suddenly exploding with public confrontations and announcements of defection. Under what structural (diocesan) circumstances did these explosions occur? What were some of the primary issues of conflict? How did the official Church react? And what fuller interpretation or meaning can we give to these events?

We emphasize structural or organizational innovation. After the period of the Second Vatican Council, the changes finally come to fruition. They take the form of innovations, namely, the introduction of new elements into the social system (Szafran 1977). New elements in organizations may consist merely of further differentiation, involving a new way to perform old tasks (Olsen 1978), or they may entail expansion and restructuring for the accomplishment of new goals (Etzioni 1961). To Max Weber (1947, 1954, 1958), the developments of bureaucracy and rationalization were innovations. To Leslie White (1949), inventions—the new joining of separate cultural elements—were also innovations.

Innovations can be summarized as new theological outlook, or ideology, such as the change from triumphalism to a humbler stance (Brown 1969) or from the siege mentality to ecumenism; restructuring, such as national episcopal conferences, shared pastorates, priests' senates, parish and diocesan consultative councils, and grievance procedures; and new technologies (new ways of performing religious practices) such as liturgical reform, the reemphasis on biblical preaching, and new approaches to religious enrichment, including adult education, marriage encounter, and charismatic renewal.[2]

We will examine innovations to understand the patterns of acceptance and to explain the struggle to implement them. Which types of innovations come first and most easily in such an organizational setting? Do new technologies precede new structures and ideologies, as often happens in societal changes (Lenski and Lenski 1987)? Which innovations seem to occasion the greatest struggle in implementation? Do most of the conflicts take place between innovators and traditionalists?

An emergent theme of this book is the social movement for change. This movement, occurring within the Catholic Church and pursuing change of the Church, provides the concepts and processes that will aid the analysis of the whole period under investigation, inspire pertinent questions for the empirical analyses, and help illuminate the findings. And, it will help explain the dynamic impetus for change.

For several aspects of this study, American Catholicism will not provide a satisfactory laboratory. To understand what has happened to the Catholic Church in the United States, one must look at worldwide Catholicism, because that was the locus of the major catalyst of change, the Second Vatican Council. The focus of the theory of change developed here is worldwide Catholicism, but with special application to the United States.

Mailed Survey. In 1971, 1,279 questionnaires were sent to priests, in almost all dioceses in the United States, who occupied ten structural positions in each diocese. These priests reported on the conditions of the diocese during the immediate post–Vatican II years (1965–1971); 74 percent completed usable questionnaires. They estimated such items as degree of conflict between priests and bishop during that era, the type and extent of punishment, the style of episcopal leadership, the extent of ideological agreement among clergy, and diocesan social unity. From this survey came a profile of diocesan clergy relations during that era and a plausible picture of causal mechanisms linking clergy conditions to priest-bishop conflict and priest resignations.

Personal Interviews. In the latter phase of the post–Vatican II period (1978–1979), Seidler conducted personal interviews with diocesan clergy who were members of the priests' senate or the Diocesan Office of Pastoral Planning or who were involved in pastoral planning. These interviews were conducted in a small number of dioceses selected to roughly represent the regions of the country. Dioceses included San Francisco, Hartford, Denver, Baltimore, Columbus, and Chicago. In each diocese, the aim was to discover how the process of change and adaptation among the clergy was progressing. What important structures had emerged? To what extent were diocesan priests continuing to gain professional autonomy and respect? To what extent were mechanisms of innovation effective or ineffective? To what did the informants attribute the diocesan success or failure of the movement engendered by the Vatican Council? From these interviews we were able to sketch a theory of organizational adaptation and change, as well as a set of propositions about diocesan conditions that may be tested on a larger sample in the future.

Chapter Two

A Survivor Organization
Faces Crisis

To begin this study of Roman Catholicism, we will take a preliminary look at the pre–Vatican II Church. Past changes and resistances to change within the Church, combined with forces of modernization that developed in the recent past, will form an introduction to contemporary change.

Organizational Features of Worldwide Catholicism

A few characteristics of worldwide Catholicism, as it existed before the Second Vatican Council (1962–1965), seem especially pertinent.

Worldwide Catholicism had (and still has) a strongly unified and coherent international culture. Its belief system was shared across national boundaries and other social divisions, and its official theology and related doctrines constituted a remarkably coherent cultural system, as a result of centuries of scholarly thought and Church interaction with a multitude of crises, heterodox beliefs, and political situations (Ahlstrom 1975:310). Such coherence helped to solidify its hold on members.

Worldwide Catholicism has been hierarchic (Foy 1978:182; Fichter 1974), that is, a multilayered organization in which each level reported to the next, all the way to the pope. At each level the commanding position was occupied by a sacred person—priest, bishop, pope. Byproducts of this system, which some called feudal (Rynne 1968; Murphy 1981; Kaiser 1963), included relative uniformity (Fichter 1974), centralization (Fesquet 1967), domination by the Roman Curia (Murphy 1981), a lack of consultative input, and the absence of intermediate structures, such as national conferences of bishops, priests' councils, personnel boards, and pastoral councils (Murphy 1981; Rynne 1968; Szafran 1977).

A corollary to the point made above, the structure of worldwide Catholicism has tended to be corporate, with only slight indications of federalism (Kim 1980:87). The official Church allowed informal adaptations to local custom, but the leeway was small. For example, some writers have noted how the American Church gradually embraced the concept of pluralism, first for practical reasons and then theoretically (Ellis 1963; Cogley 1973; Greeley 1967). Yet the pope eventually condemned this trend as an aspect of Americanism (see chapter 4). Rome also refused to allow missionaries to adapt local language and customs extensively. For example, after missionaries in China had decided that ceremonies reverencing ancestors were basically nonreligious and could continue, the Vatican ordered them to reverse their policy (Bangert 1972:157–161, 334 ff.). Yet Rome usually allowed minor adaptations such as the special honoring of local saints. Also, some writers have indicated that American bishops garnered unusual independence, largely for geographic reasons (Haughey 1971). Such limited local adaptation implies that, as Kim notes (1980:87), there are no national churches. Instead, the Catholic Church of each country exists as a subunit of international Catholicism.

The accountability structure has tended to be short and one-directional. For all practical purposes there were only three levels of mainline leadership: pope, bishop, and pastor (Kim 1980; Spencer 1966; Foy 1978:182). In addition, decisions flowed downward, whereas formal accountability was always upward; for example, priests always reported to bishops (Kim 1980:88). This structure not only produced unusually large spans of control (Spencer 1966:100) but was noteworthy for other reasons. It implied a lack of formal delegation. Though there were plenty of commissions and other governing bodies, decisions were typically made at these three key points. It also tended to invest extensive power in the hands of the individuals who occupied these positions (Spencer 1966; Vallier 1969). Finally, by neglecting an upward flow of information, it removed an important means of obtaining accurate and relevant information for decision making (Kim 1980:89).

The Church has acted as a monopoly in two respects. It has operated as a practical monopoly for religious salvation (Hirschman 1970:57–75). Even though adherents could have chosen to defect, especially in parts of the Western world where other Christian denominations constituted strong alternatives, Catholics normally did not take that option. As Greeley notes (1977: 143), apostasy rates were generally quite low before the Council. In addition, the Church preferred to have real dominance, as indicated by concordats and other Church-state arrangements giving preferential treatment to Church members (Ellis 1963; Fesquet 1967).

Local variations in belief and religious ideology have been allowed and even encouraged to exist within the limits of doctrine. For example, certain regions cultivated special devotions to saints and to various Marian cults or manifestations of Mary, such as the Black Madonnas of Spain, Switzerland and Czestochowa, Fatima, Guadalupe, and Lourdes. As Gerlach and Hine (1970) maintain about religious movements, and as also seems true of more established religious groups, a split-level belief system developed. Official doctrine and belief of the members did not coincide perfectly. In addition, theological explanations for religious mysteries, such as predestination, grace, and free will, varied by theological tradition and even sometimes by religious order. Groups also differed in moral theology. Such variations can have real consequences: for example, some Catholics in the late 1960s were told by their priests that they could practice birth control; others were told (by other priests) that they could not.

Past Adaptation and Resistance

History belies the oft-repeated notion that Catholicism remains forever unchanged. Although pre–Vatican II Catholicism exhibited traits that discouraged change, the overall history of the Church displays other traditions and tendencies.

In early centuries, Christianity passed through a number of challenging situations, including hostile political regimes, conflict between Christian communities, and bitter competition among doctrines vying for orthodoxy (Newman 1960). The Church, of course, changed as it grappled with these challenges. It developed formal mechanisms to decide orthodoxy (Hughes 1961); it created informal structures to elude oppressive governments; and it suffered schism. It also met the well-known organizational dilemmas (O'Dea 1969; Nottingham 1971) and grew from a sect into a church (Troeltsch 1931; Niebuhr 1929), even forming alliances with empires and states (Yinger 1970). Finally, it saw its own spinoffs—new sects and various religous movements— drastically alter the religious scene, giving rise to new religious communities and protracted struggles over religious territorial ascendancy.

The Roman Catholic Church has often developed itself by imitating prevailing social structures. Having roots as a sectlike opposition group in the Roman Empire, it transformed itself to an established church under the reign of Constantine (Niebuhr 1929), soon incorporating a hierarchic structure. In the Middle Ages it developed the style of a feudal organization (Francis 1951:526; Kim 1980:86), and from the sixteenth to twentieth centuries as religious orders gradually became more centralized (Cabrol 1918:705), the Church generally took on the bureaucratic traits of contemporary society (Eisenstadt 1968:73).

Another adaptation might be called culture incorporation: the Church borrowed ideas from contemporary society and included them in its theological and moral thinking. For example, the Church developed a patriarchal mentality, reflected in male leadership structures and in liturgical descriptions of God as masculine (Reuther 1975, 1977). This outlook made sense in Roman and medieval times when political, economic, and family structures were all male-dominated (Berger 1967). In addition, the Church's early condemnation and later allowance of usury (charging interest for borrowed money) demonstrate its incorporation of contemporary understandings. Before the development of capitalism, usury was understood by the Church as extortion. After capitalism developed, the Church relaxed its prohibition, only forbidding excessive interest rates. In a related form of adaptation, behavioral imitation, the Church has often mimicked the prevalent actions of its social milieu. While knights fought to win territory for their feudal lord, the Church sponsored the Crusades to win the Holy Land for its Lord (Francis 1950:526).

Roman Catholicism also changed through evolutionary processes; that is, largely by internal mechanisms that allowed it to cope more effectively with the environment (see Lenski and Lenski 1987). One such mechanism, cultural elaboration, is based on environmental interaction. When faced with new societal pressures and alternative interpretations, the Church often elaborated its doctrine in greater detail (Newman 1960). In the early Christian era, a number of credal doctrines, including those about the nature and person of Jesus and about grace and salvation, were formulated in response to such heresies as Pelagianism and Arianism (Hughes 1961; Newman 1960). Such cultural elaborations constitute the subject matter of Newman's famous treatise (1960) on the development of Christian doctrine.

Another evolutionary mechanism is innovation or invention. Though this mechanism overlaps the notion of cultural elaboration, inventions underscore the novelty and breakthrough of new structures and principles of action (White 1949). In addition, invention is at the core of evolutionary processes (Lenski and Lenski 1987). The Church created new principles of morality during the earlier phases of industrialization, as evidenced in Pope Leo XIII's encyclical *Rerum Novarum* (Condition of the Working Classes) of 1891 (Foy 1978:179). Cultural inventions of the Church include a prelude to ecumenism, developed by American theologians (Murray 1960, 1965). This was the notion that pragmatic cooperation with those of other faiths for social goals is a good to be pursued. Such practical cooperation did not imply the acceptance of others' beliefs. Though this idea sounds prosaic in the 1980s, it was revolutionary in Catholic circles in the nineteenth century (see the brief treatment of Americanism in chapter 4). The Church also continuously created new internal structures to fit contemporary needs or to match the contemporary situation. For example, a myriad of religious subgroups developed over the century, usually as a result of a special invention to cope with the social milieu (Cabrol 1918:694; Francis 1964).

Revitalization, another common path to change, entails a return to the essence or early interpretation of the faith along with special application to the contemporary world (Wallace 1956). Ecumenical councils, including the one opened by Pope John XXIII in 1962, were often attempts at revitalization (Hughes 1961; Murphy 1981). The Council of Trent (1545–1563), for example, attempted to turn a Church that had become secularized in many ways back into a more spiritual direction. That council produced a series of changes, such as institutionalizing seminary training and regulating clerical life (Hughes 1961:3132–3322; Schaff 1950). In addition, religious orders and congregations often arose from an attempt to revitalize the Church. Francis of Assisi, founder of the Franciscans, reintroduced the ideals of simplicity and identification with the poor in his contemporary version of basic Christian values (Cabrol 1918:702; Francis 1964:527).

Byproducts of this religious movement for reform included a new religious substructure in the Church that "swept aside all the barriers of segregated life and denounced the traditional means of economic support which had lent to the older orders their solid foundation." Often, such movements found themselves in conflict with the hierarchical organization of the Church, apparently for preserving the charismatic aspects of the original movement (Francis 1964:527).

On the other hand, the Church has also frequently resisted change. Through the ages it has condemned some contemporary currents of thought, such as Arianism, Pelagianism, Monophysitism, Jansenism, key beliefs of the Protestant Reformation, Americanism, and Modernism (Appleby 1984; Cogley 1973; Gannon 1971; Greeley 1967). Also it has resisted change simply by not acting. Holding firmly to its past traditions, supported by a belief in infallibility and in the certitude and unchanging nature of past pronouncements, it often continued in relative stability (Ellis 1972; Hasler 1981).

Adaptive Mechanisms

The Roman Catholic Church seems to have a special instinct for survival. As scholars have long noted (Demerath and Hammond 1969), Roman Catholicism has been remarkable in its ability to roll with large historical currents while defending a traditional core of doctrine. As noted above, it has changed itself over the centuries and adapted to circumstance. Thus, it has survived.

Several organizational mechanisms and characteristics have apparently fostered change and aided this survival. One is the council, called the ecumenical or general council, wherein all top administrators (bishops) are summoned to a general and often quite prolonged meeting (Foy 1978:164). The council, used in early ages to settle doctrinal disputes, has served broader purposes as well (Hughes 1961). For example, the Council of Trent (1545–1563) and the Second Vatican Council (1962–1965) addressed issues of revitalization, updating, and correcting internal abuses (Hughes 1961; Murphy 1981; Fesquet 1967). As Foy noted (1978:164), an ecumenical council "has supreme authority over the Church in matters pertaining to faith, morals, worship and discipline." These councils, which include representatives from every Catholic diocese and other comparable units throughout the world, often make the adaptations that relieve a crisis and secure the Church's societal niche (Hughes

1961). Though called infrequently—about once a century (ibid.)—the ecumenical council is an available mechanism and can be mobilized when needed.

A second mechanism is the extraordinary decree. Popes have always given decrees of various sorts—apostolic bulls, encyclical letters, epistles, and other communiqués (Foy 1978:178–179, 352). These cover a range of topics from canonizations to doctrine and discipline. Often such pronouncements deal with contemporary conditions, spelling out new church initiatives or solutions. For example, Pope Leo XIII (1878–1903) issued numerous encyclicals formulating his social doctrine, touching such issues as the relations between capital and labor, the African slave trade, socialism and economic liberalism, liberty, and the family (ibid.:172). His letter of 1891, *Rerum Novarum*, is often hailed as the first strong Catholic utterance for social justice in industrial relations. Popes following him expanded this social doctrine in their own formulations, such as *Quadragesimo Anno* (Pius XI 1931), *Christianity and Social Progress* (John XXIII, 1961), and *Development of Peoples* (Paul VI, 1967) (Foy 1968: 246). Probably Pope John's best-known social encyclical was *Peace on Earth* (1963), a bold new formulation for world peace.

A third feature promoting adaptation, change, and survival is something the Catholic Church shares with the rest of Christianity, namely a strong intellectual component. This element is reflected in the importance of the belief dimension (Glock and Stark 1966; Hoge and Carroll 1975; Roof 1978; Weigert and Thomas 1969). It contrasts with religions that underscore different dimensions, such as mysticism and action among Hindus (Bendix 1962; Coleman 1984) and ritual and law among Orthodox Jews (Himmelfarb 1975). The Catholic Christian church has normally supported a strong contingent of theologians and philosophers, from the early church fathers to the scholastics of the Middle Ages to the present array of Catholic theologians. Such an emphasis has produced important intellectual syntheses between religion and social environment. Those include the Thomistic synthesis of the thirteenth century, based on Aristotelian categories; the treatise (during the dominance of evolutionary theories) on the development of Christian doctrine by John Henry Cardinal Newman; *The Phenomenon of Man* (another evolutionary synthesis) by theologian-paleontologist Pierre Teilhard de Chardin (1965); and the more recent phenomenologically oriented synthesis of Bernard Longergan (1957, 1972; Crowe 1980). Such syntheses, merging theology and contemporary thought, have functioned as adaptive mechanisms.

Fourth is the intriguing structure and history of religious orders, or, more precisely, of life in religion (Francis 1964:518). Life in religion implies that persons committed to it "accept certain obligations considered as being morally superior and conducive to a state of greater spiritual perfection, in addition to the duties shared by all members of the Church" (ibid.). The term *religious orders* often includes all structured life in religion, as approved by the Church (Francis 1964; Cabrol 1918).

Almost by definition, new religious orders bring a potential for charismatic innovation (Weber, cited in Eisenstadt 1968). New orders usually originate with a charismatic leader who has a vision of a new structure or a new mission that does not fit existing structures. Thus, new orders almost automatically bring something novel into the Church. Of course, the Church, by establishing guidelines for life in religion and by scrutinizing each application for official status as a religious order, intends to tame or channel that charisma toward officially approved ends (Etzioni 1961; also Weber, cited in Eisenstadt 1968). Still, the potential for innovation remains.

The sheer number of religious orders is also noteworthy. In the United States alone, according to the listings in the *Official Catholic Directory* of 1969, there were 164 religious orders of priests, 28 religious orders of brothers, and 464 religious orders of sisters, not counting religious groups devoted to missionary activity. In all there were over 22,000 religious priests (37 percent of all U.S. clergy), 11,755 religious brothers, and more than 167,000 women religious (*Official Catholic Directory* 1969). Though all of these together constituted less than one-half of one percent of the Catholic population in the United States, their influence, through teaching, preaching, and other ministries, far exceeded their numerical strength.

Innovation does not flow automatically from all religious orders. Some, established long ago, have succumbed to the establishment mentality, as sects and social movements often do (Niebuhr 1929; Toeltsch 1931; Turner and Killian 1972). Yet the laws of probability suggest that at least a few of these religious orders will occasionally produce significant innovations. In addition, the following characteristics, combined with the numbers, increase the likelihood of innovation.

New religious orders have emerged almost continuously from the early years of Christianity to the present (Cabrol 1918; Francis 1964). Though not all of these have endured, many have left their stamp on the Church. Newly created religious congregations have often introduced striking new ideas and structures; they helped keep the Church updated and relevant.

A number of religious orders specialize in professional and semiprofessional pursuits, such as teaching and scholarship, counseling, medical services, preaching, and communication, along with their particular style of prayer or devotional life (Cabrol 1918). Such characteristics produce different viewpoints from tradational mainline administrators (bishops and pastors) and even lead to conflicts with local bishops and diocesan structures. The professional orientation of religious orders also produces innovations, at least on occasion, because the professionals' goals, expertise, and service orientation distinguish them sharply from administrators (Blau and Scott 1962).

Religious orders are attached at the top of the organizational chart (Kim 1980:92). Attachment at the top means that a religious order is responsible to the pope through its own leader and not through intermediate members of the mainline Church hierarchy (pastors and bishops). Such attachment gives orders greater flexibility to continue the charismatic spirit of the founder. By contrast with the administrative mentality and conservatism of the Roman Curia and other Church bureaus and commissions (Murphy 1981), which are also attached at the top, religious orders are not necessarily subject to the same pressures for bureaucratic and administrative thinking (Blau and Scott 1962). Furthermore, they are generally free from the governing policies of local bishops, in whose territory they operate, and so they are relatively free to perform their mission as they see fit. Thus, attachment at the top, an aspect of the religious exemption mentioned above, helps to reinforce the continuation of innovation.

To return to our list of mechanisms that promote change and survival, a fifth feature is the incorporation of diversity. We have already noted that certain variations were tolerated in this organization. Under the same broad organizational roof have existed hermits and social activists, Franciscans and Renaissance popes. Beyond this tolerance, the Church has made the incorporation of diversity into a strategy. By contrast with the Protestant tradition, which split and formed separate religious bodies, Roman Catholicism has more often than not incorporated the potentially disruptive (Yinger 1970: 251–281). A contemporary example is the Pentecostal or charismatic movement, which remained within Catholicism while splintering off from American Episcopalianism (Harrison and Maniha 1978). Past examples include the original Jesuits, attacked and controversial at their beginnings (Harney 1941:44) and hated by a variety of civil and religious leaders who had the order suppressed in the eighteenth century, only to be restored by a new pope early in the nineteenth century (ibid.:chaps. 12–13).

Retaining dissent and diversity within the structure can obviously promote change. New ideas and new structures enter the system and eventually can affect Church planning, goals, and atmosphere. Instead of cutting off the dissent or implied criticism of diverse groups (Gerlach and Hine 1970), this strategy seems a functional way of using dissent and criticisms for periodic updating and survival.

Of course, there have always been limits on Catholic tolerance for internal dissent. The East-West schism of the eleventh century and the Protestant Reformation of the sixteenth century show what happened when the limits of toleration were reached. In addition, that tolerance has waxed and waned over the centuries. Periods of waning include the Inquisition, pre-Reformation times, and the nineteenth and early twentieth centuries, as we shall see.

A sixth and final characteristic fostering change and adaptation is the toleration of localized environmental situations—a subcategory of the toleration discussed above, but one that deserves separate consideration. Here we refer to the quasi-political posture taken by the local Church, depending on its numerical size, the political regime of the country, and other factors (Martin 1978). In medieval Europe, Roman Catholicism was part of the established order. In Africa and large parts of Asia it has been mainly a missionary church. It has adapted to a pluralistic, free setting in the United States and to a kind of Cold War situation in Poland. It survived underground in the early days of Christianity and in Elizabethan England, and more recently in Mexico and in Eastern Europe. It has often flourished in close partnership with the regime, as in Franco's Spain, but it has also formed a major source of opposition to the establishment, as in the Latin American Bishops' statement at Medellin, Colombia, in 1968. In that statement the bishops sided with the poor and placed blame for social injustice on Latin America's social, economic, and political structures (Brown 1978:207 ff.).

Such a diversity of local environmental niches can occasionally produce change for the worldwide Church. Medieval ties with the establishment, sometimes called Caesaro-Papism, probably established a norm for future attempts by the Vatican to establish concordats and other official support. More recently, the experience of American Catholicism, flourishing in a religio-political climate of toleration and nonestablishment, formed the major basis for the decree of the worldwide Church embracing feedom of conscience (Fesquet 1967; Rynne 1968). The American setting produced not simply a random change, but rather an adaptation that brought the Church into line with contemporary thinking on Church activity both in Western Christian nations and in non-Christian regions.

These six factors suggest the potential for change within Catholicism. At the same time, they do not compel change. Other factors must also come into play before the organization actually changes.

The Growing Crisis

The growing crisis of the post–Vatican I era developed because of two important factors. The Church continued an orientation based on antimodernism, infallibility, and feudal structures. Features of the modern, democratic, and industrialized world penetrated the Church at a growing rate.

The Church of the late nineteenth and early twentieth centuries supported uniformity rather than variability; tradition instead of innovation. Several developments apparently furthered this orientation.

There was the legacy of a previous Ecumenical Council, Vatican I (1869–1870). Vatican I proclaimed papal primacy and infallibility and was adjourned prematurely before papal power could be balanced by the proclamation of other sources of authority (Ellis 1963). The theme of papal infallibility remained dominant into the twentieth century (Ellis 1972; Hasler 1981; Küng 1961). There were several consequences.

Church leaders emphasized tradition over scripture, stifling one source of revitalization (Vawter 1959; Kurtz 1986). Obedience to Rome became a primary virtue (Dulles 1974, 1977; Hasler 1981; Kurtz 1986; Küng 1961; McBrien 1973), and religious innovation took a back seat. Siege mentality waxed as adaptation waned (Brown, 1969; Hasler 1981; Novak 1964; Rynne 1968).

The Church developed a bureaucratic centrism during this period. Life in the Church had gradually grown more centralized and bureaucratized during the preceding several centuries (Cabrol 1918:705; Weber, in Eisenstadt 1968:73). The nineteenth-century proclamation of papal infallibility both reflected and advanced this tendency of archconservative Vatican congregations, which regulated writings about Church doctrine, clergy life, marriage issues, and so forth (Murphy 1981; Rynne 1968; Kaiser 1963).

Bureaucratic centrism obviously tended to block innovation. The Sacred Congregation for the Doctrine of the Faith (formerly called the Holy Office) often banned books and disciplined theologians (Hebblethwaite 1980). The Sacred Congregation of Rites demanded near absolute worldwide uniformity, even in the minutest details.[1] The Vatican tended to carefully select each bishop on the basis of his adherence to Roman policy (Greeley 1977:158–159). Thus, the climate for creative ideas and innovation was extremely poor. The basis for a monolithic structure had been built.

Additional consequences of this tradition arose in the United States. The Church often functioned as a haven for immigrants (Greeley 1972; Handlin 1951). The Church was a protective institution, a refuge for those who suffered discrimination because of their religion or language or ethnic origin. It also nourished the new Americans, imparting a sense of identity and worth as they faced a strange and difficult reality (Ellis 1969; Greeley 1972). In such a setting, one does not change the Church. One loves it and serves it.

In addition, as Ellis (1972) has sketched it, the seminary education of United States clergy strongly reflected the conservative theology of its French, Irish, and Roman sources. Trained in isolation, with a largely ecclesiastical orientation devoid of emphasis on Scripture or social issues and strong on apologetics, generations of seminarians came narrowly educated to the active ministry. They had missed the academic development of intellectual curiosity, openness to the truth of other religions, and concern for the social gospel (ibid.). The seminary tended to cultivate an organization-man mentality in the new clergy. These seminarians would toe the line; they would rarely venture into realms that might bring innovation.

In the pre-Vatican era, a rather conservative hierarchy (NORC 1972; Fichter 1968, 1974) controlled American priests tightly (Fichter 1968). They used a variety of rewards and punishments to keep them in line, from desirable pastorships to special assignments, from calling on the carpet to suspension.[2] American priests were subject to pressure to move in line with the ruling traditionalist mentality.

Observers have summarized the dominant orientation reflected by all of these factors as the siege mentality (Brown 1969; Kaiser 1963; Rynne 1968; Fesquet 1967). The hierarchy feared for the purity of Catholic doctrine, which might be tarnished by the infusion of secular thought, by too much speculation, too much freedom, too much reading of non-Catholic sources (Ellis 1972). During that era, safe versions of investigation emerged—Catholic sociology, the Catholic version of evolution, Catholic solutions to poverty or population problems.[3]

These developments strongly implied a distrust of science and free scholarship (Ellis 1972; Kurtz 1986). The Inquisition continued, though it was called the Holy Office in the decades preceding Vatican II. Books were banned and eminent theologians were scrutinized for orthodoxy (Hebblethwaite 1980; Küng 1961). The defensiveness even extended to the religious education of children, who were not exposed to the Bible and were discouraged from raising questions; rather, they were rewarded for giving pat answers to standardized questions.[4]

In sum, the Church of the nineteenth and early twentieth centuries embodied at least two types of images (Morgan 1986). In ideology or mentality it was traditionalist and defensive; in structure it was bureaucratic and centralized.

The Penetration of
Modern Life

Modern life was coming gradually to the Church, despite the monolithic and defensive ascendancy. This penetration of modern life brought a crisis and eventually triggered change in the worldwide Catholic Church. Crisis-bearing trends reflecting modern life originated from technological developments, changed social patterns, and contemporary ideological trends.

Technological developments of the industrial age affected all the churches profoundly, including the Roman Catholic. Improvements in communication and transportation undermined the reigning ethnocentrism of European Christianity (Dillenberger and Welch 1954). Contacts with Asia and Africa increased, and anthropologists helped the West open its eyes more realistically to the culture of indigenous peoples. The industrial growth of the United States brought respect as a world power. Suddenly non-European continents exerted an influence on the churches.

Such realignments of power and perspective challenged Western Christian absolutism, at least implicitly. Some Christians realized that the world presented a competitive market for religion (Berger 1963) and that the competitors were not voodoo, idolatry, and superstition, but sophisticated religions, such as Islam and Hinduism (T. Merton 1967). As a worldwide minority, could Christianity or Catholicism claim a monopoly on spiritual well-being? Should Christianity continue mainly to seek conversions in a Western colonial mode, or should it extend greater respect to non-Western peoples and cultures (see Greinacher and Muller 1979)?

Archaeological investigations also modified religious explanations and overviews (Albright 1949, 1966; Bright 1959; Jones 1966; McKenzie 1956; Pritchard 1958; Wright 1961). The discoveries of ancient Troy, Peking Man, and the Dead Sea Scrolls enlarged our understanding of earlier civilizations, the development of the human race, and scriptural reliability. The new technique of carbon dating added precision to the calculation of ancient events. Biblical scholars reinterpreted the time of creation, moving it into the distant past and rendering symbolic the interpretation of the biblically stated number of years since Adam and Eve (Vawter 1956). Evidence also mounted concerning the Flood and the fall of Jericho, confirming their historicity but placing them in earlier periods than those calculated from the Bible (Albright 1949; Bright 1959; McKenzie 1956; Pritchard 1962; Vawter 1956; Wright 1961). Naturalistic interpretations also abounded. Could the parting of the Red Sea be attributed to occasional earthquakes? Was the Star of Bethlehem a rare convergency of several planets? What was the nature of the miraculous?

Technological developments in literature also had profound effects. Improvements in the reproduction of manuscripts—printing, photocopying, and microfilm—increased access to ancient literature and history. Literary scholars began to decipher ancient tongues and understand ancient literary forms. They gained access to the Gilgamesh epic and other pertinent literature of the Fertile Crescent (Heidel 1949); these in turn cast new light on the biblical accounts of creation, of Abraham, Job, and Jonah (Heidel 1949; McKenzie 1956; Vawter 1956). Scholars understood better the contemporary myths that biblical accounts were meant to combat. They also saw how parallel literary forms were incorporated in the Bible.

Other technological innovations produced new social patterns that altered religious conceptions. Medical advances, combined with industrial technology, produced shorter working hours, more leisure time, and greater longevity. Consequently, personal fulfillment became a more salient value, at least for the burgeoning middle classes (Greeley 1973). This value modified the former interpretation of salvation, namely, a fatalistic forebearance while waiting for the next life. Similarly, the development of new contraceptives and the extended stages of women's life cycle, before or after childbearing years, paved the way for new attitudes about sexuality. Was not the previously proclaimed secondary function of marital intercourse—mutual happiness and support for the marriage bond (Zalba 1938)—as important as the childbearing function (Callahan 1968)?

A host of additional technological innovations and altered religious viewpoints could be cited. Many of these changes, however, appear to have occurred through the mediation of new social structures, themselves created by technological advances.

Several emerging social structures implicitly tested any monocratic leadership. These included the growing dominance of democratic civil governments and the gradual extension of suffrage to women, blacks, and other less privileged groups (Lenski and Lenski 1987). The common people's increasing opportunities for education, which legitimated their participation in political decisions, also undercut a feudal ecclesiastical system—a system more suited to the untrained masses. Even some aspects of bureaucracy that the Church embraced (Weber, in Eisenstadt 1968) contradicted autocratic principles. For example, the emphasis on accountability (ibid.), when applied to the highest levels of authority, suggested that leaders respect rather than disregard the will of subjects. In addition, bureaucracy's need for input from accountants and financial advisers belied the possibility of elite rule without consultation.

The dramatic growth of urban areas during the first half of the twentieth century (Lenski and Lenski 1987) was another structural factor. Urban life and urban problems called for new approaches by the Church to evangelization and social action (Suhard 1948; Suenens 1965). These approaches would differ from those fashioned during a period of agricultural dominance.

Worldwide changes in population structure created new issues for the Church. As Greeley points out (1973:139): "In our era the problem is not underpopulation but overpopulation; marriage is no longer an important institution for the transmission of property; infant mortality rates are low, life expectancies are long, and the amount of time a child is dependent on his parent has trebled over even a century ago. . . . The position of women in society is changing drastically."

Women could now expect to spend a significant portion of their lives without mothering responsibilities, even if they stayed at home while the children were young. These changing structures challenged the assumption of traditional Church teaching about family life, birth control, family planning and size, and women's place in the home.

The emergence of new nations and the era of development in Africa, Latin America, and the Far East radically changed the relationship between these peoples and the Church. Old missionary patterns were undercut. There were new cries for indigenous Church leadership, along with greater respect for local custom and ritual (Greinacher and Muller 1979). Even ecumenism received a boost from the reexamination of missionary policy (Baum 1962, 1964; Dillenberger and Welch 1954).

In the United States, social patterns also triggered change. Social classes were realigned; American Catholics moved more solidly into the middle classes (Greeley 1977). By 1960, when the election of President John Kennedy symbolized the acceptance of American Catholics, the traditional apologetic and defensive posture of the Church seemed inappropriate. In addition, as noted elsewhere, the success of Catholicism within a structure of religious pluralism suggested the need for adopting the principles of religious tolerance and freedom of conscience (Murray 1960).

Unique historical events also undermined traditional religious practices. After World War II and the Nazi atrocities, European religious denominations worshipped and worked together (Dillenberger and Welch 1954; Ahlstrom 1975). In the United States, a common support for civil rights led Catholic and other religious groups to cooperate in freedom rides, marches, and other matters of social justice. Thus, war, the Holocaust, and civil rights issues helped to tear down traditional religious defenses and interfaith barriers.

New ideologies contradicted traditional Catholic principles. Some of these values—such as liberty and equality—had been gathering strength for centuries (Greeley 1973). Others, such as personal growth and development, blossomed only in the last half century (Yankelovich 1981). Greeley (1973) calls the personalist revolution one of the most important cultural developments of our century. By this term he means the call for individuals to become more fully themselves. This revolution is reflected in progressive educational theories and in the demands of adolescents and rising minority groups.

The personalist revolution had several possible ramifications: inconsistencies between personalism and the severe side of traditional Church teaching (sin, penance, purgatory, and hell) and clashes between obedience-oriented members of the hierarchy and lower-level Church participants who embraced self-fulfillment.

Another value—professionalism (Wilensky 1964)—was gaining new emphasis within a Catholic subgroup that included Catholic clergy and men and women religious. Although priests and men and women religious had ranked for centuries with doctors and lawyers as part of the professional elite, something seems to have happened along the way. By the twentieth century, Catholic clergy and religious were in an anomalous situation; they possessed only some of the traits of professionals (Vera 1982). Notably lacking were expected levels of professional autonomy (ibid.) and occupational satisfaction (Hall and Schneider 1973). In addition, their realm of expertise had shrunk in recent decades by the encroachment of secular experts in counseling, psychology, social work, and other areas.

The new emphasis on professionalism posed a potential threat to the status of pre-Vatican clergy and religious. If they caught the new professional spirit, they would begin the quest to recapture lost professional traits. They would push against the traditional tide for increased professional autonomy, greater training in related secular sciences, and whatever else would further their occupational satisfaction.

Conclusions

At least until the mid-twentieth century, worldwide Catholicism has been a survivor organization. Using some unknown ratio of adaptation to resistance, it continuously evolved, adapted, and incorporated enough aspects of contemporary cultures to maintain relevance. At the same time, it retained its identity sufficiently by revitalizing itself and by resisting extreme forms of accommodation.

Through a large part of its history, the Roman Catholic Church exhibited a strong potential for adaptation and change. We noted this especially in its mechanisms for change, such as the general council, the power of popes, the exemption of religious orders from mainline authority structures, and the inclusion of diversity, whether by incorporating new religious movements or by legitimating new religious orders, themselves often the product of a new religious movement. In fact, growth of this church, as a strong and stable organization, seems due in large part to its ability to adapt through these and other innovation-supporting structures.

This potential, however, was counterbalanced in the nineteenth and early twentieth centuries by forces that strongly resisted change. Thus, the Roman Catholic Church of the era between the Vatican Councils (1870–1962) developed a style peculiar to a unique historical situation, which included the advances of industrialism with its accompanying tides—democracy, education, and self-fulfillment. It also included the Protestant Reformation and a strong rush of modern ideologies and reinterpretations that directly challenged the Church's European hegemony, its belief system, its internal structure, and its relationship to the whole world. The Church's style, developed partly in reaction, was to play it safe, to be defensive, to close the door on potential outside influences.

In part, also, the Church's style was the logical result of its position as a carryover organization—that is, one whose form and orientation were developed in accord with an agrarian level of development (Lenski and Lenski 1987). The Church's well-honed patriarchal structure, feudal aspects, top-down authority style, and desire for a monopolistic control over people's allegiance all constituted adaptations to an agrarian system (ibid.). It is easy to understand the Church's initial and prolonged reactions to modern developments. They reflected its long and meticulous formation during the many centuries of agrarian dominance.

Many factors must be considered to explain why the Catholic Church eventually modernized with Vatican II. The Church's potential for change is only one of those factors. Indeed, even with that potential, the Catholic Church maintained an antiaccommodationist stance for almost five full centuries, whereas Protestantism and other movements adapted to contemporary forces. The Church's potential for change, combined with its resistant tendencies, poses the question more sharply: why did the Church give in at last to modernity?

The rising crisis in the Church does not explain why the Church finally moved toward modernization. Latent inconsistencies and deprivations, even when perceived, do not always lead to social movements, revolution, or change (McPhail 1971; Tilly 1978; Oberschall 1978; Jenkins and Perrow 1977).

How and why did Catholicism change? What form did the change take?

Chapter Three

Contested Accommodation

To explain the changes within Catholicism, analysts have readily applied a whole range of concepts: rationalization, secularization, modernization, and so forth. The turmoil within the Church continues, and an observer may question the degree to which most of these concepts aptly describe the processes taking place.

What seems necessary is a complex explanation—one that portrays processes especially at the macro and meso levels. At the same time, a helpful explanation would recognize the unfinished character of the changes and even underline some of the anomalies, uncertainties, and conflicts.

Contested accommodation, a complex and unfinished process, describes the macro level of change within Catholicism, especially in the United States, more aptly than do simpler terms such as accommodation, assimilation, updating, secularization, and so forth. The theory proposed here is a conscious attempt to combine functionalist and conflict assumptions, following the leads of van den Berghe (1963), Lenski (1966), and Olsen (1978). A functional outcome (accommodation) is seen here as contingent upon power struggles and as a partial process, not the automatic fulfillment of societal needs (Parsons 1951). With Olsen (1978) we hold that social change comes from the exercise of power by an organization or its subunits in an effort to cope with social tensions. In Catholicism, pope, bishops, theologians, and others struggled, often with each subunit acting contrarily to the others, but all for the sake of coping with tensions caused at least originally by the surrounding secular culture.

Organizational Updating

Organizations whose values and structures are not isomorphic with the surrounding milieu tend to incorporate features of the host culture, at least to a limited degree, when the following conditions are met simultaneously: the social environment heavily penetrates the organization, resulting in structural strain (Smelser 1962) or a sense of crisis; prophetic leaders construct new and plausible visions of religious reality incorporating old and new structures and values; and by accident, luck, or the force of key personalities, the battle situation favors the forces of change.

In the Catholic case, environmental penetration gradually increased from the late nineteenth century onward. There were many points of strain—the modernist controversy at the turn of the century, the long struggle over biblical scholarship, the growing antiestablishment movements to reform worship and to liberalize the Catholic social consciousness.

A crisis emerged in the middle decades of the twentieth century when, despite much encouragement toward *aggiornamento* by the official church (Foy 1978), avant-garde theologians and biblical scholars were still showered by strong negative sanctions. The crisis came to a head following the Second Vatican Council, when a variety of traditional and liberal reconstructions vied for ascendancy.

Key personalities and accidents of history greatly aided the changes in Catholicism. These included Pope Pius XII, who supported biblical scholarship, and Popes John XXIII and Paul VI, who favored general but substantial change in line with the Council. The greatest accident of history was World War II, but other events, such as the growing importance and independent status of the developing nations, also promoted change. At the diocesan level, however, bishops were powerful enough to promote or forestall changes, at least during the 1960s (Seidler 1972).

This argument implies that forces of traditionalism—the Vatican bureaucracy, the weight of past interpretations and socialization, ingrained habits, and the use of strong sanctions at local and international levels to enforce traditionalism—tended to dominate. The principle of social inertia favored a traditional paradigm, despite strong currents of change, until key protagonists were able to turn the tide.

Accommodation Amid Conflict. Contested accommodation refers to specific processes described below, which may remove conceptual ambiguity. Many sociological concepts of change—religious revival, cultural adaptation, synthesis—imply a completion and neatness of the process and thus oversimplify (Haughton 1979; Wallace 1956; Dulles 1977). Contested accommodation, however, connotes the unfinished and ambiguous nature of change.

Another reason for choosing this term is its approximation to reality. Accommodation connotes two aspects of reality, both a rapprochement to the surrounding culture and a maintenance of social distance (Park 1952). Many changes suggest a limited acceptance of the dominant culture. These include the new emphasis on the church's pastoral role, charismatic renewal, and increased optimism about the faith. Surveys reveal strong levels of Catholic participation and belief (Gallup and Poling 1980). In addition, leading theologians in America define the task of current Catholicism as one of limited accommodation. Dulles (1975:64) urged the Church to pursue modernization, but without adopting uncritically the "latest fruits of Western Civilization." McBrien (1981:chap. 11) described Christ as not only of culture, but also in part against culture, above culture, and a transformer of culture. In a protest against dominant values, the American bishops condemned the buildup for nuclear war.

Calling on terminology from social ecology and organizational theory, one might regard the outcomes to date as an example of partial isomorphism (Hawley 1968; Hannan and Freeman 1978). The Catholic Church imitated its social milieu by incorporating structural forms (wider collaboration) and values (self-determination, tolerance, freedom of conscience) that matched predominant structures and values of the surrounding environment. At the same time, the isomorphism was only partial, as the Church fell short of totally embracing these structures and values. At least in the United States, for example, the use of participative structures has been quite limited,[1] and the pope still reigns as a kind of monarch. Even in the worldwide Church, not least in the Vatican curia itself, wider participation has been limited. Vaillancourt (1980) and Nichols (1981) note the apparent collegiality and participative format of the post–Vatican II congresses of laity and the synod dealing with family, but in actuality, they report, the traditional Church bureaucrats are still in charge.

We call the accommodation contested to signify several layers of struggle. Theologians and others battle over the degree to which the Church should adapt itself to the modern world (Gilkey 1975; McSweeney 1980; Dulles 1977). Debate over the Hartford Appeal reflected this struggle,[2] as did the Church sanctions leveled against such theologians as Teilhard de Chardin, Hans Küng, and Edward Schillebeeckx.[3] The early post–Vatican II era even saw a generalized contest between theologians, who tended to be more progressive, and the relatively conservative bishops, especially in the United States. An authority battle or power struggle has flourished since the Second Vatican Council, as bishops and pope have often tried to restrain progressive members, especially clergy, from becoming too secular in dress, life-style, ritual, and political activity (Seidler 1981). There is another power struggle over Church accommodation. Traditionalists, following Bishop LeFevre, believe that official Catholicism has capitulated to secularism and proclaim themselves the true Catholics (McSweeney 1980). Finally, the 1970s saw an internal battle over the independent power of charismatic Catholics (ibid.). These battles have erupted over the degree of accommodation that is appropriate for the Church.

In addition, the outcome of *aggiornamento* has been far from inevitable, as the single term *accommodation* might imply. Changes were disputed at every step along the way. To remember the drama and suspense, one need only recall the attempts by the Vatican bureaucracy to undermine aggiornamento, the pendulum swings at the Vatican Council, the key actions of cardinals such as Lienart of France, whose early council motion for a recess allowed for broader representation on the many commissions—thereby giving aggiornamento a fighting chance (Brown 1969:162)—the famous Frings-Ottaviani exchange,[4] and the behind-the-scences politicking of theologians (Brown 1969; Rynne 1967). One should also remember the key role played by Pope Paul VI in allowing aggiornamento to proceed and the icy waters thrown on much of it by Pope John Paul II. The process of change has had its cliff-hangers, its ups and downs, its power struggles.

This power-contending emphasis (Snyder and Tilly 1972) suggests the importance of key actors. Certain contenders for power strongly shaped the timing, direction, and speed of the Church's adjustment to the modern world. Without Pope John XXIII, Cardinals Frings and Lienart, and others, there might have been no updating of the Catholic Church at that point in history. A theory of accommodation, to be realistic, seems to need supplementing by the theory of groups contending for power and leaders who would support and manipulate situations to promote or resist change.

In the Catholic case, power contention seems to follow a pattern described by many authors: the major protagonists are often members of an elite (Pareto 1935; Snyder and Tilly 1972). Yet, as in other great upheavals, the common person, or laity, has played an important supportive role. In both charismatic and traditionalist movements, lower-level Catholics have attempted to help chart the meaning of aggiornamento (see McSweeney 1980).

Lay Catholics have also challenged pastors and bishops over school closings, financial accountability, charismatic practices, and other issues salient to them (see *National Catholic Reporter*, passim). Nevertheless, contention for power seems almost by definition to involve mostly upper-level members, those with the most power to lead the Church or define its role.

The Inadequacy of Delegitimation. Delegitimation of traditional authority is a very important aspect of the transformation (Hebblethwaite 1975; Gilkey 1975; McSweeney 1980). The new structures meant the demise of the monolith, the undercutting of an authoritarian style of leadership. New interpretations of scripture and doctrine helped to erode a blind and rigid obedience. Such new structures and interpretations, along with the new emphasis on freedom of conscience and free inquiry, facilitated the delegitimation of traditional authority.

Delegitimation of such authority seemed to occur as a byproduct of larger processes. Gilkey (1975:45ff.) sees the lessening of Church authority as an important consequence of modernization, not as the main event. The larger processes included accommodation to the milieu, with rational thinking and freedom gaining in prominence. In addition, the accommodation meant incorporating many other bases of decision making such as science, technology, psychology, and non-Catholic mysticism, all of which partially undercut traditional authority.

Yet, the concept of delegitimation is much too limited and negative. It neglects the positive side of the coin—the increased emphasis on other forms of authority within the Church. For example, participative or consultative authority increased with the new structures. Rational authority also expanded because of increased secular and specialized knowledge within the Church, as ecclesiastical leaders supported their planning and guidance with knowledge gained from economics, psychology, and administrative science. Perhaps most important, charismatic authority of nonelite Church members grew by leaps and bounds, especially through the Pentecostal movement.

Finally, the term *delegitimation* seems to add a note of finality or linearity that goes beyond present evidence. Traditional, even supernaturally based, authority (see Gilkey 1975) still appears to permeate a large portion of Catholicism today. A 1983 Gallup poll showed that Pope John Paul II was the second most admired man (*Emerging Trends*, March 1983), a finding that hardly seems plausible under a delegitimation hypothesis or even a purely rational foundation of authority. Greeley (1977) reported extremely high ratings by Catholics of pope and parish priests, along with other signs of loyalty to the church, despite the loss of legitimacy on such doctrinal matters as papal infallibility and the eternal punishment of sinners. Delegitimation is only a partial explanation at this point, and it may even be largely a transitional phenomenon.

In sum, the Catholic Church of the twentieth century has undergone such basic change in official self-understanding, religious behavior, ritual practice, and orientation to the world, that the transition has been called revolutionary (Brown 1969: Pelikan 1983; Ellis 1969). Catholicism has generally accommodated to its surrounding milieu, largely by incorporating contemporary structures (such as broad participation) and principles (such as freedom of conscience), and by building on the advances of science (as in biblical criticism). Yet the accommodation has been neither complete nor automatic nor peaceful; it has been partial and conflict-laden. It arose in conflict and progressed through a power struggle in which dominant forces of liberalism won major victories. Currently, the struggle continues among forces that are attempting to control the direction the Church will take in the future. This constellation of events will be called contested accommodation.

Aggiornamento as Process

Enough has already been said about *aggiornamento*, or updating. John XXIII wished to allow the church to speak contemporary language, but what constitutes the process? Evolutionary updating, religious reconstruction, and power contention are focal concepts. Evolutionary theorists seem to focus on the process and form of change.

Evolutionary processes, whether occurring in organizations or whole societies, include internally generated upgrading (Parsons 1966; Lenski and Lenski 1987) and social selection (Lenski and Lenski 1987), enhancing the probability of survival. Internally generated upgrading distinguishes evolution from changes introduced by simple diffusion or outside coercion. Though outside pressures may trigger internal mechanisms, in evolution the real causes of change are generated internally. At the societal level, major internal mechanisms are invention (ibid.), a value change (Parson 1966), and differentiation (Eisenstadt 1964). In the Catholic case, invention seems to be the main analogue (see below), though value change and differentiation also occur.

Social selection is the analogue of natural selection. The fittest organizations, those with updated technologies and structures that can articulate with the social milieu, will have the best chance of survival. Evolutionary processes imply the importance of successful interaction between an organization and its social environment.

Evolutionary updating implies a special form or pattern. Here, that pattern is a movement from structures and values that typify a less technologically advanced (Lenski and Lenski 1987) or less differentiated (agrarian) society (Eisenstadt 1964) to those most often found in more advanced or more differentiated (industrial) societies and organizations. Participative structures and self-determination are most characteristic of contemporary industrialized societies (Lenski and Lenski 1987), and they have developed over a long period of time (Greeley 1973). In addition, cooperation and the ecumenical spirit seem partially to be demanded by the contemporary small-world phenomenon created by rapid communications and transportation. Participative decision making in the Church, freedom of conscience, and ecumenism may be considered elements of updating that enhance the Church's articulation with its social environment.

Yet the Catholic Church incorporated participative structures and contemporary values only according to the reintegrations or inventions of theologians and other religious thinkers, and only after long decades of resistance. In addition, contemporary values and structures were only partially accepted; for example, all the democratic structures take the form of advisory boards, not legislative bodies. The major impetus to change seems to have come from theological and scholarly inventions, the new combinations of old and new sociocultural elements (White 1949; Lenski and Lenski 1987).

Evolutionary processes appear to operate differently on religious institutions than on whole societies. In the case of Catholicism, the embracing of structures of modern societies occurred rather emphatically in the last half of the twentieth century, long after such structures were incorporated at the societal level. Apparently, the accommodations made by religious institutions and other organizations, by which they incorporate structures compatible with modernity, occur (if at all) whenever the internal dynamics and other circumstances of each organization allow. Organizational response seems the key factor (McSweeney 1980), not technology (Lenski and Lenski 1987; White 1949) or differentiation (Parsons 1966; Eisenstadt 1964). Organizational change proceeds throughout a society in hit-and-miss fashion, affecting first one segment and then another.

In the Catholic case, a double principle seems to have operated. In temporal terms, these imitative changes were derivative and secondary; that is, they occurred after Western democracies took on the traits. In its own history, however, Catholicism was propelled forward by internal forces of change. This change was anything but derivative; the religious reconstruction involved a unique configuration of structures and values hammered out over a long period by Catholic theologians and others. In addition, the changes were more than passive settling into a secular culture. They appear to be the consequence of internal pressures that bubbled to the surface long after they were developed and encouraged by progressive segments of the Church. These shifts were initiated partly by cultural and environmental factors, such as urbanization, rationalization, and secular scholarship, but when transformed into the inner life of the Church they took on a life of their own and became dynamic forces for change.

Looking more closely at the Catholic Church itself, one might note processes of religious reconstruction. Theologians have been engaged heavily in it, especially since the Council, but before it as well. Many writers (Dulles 1974, 1977; McBrien 1969, 1973, 1981, 1982; Küng 1976; Gilkey 1975) reflect attempts to capture the essence of reconstruction (Wallace 1956)—a coherent merger of contemporary and traditional religious elements, coalesced into a new vision of Catholicism.

Key processes—environmental penetration, religious erosion, and ideological reconstruction—in part elaborate this reconstruction, the new paradigm sought by the Church, and in part explain why and how it occurred.

A changing world affected Catholicism during the late nineteenth century and the first sixty years of the twentieth century. Technological developments in transportation and communication brought Africa, Asia, and other missionary lands into more direct and immediate consciousness (Dillenberger and Welch 1954). Archaeological investigations were incorporated into biblical interpretations (Vawter 1956; McKenzie 1956, 1979). Medical advances and contraceptives affected longevity and sexual possibilities. Participation in education and suffrage increased; economic advances were made; urban problems grew (see Lenski and Lenski 1987). The values of self-fulfillment, liberty, and equality expanded gradually throughout the world (Bell 1973; Janowitz 1978; Lenski and Lenski 1987). These and other socioenvironmental forces had a major impact on the consciousness of Catholicism.

Environmental penetration had consequences. On the other hand, speedier transportation and communication aided missionary activity by improving access to foreign lands. Archaeological discoveries often confirmed events reported in the Bible. On the other hand, this penetration also presented challenges. Scientific advances challenged the literal interpretations of biblical accounts, such as the six days of creation (Vawter 1956). Many factors, including increased education, contraceptives, knowledge of population problems, and the value of fulfillment, all helped erode the apparent obedience to traditional church encouragement of large families and opposition to birth control (Noonan 1965). The new emphasis on individual self-fulfillment (Greeley 1973; Bellah 1985; Yankelovich 1981; Bell 1976), along with education and middle-class living, undermined many traditional Catholic values. Consequently, many aspects of American Catholicism were eroded: absolutism, blind obedience, centralized authority, and the hierarchic underpinnings (Greeley 1973).

Finally, the new context generated an array of new ideas. Because of environmental penetration, almost everything Catholic, from missionary activities to sexual norms, appeared in new light. Because of new challenges to traditional Catholicism, scholars looked for new ways to conceptualize the Church. Catholic thinkers were catapulted to ideological reconstruction by the wealth of new ideas available to them (White 1949) and the momentum triggered by the undermining of traditional understandings, combined with a desire to preserve a viable Catholicism (Dulles 1974, 1977; McBrien 1973).

Ideological reconstruction occurred in various ways. Theologians advanced a religious version of secular values and systems, such as consultativeness or a search for community. They simply borrowed terms from social science to expand religious understandings, or they examined contemporary challenges in light of the values and structures of early Christianity.

Ideological reconstruction appears to be a long process of debate and refinement, as noted by the following example. In 1931 the Catholic ecclesiologist, Arnold Rademacher, applied Toennies' categories, *gemeinschaft* and *gesellschaft*, to the Church (Dulles 1974:44). French theologians Yves Congar and Jerome Hamer discussed the Church as community or communion (ibid.:45). In some of this discussion, the long-standing definition of Church offered by Robert Bellarmine, underscoring the institutional side of Church, was expressly rejected. Thus new ideas emerged to replace the old. Yet there ensued a long refinement and debate over which term best represented the theological reality—the mystical body of Christ, championed by Pope Pius XII in the encyclical *Mystici Corporis Christi* (1943), or the people of God, the cornerstone of the Vatican II document on the church (Abbott 1966). Should institutional aspects be emphasized to the same degree as community aspects? Should the relation to Christ be specified more clearly, as in the term *body of Christ*, or should the fellowship of believers be noted more emphatically, as in *the people of God?* (See Dulles 1974 for an extended discussion of this matter.) The growth of participative institutions (a contemporary phenomenon) apparently influenced this discussion, and it entered the writings of many theologians (Küng 1976; Dulles 1974; McKenzie 1966; McBrien 1973). New ideas and controversy produced refinements, and the great traditions—Bible and the community context of early Christianity— played a part in the development of new understandings.

Ideological ferment occurred in many realms of thought before the Vatican Council. The Social Gospel and a growing social science merged with biblical and ethical scholarship to produce the great social encyclicals, from Pope Leo XIII's *Rerum Novarum* in 1891 to Pope John XXIII's *Mater et Magistra* in 1961. The eucharist and the whole secular world were brought together in Teilhard's *The Divine Milieu* (1960). Worship and citizen participation merged as the liturgical movement promoted the vernacular and increased participation from the pew (see Ellis 1969:136–138).

Since the Vatican Council, ideological reconstruction has continued and multiplied. Most notable have been theological attempts to integrate the divine and the human. Karl Rahner (1961, 1969) interpreted sin, grace, and redemption with insights from contemporary philosophy. Hans Küng (1976) developed a theology "from the ground up" (that is, based on human experience). In McBrien's view (1969), the existential approach has become dominant in theology, in contrast with the Ptolemaic theories of the past. Dulles (1977) approved the situationist theory of theology rather than the logical approach of the past. Schillebeeckx (1963) used contemporary notions of symbols to interpret the sacraments.

Ideological reconstruction constituted a tremendous output of energy aimed at redirecting the Church. Apparently, the immediate goal of many was to bring consistency between theology and the contemporary world. Different theologians concentrated on different aspects of the religious realm— worship, doctrine, social action. At first their separate activities remained somewhat isolated; yet eventually their visions of a reformed church coalesced into a more generalized intellectual movement for change within the Catholic Church, especially after Pope John XXIII made possible fresh ideas and reform. (For a detailed discussion of this movement for change, see Seidler 1979b.)

Ideological reconstruction helped to provide the momentum for change. It presented fresh visions, images of a church consistent with contemporary understandings, and practical solutions to the felt restriction of the traditional church. Through it, energy for consistency became a powerful force for change.

This religious reconstruction has been largely a segmentary vision, not a unified or completed *Summa Theologica*. Some aspects, such as the new decree on freedom of conscience, were adopted at the Vatican Council, but only after a council battle and after long years of reflection by such theologians as American Jesuit John C. Murray. Other ideas, such as new understandings of creation or eucharist, gradually suffused the Catholic Church but never fully conquered the minds of many Catholics. In short, there is no universal acceptance of a common Catholic theology (see Küng 1976; Tracy 1981).

There are several brands of ideological reconstruction, all vying for ascendancy within Catholicism. The most prominent, described above, was basically ratified by the Second Vatican Council. Other reconstructions include traditionalist Catholicism, whose vision of the ideal church is that espoused at the Council of Trent (McSweeney 1980), and charismatic Catholicism, which encourages liturgical reform via Pentecostalism and communal living but discourages social activism, emphasizing primarily a concern for personal morality (ibid.).[5]

Even within the reconstructing mainstream there are competing formulations and emphases. One emphasis, perhaps symbolized by Daniel Berrigan and the activist Catholics, might be called political Catholicism (ibid.). An even more radical emphasis, which seeks more rapid and more basic changes in authority structure (Davis 1967; Ruether 1975, 1977), may be called antiinstitutional Catholicism. Still the main reconstruction remains, in our observation and research, an updated or contemporary Catholicism—a general emphasis on reformulating to retain the essence of Catholicism while accommodating to the contemporary scene.

The days before Vatican II were filled with attempts by church officials to limit or exclude environmental penetration. Leo XIII in 1879 and Pius X in 1907 issued encyclicals to counteract or condemn modernism. Pius X demanded that all clergy take an oath against modernism—a practice that remained in effect until the 1960s (Meyer and Albright 1987). The Holy Office and the *Index of Forbidden Books* continued to be effective tools against secularism. In the 1940s and 1950s, frequent warnings were issued about the dangers of attending secular universities, where, it was said, sciences were not presented in the proper religious framework, and faith often withered.

In one period, which reached its height in 1912–1913, Catholic integrists organized in Rome to lead the attack on liberalizing and modernizing Catholics (Aubert 1978:200–203). Integrists were zealots who believed in a strict adherence to all papal directives and traditional church teachings (ibid.:200). Organized by Monsignor Umberto Benigni and apparently with the knowledge of Pius X, they shaped a kind of ecclesiastical secret police. This international antimodernist network ran a campaign of denunciation, especially of theologians and biblical and Christian journals (ibid.:200–203; Poulat 1969a, 1969b; 1977). Called a witch hunt, its excesses generated strong opposition during the last days of Pius X (Aubert 1978:203).

As modernity impinged more heavily on the world, Catholic traditionalists fought against it with a heavy hand. Official reactionary policies of the Church of the late nineteenth and early twentieth centuries may rarely have reached the extremes of integrism, but fundamentalist policies endured until the Second Vatican Council (Brown 1969; Hennesey 1981). In this context, the council itself can be seen as a reaction to fundamentalism within the Church.

Post-council discussions have also endured an atmosphere of contention for power between liberal and traditional theologies. Liberals, soaring on the wings of Vatican II victories, pushed through a complete set of reforms in liturgy, sacramental understanding, ecumenical dialogue, and other areas. Though empowered to do so, they may have demanded too quick and too uniform a movement forward, e.g., biblical translations referring to Mary as the young girl instead of as virgin were said to be secularized. Traditionalists also complained that divine mystery was removed from the liturgy; they believed that the essence of Catholicism was diluted. Even the 1980s conflict between Jesuits and Pope John Paul II reflects the same power struggle. The Pope, in an unprecedented move, took over control of the Jesuits' transfer of leadership because the Jesuits had become too liberal (see *Time*:November 9, 1981).

In some ways the battle remains the same—conservatives and liberals contend over whose interpretation will prevail. Yet in other ways, the terms have changed. In the early twentieth century, the main question was, Shall the church allow any environmental penetration? Today the questions are, Assuming the legitimacy of environmental penetration and its endorsement in Vatican II documents, whose interpretations will prevail? Whose reconstruction of old and new elements will stand?

Chapter Four

Aggiornamento as a Social Movement

Social movements are generally defined as collective demands for change, or for resistance to change in some aspect of the social system, often dramatized by noninstitutionalized means (Gusfield 1968; Turner and Killian 1972; Vander Zanden 1960; Wilson 1973:8). Some of these movements are well organized and some are not, often depending on their developmental stage, but none is completely institutionalized or incorporated into the contemporary social structure. Social demands for change, when so incorporated and legitimated, often reside in other collective entities, such as political parties or interest groups.

Most social movements proceed, more or less, through four stages: laying the foundation, mobilization, legitimation, and implementation.

These headings have been distilled from the writing of various authors. This series of stages in not the only one or even the best; there are many other ways to summarize the phases of a movement. In addition, no "natural history" of a movement (Smelser 1963) or even a rigid life cycle (see Turner and Killian 1972:252 ff.) is implied. Furthermore, stage two need not precede stage three; the order may be reversed, or the two stages may occur simultaneously. In fact, as will be seen below, the example of the Catholic Church alone would help one discount any such rigid temporal interpretation. The stages listed here are intended only as an ideal typical model—a tool to help us understand what happened in Catholicism.

Stage one, laying the foundation, is characterized by structural strain (Smelser 1963) and by the development of usable communications networks (Freeman 1983:11), potential leadership, and key notions that later will become part of the accepted ideology of the movement. Most of these conditions were met by the minimovements and trends within Catholicism during the period before Vatican II.

During stage two, mobilization, several things occur. The issue of change becomes more public (Blumer 1971; Turner and Killian 1972:252ff.; Smelser 1963) as movement leaders emerge and the problems become more widely recognized. Along this line, a movement ideology becomes more coherent, as reflected by slogans, chants, symbols, and other simplifications (Lang and Lang 1978; Turner and Killian 1972:270; Smelser 1963). These outward signs suggest that many topics of change have coalesced into an overarching theme. The movement ideology is also articulated in some detail (Lang and Lang

1978:100; Wilson 1973), as the ideology now contains a diagnosis of the problem (Wilson 1973), a target for blame (Lang and Lang 1978:102), a prognosis and solution, and a rationale (Wilson 1973). Such movement developments help to accomplish the central feature of mobilization—namely, to employ a variety of people and tools that have the power to push the movement goals forward. This important phase in a social movement (ibid.:89) brings "the affected group into action" (Smelser 1963:17). The commitment of these affected people thus becomes a resource for the movement. Other resources include money and physically persuasive objects, organization, power, visibility, and legitimacy (McCarthy and Zald 1973, 1977; Tilly 1978; Gamson 1975; Bromley and Shupe 1979). In addition, mobilization often nourishes a latent or public countermovement (Mottl 1980). In this climate of movement and countermovement, each struggling for a wider constituency, resistance and confrontations often abound (Spector and Kitsuse 1973; Snyder and Tilly 1972). In Catholicism, mobilization of this type began during the Second Vatican Council and reached a high point during the late 1960s.

Stage three, legitimation, occurs when the appropriate governing body recognizes the issue and alters its approach, thus solving the problems articulated by spokepersons of the movement (Spector and Kitsuse 1973; Blumer 1971). During this period, the focus is especially on officials, as interest groups address the legislators in an attempt to educate and mobilize them, lobby in favor of the cause, and apply other political pressures to the officials. Continuity is maintained with the previous mobilization period. In stage three, however, the governing body recognizes the issue as worthy of official discussion and problem solving. The issue passes into official hands in many senses (Spector and Kitsuse 1973). This stage reflects official legitimation only; local authorities and the general population may still not recognize the issue or desire to make any changes. Often, however, the general population has recognized the problem sufficiently to force local officials to address it.

Stage four, implementation, follows logically from official legitimation (ibid.). In this period, officials translate the new ideology into legislation and practical programs and try to enforce them. The new laws meet the challenge of feasibility and public acceptance. During this stage, officials presumably educate the people to accept the new laws by explaining their meaning and showing their legitimacy.

Conflicts may arise in several ways. Progressive leaders may push people too fast toward the new ideas, or conservative leaders may drag their feet. Reaction by the masses—riding the new wave too enthusiastically or refusing to comply—may also cause conflicts. Finally, movement devotees often note that the original movement goals have been coopted or achieved only partially through this long process. At this point, they often renew the movement in the hopes of hitting the mark more squarely next time (ibid.), and so the stages begin again.

How well do these stages illuminate Catholicism? In what time periods did the movement take place?

It is assumed that similar movement periods occured in many other countries. Indeed, an examination of the leading theologians cited in this country shows that ideas of change were shared cross-nationally. In addition, precursor movements, such as the biblical and liturgical movements, began in Europe and diffused to the United States and elsewhere. Movement ideology, leadership, and organization were heavily shared cross-nationally, and movement stages were roughly contemporaneous. Worldwide Catholicism, especially Catholicism of the Western world, can be perceived with some modification, as proceeding through the stages described here.

These stages may not apply to segments of the Third World, behind the Iron Curtain, or in other exceptional settings. Such situations may have required local Catholic communities to put their energies elsewhere.

A word of caution: The exact cutoff points for the periods described below are somewhat arbitrary, but we suggest dates as rough dividing points between stages.

Backdrop for the Movement

During the long period from the closing of the First Vatican Council (1870) until Pope John XXIII called the Second Vatican Council (January 25, 1959), worldwide Catholicism seemed to be dominated by a siege mentality. It emphasized the papal infallibility proclaimed at Vatican I (1869–1870) and marshaled its forces to resist modernity (Cogley 1973; Ellis 1963). Particularly in the United States, the Church seemed to be caught up in a war against liberalism (Cogley 1973:185ff.).

During that period of almost a century, tension was never completely absent from the Catholic Church (Reichley 1986). In some cases it was official Church policy pitted against a number of Catholic communities and/or pastoral practices. Other conflicts developed between contemporary church practices and reform movements. The sporadic density of critical voices and the gathering countertrends reflected these tensions and illustrated the general structural strain of this period (see chapter 2).

There were hints of the movement to come from 1870 to 1920. In this premovement period before and after the turn of the century, various tensions existed, which in retrospect were clear predictors of change.

There was the majority-minority conflict at the First Vatican Council itself, which continued in somewhat abated form in the years following the council.

As some indication of the division over the definition of papal infallibility, Ellis (1963:186–187) summarized the crucial trial-balloon voting on July 13, 1870. Of forty-five American bishops, fifteen voted for the decree, four voted against, five approved with reservation, and twenty-one absented themselves. Later, fifty-five bishops from around the world sent a formal protest to the pope, explaining their absence from the final vote on infallibility; they preferred absence to voting against the pope on infallibility (ibid.:187). For that final vote, twenty American bishops were absent (some had already departed for home), and one voted against the decree, and twenty-four voted in favor.

Afterward in the United States, the reaction to the council involved a severe struggle of conscience for many bishops (ibid.:188–189). Some bishops delayed their acceptance of the constitution *Pastor Aeternus*—in the case of Bishop Domenec of Pittsburgh, for as much as a year and a half. Much of the bishops' chagrin over the decree, according to Ellis (ibid.:189), was the council's failure to explore the bishops' role in church authority. The issue of authority remained at least under the table. Ninety years later, on the eve of the Second Vatican Council, many bishops (successors to the participants at Vatican I) still wanted this issue to be aired.

Perhaps a more general tension arose between Vatican and Catholic scholars—bishops, academics, or others—on the attitude toward the contemporary world. During the days of preparation for the council, priest-theologian James A. Corcoran of the Charleston Diocese, theological representative of the American bishops to Vatican I, wrote from Rome to his friend, Archbishop Martin Spalding of Baltimore. Referring to the intent of the Vatican theologians, he said, "I believe the fundamental principles of our (American and common sense) political doctrine are condemned" (cited in Ellis 1963: 173). Regarding Alisio Cardinal Bilio, president of the dogmatic commission on which the American bishops served, he wrote: "Like too many of the rest, he (Bilio) has never looked boldly in the face of the world in which we live and to which we are coming" (ibid.:175).

When Bishop Spalding summarized the attitude of the American bishops for theologian Corcoran, again before the council began, he wrote carefully but clearly. Infallibility would be hard to limit. He wrote that freedom of worship, which was on the verge of condemnation, "is not only not censurable but commendable and the only thing practicable in countries like ours, England, Russia, etc. And so of the liberty of the press, and progress in the American and Anglo-Saxon sense, not in the Liberal European. There is a wide distinction and any attempt to confound things so wide apart would be wrong and nuatory, putting us in a false position, in fact, untenable." Spalding also thought that the proposed emphasis on the union of church and state was wholly impracticable, especially in the United States and half of Christendom (ibid.:174).

Ellis attributes the triumph of the pope and his Vatican theologians to several things. First, the definition of infallibility was the culmination of a whole century of centralizing tendencies (ibid.:188). Second, Rome lacked political realism: thus pope and Roman Curia did not comprehend the finality of the decline of absolute monarchies during the nineteenth century. In addition, Ellis maintains (ibid.:170), they confused philosophical liberalism with legitimate support of freedom of conscience, assembly, speech, and press. Third, "the Church was not able to marshal an array of first-class scholars such as the French Benedictines . . . and the Jesuit Bollandists . . . (of) the seventeenth century" (ibid.:168). In 1893 Wilifred Ward described typical nineteenth-century theological writings as "incredible and unsupported stories in history and extravagances in dogma . . . disparagement of scientific research . . . distrust of modern science and civilization" (ibid.). Regarding the generations captivated by Darwin's *Origin of Species* or Renan's *La Vie de Jesus*, there was no adequate official Church discussion.

The Roman mentality and the decrees of Vatican I gave support to those American Protestants who feared that if Catholics became a majority, the pope would demand an agreement with this country proclaiming the unity of church and state and abrogating the rights of non-Catholics. Many American bishops and theologians were upset at their predicament. As one member of the council minority of bishops said, the council majority "is composed of men who have not come into conflict with the unbelieving mind, or into contact with the intellectual mind of the time" (ibid.:184).

Soon after the council, tensions arose between Rome and some of the brightest American bishops, who were leading proponents of Americanism— a set of ideas exaggerated by monarchist opponents in France and condemned in 1899 by Pope Leo XIII (Greeley 1967:chap. 6; Cogley 1973:71–78). The foremost Americanist bishops were James Gibbons, John Ireland, John Keane, and John Lancaster Spalding. Greeley (1967:151) calls their collective thrust "a brilliant and imaginative campaign to finally Americanize the Catholic Church in the United States," a goal that was only partially successful. Greeley (ibid.) also says that "leaders of their splendor have not again appeared on the ecclesiastical scene."

To the Vatican, the Americanist crisis reflected a fundamental issue. Ahlstrom (1975:310) summarizes it in this way:

The very presence of the Roman Catholic church in the United States posed the bedrock question as to how a huge ecclesiastical institution, which had emerged from the wreck of the Roman Empire, slowly structured itself according to principles of canon law, consolidated its authority during fifteen centuries of tumultuous European history, and defined its faith at the Councils of Trent and Vatican I, was to be regulated in a pluralistic democratic state in which churches existed as one kind of voluntary organization among others, and in which its members were scattered at random so far as their social, economic, and political relationships were concerned.

The phantom heresy (Cogley 1973:74; Greeley 1967:151), a theological extension by Vaticanists of practical approaches taken in the American context, has been summarized to include the following ideas: the superiority of action over contemplation; the notion that the operations of the Holy Spirit on the individual transcend the need for sacraments and ecclesiastical authority; and the proposal that the Church should adjust or even radically change its basic teachings in order to accommodate modern science (Cogley 1973:73). Although Leo XIII did not accuse any particular person of holding these beliefs, he did use the word *Americanism*, suggesting a continental location of these ideas and leaving a bitter taste with some Americans. As Ahlstrom notes (1975:316), Americanist prelates were basically traditional; and where they were liberal, except on the church-state issue, their liberalism tended to be practical, not doctrinal.

Prominent American Catholics also promoted the modernist movement, though this program of church reform was largely known as a European movement (Appleby 1984). As Gannon put it, "The American priest . . . displayed a surprising intellectual activity . . . [though] daunted politically, socially, and ecumenically by the condemnation (of Americanism)." Intellectually, the priest "ranged farther and more freely than he ever had before, seeking to know whatever was true in the relationships between religion and the new physical and historical sciences" (Gannon 1971:338–339). Catholic authors published articles sympathetic to the new modernist ideas in progressive Catholic publications, such as *Catholic World, Catholic University Bulletin*, and the *American Catholic Quarterly Review*. These authors included Catholic Professors Pace, Lambert, Shahan, Elliot, and Kerby (Appleby 1984:15). The Roman Catholic seminary at Dunwoodie, New York, even revised its curriculum to reflect the new thinking.

Modernism overlapped the ideas of Americanism and fared no better than Americanism; it was condemned in 1907 by Pius X. Key topics included a Catholic interpretation of Darwinism; theology as evolving; reconciling evolutionary theory and creation; the need for a new apologetic to address the nonrational side of human beings; and the need for the church to embrace democracy (Appleby 1984; Kurtz 1986).

These controversies polarized American Catholics into the liberal and conservative wings that still exist (McAvoy 1969). The condemnations quieted theological speculation on the American experience, as theologians apparently sought to avoid being suspected of heresy (Cogley 1973:75). Instead, they turned to "developing know-how and letting theory be" (Ong 1957:21–22).

One can easily see that these nineteenth-century controversies were precursors of the conflict and changes of Catholicism in the 1960s, especially in the United States. Americanists, modernists, and the minority at Vatican I endorsed (with reservations) the modern world, modern science, democracy, freedom of conscience, and ecumenism, but these attempts to reconcile the Church and modernity were aborted.

Some writers have said that the period between the two Vatican councils was quite calm within the American Catholic Church (Cogley 1973:71). Yet there were constant reminders of the gap between official Catholicism and progressive thinking. The continuous activities of the Paulists, who carried forward Isaac Hecker's vision, promoting understanding of non-Catholics and asserting that belief must be given freely and not constrained (Ellis 1963: 261–269; O'Brien 1983; Langlois 1983), were a living contradiction of the more dominant authoritarian viewpoint. Then, too, the ever-present experience of living under a political system in which religion flourished challenged the reigning European assumptions that favored a union of church and state.

In the nineteenth century, the American Catholic Church also practiced consultative government, as shown in the provincial and plenary councils of Baltimore; there, bishops set policies for the American Church, subject, of course, to Rome's approval. Greeley (1967:30) notes that such collegiality among church leaders was unmatched anywhere in the world. As is commonly known, the Second Vatican Council came around to this policy for national churches in the 1960s. Here, the American way was a precursor of later changes.

The method of selecting bishops was also an American tradition (ibid.: 30-31). Starting with Bishop John Carroll in the late eighteenth century, the tradition later took the form of votes by bishops of a province (region of the country) or by archbishops of the country. An attempt to introduce grass-roots participation brought the *terna* system into play (ibid.:31), which gave certain diocesan directors and consultants the right to submit a list of three names to Rome for consideration as bishop of a vacant diocese. This privilege was abrogated in 1916 but was reinstated at Vatican II.

The period between Vatican I and the end of the First World War was filled with misunderstandings and conflicts between Rome and the Americanizers (ibid.:22ff.; Reichley 1986). According to Greeley (1967:24), this situation was inevitable, as the conservative officials of the Roman Curia could not understand the American scene. In addition, many European clergy were doubly upset when it was suggested that America provide the model for the universal church (Cogley 1973:73).

Precursor Movements and Trends

In the four decades before the Second Vatican Council, 1920–1959, the Church in America showed signs of moving beyond the state of tension and sporadic jousts with Rome. Several minimovements, often partly endorsed by the official Church and always at least partly spawning activities that broke with tradition, were underway. These included a liturgical movement, a closely related vernacular movement, a drive to implement the social gospel, and the new flowering of Scriptural scholarship. They constituted movement stage one, laying the groundwork.

Such movements of discovery and renewal became especially profound, according to Ahlstrom (1975:525), because of the adversities of war, economic distress, and tumultuous social change. "One may even speak of the adversities of affluence" (ibid.) during that era. Certainly, the major disruptions of life that occurred during the four decades preceding the Second Vatican Council helped inspire some of the movements and trends discussed below.

The liturgical movement was an attempt to revitalize Catholic participation and understanding in worship, especially at the Mass (Ellis 1969:136). In the early part of this century, few Catholics had missals, the appropriate books to follow the rites and prayers of the Mass (ibid.:137). Often, Catholics in the pews recited the rosary or read other devotional material while the priest performed his separate act in Latin at the altar. The liturgical movement sought to move Catholics from this parallel praying to more meaningful and direct participation in the drama of the Mass itself. This corresponded to the movement already underway in Europe (ibid.:136).

The liturgical movement traces its origin in this country to the 1920s. During that decade, Catholic priests began writing articles and books to help the laity understand the communal aspects of worship. In November 1926, Father Virgil Michel, O.S.B., a leader of the movement and a Benedictine of St. John's Abbey in Collegeville, Minnesota, began a monthly journal devoted to the liturgy called *Orate Fratres*, and later *Worship*. In time, the dialogue Mass (in Latin) was introduced and created a demand for missals, which jumped from an estimated circulation of fifty thousand in 1929 to several million by 1952 (ibid.:136–137). In addition, the School of Liturgical Music, founded by Pius X in 1916 at Manhattanville College in New York, fostered the serious study of Gregorian chant. In 1940 a series of annual liturgical weeks began, whereby interested parties could exchange ideas about all aspects of worship.

Though Northern European countries had initiated the vigorous liturgical movement, it also grew in the United States "from a timid trickle into a mighty tide." In addition to Father Michel, other American pioneers of the 1920s and 1930s were Gerald Ellard, S.J., H. A. Reinhold, and Martin Hellriegel. Their initiatives had tremendous consequences; the Liturgical Conference grew "from a courageous nucleus to countless thousands of members" in a period of twenty-five years (McNaspy 1966:133).

This strong liturgical movement had at least two consequences. First, a spinoff vernacular movement grew among many of those interested in liturgical reform. Second, the movement generated solid scholarly underpinnings, especially the vast research of Joseph Jungmann, S.J., and other historians.

Liturgical renewal was addressed early during the Second Vatican Council, largely because of the prior flowering of this movement. As McNaspy (1966: 133-134) puts it, "The magnificent text proposed to the Council Fathers was, accordingly, no haphazard or improvised sketch, but the fruit of serious preliminary work."

A look at the Constitution on the Sacred Liturgy, adopted in 1963, will indicate its continuity with the liturgical movement discussed above. The constitution stated, "In the restoration and promotion of the sacred liturgy, full and active participation of all the people is the aim to be considered before all else" (Abbott 1966:144, n. 14). It also encouraged the extended use of the vernacular in all liturgical rites (ibid.:150, n. 36) and the adaptation of other contemporary cultural expressions, such as local musical genius (n. 119). In addition, it emphasized reform for the sake of meaningfulness (n. 50) and return to basics, especially by making Scripture more central (nn. 7, 24, 35, 51) and underscoring the basic elements of the faith (n. 111), while downplaying devotions, images, and feasts of saints (n. 125). This document broke with the dominant practices of Catholics of the preceding centuries and followed a path similar to that taken by the sixteenth-century Reformers (Pelikan 1966).

In the 1930s and 1940s, there was an upsurge of social action by American Catholics. Activist editor Francis P. Lally (1962:48) called the 1930s the first decade of widespread Catholic social consciousness in America. Catholic social activists turned their efforts to labor and social legislation and helped pass the social reform laws of the New Deal (Hennesey 1981:259).

Though in earlier decades, especially the 1920s, Catholics retreated from social action and even obstructed it—shelving their own bishops' plan for social reform (ibid.:245; Abell 1960:228)—still some ground was broken before 1930. In 1919 the National Catholic Welfare Council (later changed to "Conference") came into being, with a Department of Social Action. An invention of American Catholics, this organization was intended to represent the American bishops and to coordinate activities of the American Catholic Church. In 1919 the NCWC issued a pamphlet, written by social activist Monsignor John

A. Ryan, entitled, "Social Reconstruction: A General Review of the Problem and Survey of Remedies." This tract triggered charges of socialism by the National Association of Manufacturers, and many Catholics fought it vigorously. Nevertheless, eleven of its twelve proposals were endorsed by the New Deal and ultimately became law. It remains a key document of the social philosophy of the American Catholic Church (Ellis 169:140–145).

Other agencies also prepared for social action. The National Council of Catholic Women helped educate social workers in the 1920s, and after 1921 it supported the National Catholic School of Social Service in Washington (Hennesey 1981:245). The National Catholic Rural Life Conference was founded in 1923; it devoted itself to the welfare of rural Catholics, receiving the cooperation of other Catholic agencies, such as the Church Extension Society and the American Board of Catholic Missions (ibid. 1969:245). In addition, the Catholic Conference on Industrial Problems organized workers, although it had little success with management (ibid.).

In the thirties, Catholic social activism flourished. That decade spawned new Catholic social activities and a dramatic upswing in Catholic participation in organizations devoted to alleviating problems of the poor and of workers.

A great impetus for the Catholic turn to activism during the thirties was the 1931 encyclical of Pope Pius XI, *Quadragesimo Anno*, advocating social reconstruction. Along with the pain of unemployment and economic collapse experienced by Roman Catholics and others, this encyclical stimulated a resurgence of social thought and action among American Catholics (Ahlstrom 1975:515).

Highlights of the Catholic social activism of the thirties include the Catholic Worker movement, started by Dorothy Day, the Association of Catholic Trade Unionists, and *Commonweal* magazine (Cogley 1973:chap. 7). Such activities were often controversial, but they expanded and drew substantial followings.

Dorothy Day, a socialist turned Catholic, set out to refute the Communist charge that Catholicism was indifferent to the social aspirations of labor (Abell 1960:246ff.; Ahlstrom 1975:517). In her monthly paper, *Catholic Worker*, she gave extremely liberal interpretations of papal social doctrines and proposed a broad program for social reconstruction. Her lay apostolate, inspired by the Catholic Worker movement (which she led), opened houses of hospitality for the poor and the unemployed in thirty cities. Believing in the priesthood of all Christians in an era of Catholic clerical domination, she also counteracted the inhumanity and depersonalization of modern industry (Ahlstrom 1975: 518). Her Catholic Workers, like Communists, "engaged in tireless indoctrination of the poor . . . (they) practiced voluntary poverty, combined manual and intellectual labor, and performed works of mercy in a highly personalized manner" (Abell 1960:247). Dorothy Day founded a farming commune in 1936, participated in strikes, and elaborated a Christian philosophy of labor, opposing both the Communist approach and that of the reactionary Christian Front.

The Association of Catholic Trade Unionists, formed in 1937 to help Catholics function in the labor movement, endorsed the CIO and responsible industrial unionism (Ahlstrom 1975:518). It inspired dozens of Catholic labor schools and gave Catholicism new prominence in labor (ibid.).

Commonweal was established as an independent journal in 1924 to provide the increasingly educated Catholic " with sophisticated comment on the affairs of the day that would reflect a humanist tradition handed down from the Middle Ages" (Cogley 1973:176). Run by lay Catholics and respected by its peers in secular journalism, it gained a wide non-Catholic readership. Until the 1960s, it remained the primary outlet for the liberal Catholic lay voice.

During the 1930s when *Commonweal* adopted bold social positions, it received a barrage of criticism for labeling the popular Father Charles E. Coughlin a demagogue and for refusing to endorse the Franco cause in Spain (ibid.:176–178). *Commonweal* Catholicism also proposed a general social philosophy, believing that the industrial order could gradually be made compatible with a personalist Christian democracy. Drawing on the papal encyclicals, it proposed changing competition to cooperation: laborers would form unions, share in profits, and participate in the management of industries, which were to be decentralized (Ahlstrom 1975:519). Although often criticized roundly by Catholics, *Commonweal* suggested solutions that were controversial at the time but were often adopted quietly by the wider Catholic community (Cogley 1973:177–178).

Commonweal's publishers, the Calvert Associates, also inspired the formation of a Catholic League for Social Justice to study and apply the eonomic teachings of Pope Pius XI. The league was approved officially by Cardinal Hayes of New York in 1932. Its leader, Michael O'Shaughnessy, an oil executive and industrial publicist, gathered a small but influential number of Catholic business leaders to work toward reforming the social order in line with the pope's social encyclical. O'Shaughnessy was a powerful speaker for the cause, and his proposals were endorsed by such Catholic organizations as the Holy Name Society in Chicago, the National Council of Catholic Men, and the National Catholic Alumni Federation (Abell 1960:242–246).

Beyond the highlights of the 1930s, Catholics made other forays into the social sphere. Labor priests counseled union members in their relations with management and fellow workers (Ellis 1969:146). Catholic ruralists suggested that farm workers should have a share in the land (Hennesey 1981:264). In some places, Catholic bishops and other Church leaders acted early in the movement for racial equality. In 1936, for example, Catholic University opened its doors to blacks, eighteen years before the Supreme Court ended school segregation. In St. Louis, Raleigh, and Washington, D.C., bishops also prefigured the Supreme Court's decision, thus "anticipating the most enlightened public sentiment" (Ellis 1969:147–148).

These and other social activities suggest a new thrust in Catholicism. A significant and visible segment of Catholic leadership promoted its own version of the Social Gospel revival (see Ahlstrom 1975:412). Thus, a strong current of Catholic thought moved away from pietistic conformism and isolationism and into active engagement with the larger social world. Catholics in America were gaining maturity and self-confidence (Ellis 1969; Ahlstrom 1975; Reichley 1986), but this social awareness remained a minority sentiment among American Catholics (Hennesey 1981:269).

This movement reached theoretical fruition and fuller legitimacy at the Second Vatican Council. Throughout the completed documents, one notes the dominant place given to reforming the temporal world, whether in the constitution on laity, on the priesthood, or on ecumenism. In addition, the Pastoral Constitution on the Church in the Modern World, itself a breakthrough for Catholicism (Brown 1966), states that "the social life is not something added on to man." For this reason, "man's social nature makes it evident that the progress of the human person and the advance of society itself hinge on each other" (Article 25). The Church's official policy no longer condoned a religious individualism that avoided social issues.

One could trace the revolution in Catholic biblical scholarship to *Providentissimus Deus*, Pope Leo XIII's encyclical on biblical studies of 1893. Probably the strongest official momentum, however, came from Pius XII's 1943 encyclical *Divino Afflante Spiritu*. Not only could Catholic biblical scholars come out of the closet thereafter, but they soon stepped into the midst of the biblical renaissance that was prominent in Protestant scholarship during this period (Ahlstrom 1975:522; Kurtz 1986).

The Catholic Scriptural renaissance has several consequences. A whole range of critical questions was opened to research—questions already posed by Protestant scholars and questions raised naturally about previously declared theological definitions. For example, how does one reconcile the hierarchical authority of pope and bishops with the authority proposed in the New Testament (McKenzie 1966)? Is the term *transsubstantiation* consistent with biblical accounts of the Eucharist (de Baciocchi 1955; Powers 1967)? Can a profound biblical reflection cast light on our understanding of almost all aspects of faith: the centrality of Christ, religious freedom, Mariology, prayer, sacraments, the church, preaching, and so forth? Theologians are still addressing these concerns (Küng 1976; McBrien 1973, 1981; Dulles 1977).

Another consequence of the renewed biblical emphasis was the Bible movement, which reached out to the larger Catholic consituency. Father Pius Parsch, leader of the Bibelbewegung in Austria, was enormously influential in popularizing the use of the Bible in this country after World War II. In the United States, American bishops, such as Edwin V. O'Hara of Kansas City, and influential parish priests, such as Monsignor Hellriegel of Saint Louis, strongly promoted biblical preaching (Ahlstrom 1975:521). In addition, the liturgy movement promoted the Bible by its emphasis on the centrality of scripture.

Vatican II strongly endorsed the biblical perspective. One needs only to peruse the documents (Abbott 1966) to note the frequent Scriptural citations. More important, key definitions incorporated the new biblical perspective. The scholarship of the Bible movement bore fruit; for example, the Dogmatic Constitution on the Church conforms to solid biblical notions (Dulles, 1966). Accordingly, the bishops call the church the people of God (#4), the flock (#6), the body of Christ (#7), a community of faith (#8). They also speak of the liturgy as a function of a holy people, and not private functions (Constitution on the Sacred Liturgy, #26), incorporating the renewed biblical insight. The bishops state explicitly the importance of sacred scripture in the celebration of liturgy (#24); they justify ecumenical activity largely by recalling numerous biblical passages (Decree on Ecumenism, #2 and #3); they propose for imitation the early Christian communities, as reflected in the New Testament (Decree on the Appropriate Renewal of Religious Life, #15). In their Declaration of Religious Freedom, the bishops present a detailed biblical account of Christ's acceptance of such liberty (#11). Finally, biblical accounts of Apostolic authority clearly underlie the new notions of episcopal leadership (Decree on the Bishops' Pastoral Office in the Church, #1).

Three other American developments also contributed to the movement for change, expressed in the United States during and after the Second Vatican Council. These were the rediscovery of the Church, an enlivened historical consciousness, and an ecumenical longing.

The years before Vatican II brought Catholics to a new awareness or rediscovery of the corporate nature of the church and its status as an organic entity. Although this development overlapped with the liturgical and biblical movements, it was a distinct theological thrust as well, and it deserves separate treatment (Ahlstrom 1975:520–521).

In 1943 Pope Pius XII issued the encyclical *Mystici Corporis*, in which he developed the notion of the body of Christ, originally stated in the New Testament epistles of Paul. As Paul said, Christians are members one of another. In America, where individualistic conceptions of church were dominant, this corporate thinking was almost radical. The encyclical, following the thinking of nineteenth-century German theologian J. A. Moehler and twentieth-century scholar Karl Adam, had tremendous consequences. It was quoted everywhere in Catholic schools and pulpits, and it spurred the liturgical movement (ibid.:521).

One important outcome of the rediscovery of church was a new serious concern for the place of the laity (ibid.). Treatises on the laity blossomed, especially by European authors, but also by Americans (Congar 1957; de la Bedoyere 1961; Phillips 1955; Cushing 1960; Callahan 1963). Professor Leo R. Ward (1959:7) remarked that, except for the Church's emergence from the ghetto period, the new attitude toward laity was the most important new direction in contemporary American Catholicism. The lay apostolate came to be felt increasingly in social action, retreat centers, interracial relations, and local parishes (Ahlstrom 1975:521).

In fact, one could speak of a lay movement. Sources of lay vigor noted by Daniel Callahan (1963:105–111) included an ideology derived mainly from the mystical body concept, participation by laity in the late forties and early fifties in such organizations as the Christian Family Movement, Young Christian Workers, and Young Christian Students; increased lay education; and a perceived inconsistency between the freedom experienced inside and outside the Church. These and other factors contributed to increased lay involvement in church affairs and a demand for greater rights and responsibilities within the church. Such a movement came after the quiescent lay period of the early twentieth century. It reflected earlier vigorous lay orientations of the Americanist period, which had been repressed at the turn of the century (ibid.:chap. 3).

New writings on the church flourished (e.g., Suhard 1948; Congar 1960; Norris 1962). Constructed on a scriptural foundation (Norris 1962), they developed the ramifications of the new corporate thinking to a range of theological issues, including social action (Suhard 1948), the laity, authority, salvation, and other important topics (see Burns 1964).

The Second Vatican Council eventually incorporated this thinking, as seen by the numerous decrees in keeping with the corporate notions of church, such as the Dogmatic Constitution on the Church, the Pastoral Constitution on the Church in the Modern World, the Decree on the Apostolate of the Laity, and by related decrees on the liturgy, ecumenism, the missions, and Christian education (see Abbott 1966). Protestant commentators (e.g., Brown 1966; Wedel 1966), steeped in this orientation to church and laity, praised highly (with minor caveats) the council's incorporation of these notions.

After World War II, American Catholics turned noticeably toward serious historical research, heightening their awareness of the way in which "the past inheres as a vital reality in the present." This was a decided shift from the attitude of the early twentieth century; that era was dominated by the condemnation of modernism and Americanism, both of which movements aimed at historical understanding. The renewed concern with historical understandings was exemplified by the surge of interest in Teilhard's writings, especially *The Phenomenon of Man* (Teilhard 1965), which attempted a synthesis of theology and evolutionary theory, and by the popularity of John Henry Cardinal Newman's approach to the development of doctrine (Ahlstrom 1975:522). Newman's book, *An Essay on the Development of Christian Doctrine*, was first published at the time of his conversion to Catholicism in 1845 and proposed for his own judgment a set of evolutionary criteria for Christian doctrine (Newman 1960). In that era, the book was the object of suspicion by Catholic theologians, but by the 1940s a Newman cult had expanded from Europe to the United States and elsewhere; in the period immediately before the Second Vatican Council, Newman was read by Catholics for guidance, not for refutation (Weigel 1960:14–15).

This historical consciousness underlies prominent notions of Vatican II. As expounded in the documents of the council, the Church is a pilgrim Church, whose members can sin and which is in need of continuous reformation (Decree on Ecumenism, #3 and #6). Such concepts eradicated the image of the Church as the seamless and timeless robe of Christ and focused on the empirical Church moving through time (Brown 1967:123ff.). Thus, the council propelled Catholicism squarely into the arena of ecumenical discussion with Protestants who were long accustomed to thinking of the Church in historical terms (ibid.:chap. 7).

Among Protestants, the beneficial programs of the World Council of Churches, organized in 1948, and the "bold and imaginative speaking and writing of Protestant leaders like Eugene Carson Blake" deeply impressed religious-minded Americans. Among Catholics, Pope John XXIII, with his aim of Christian reunion, was extraordinarily influential in encouraging ecumenism (Ellis 1969:181). In addition, spreading secularization and other social problems moved Christian (and Jewish) communities to work together. The movements mentioned above (liturgy, Bible, social gospel) also brought together those of diverse faiths into cooperative efforts (see Ahlstrom 1975: 520–525).

As a result, American Catholics longed for a more ecumenical climate, especially after the long years of the defensive posture. According to Ellis (1969:182), "Thousands of Catholics had been waiting for a long time for a signal from their Church that they might fraternize more closely with other Americans." They received that signal in 1964 in the council's Decree on Ecumenism.

These movements and trends were not completely disparate. Monsignor Paul Furfey, a well-known analyst of the period, wrote in 1936, "The Liturgy is the perfect expression of the new social Catholicism. The new movement is founded upon faith and the Liturgy is the public expression of our faith" (Hennesey 1981:266). The liturgical movement was rooted largely in insights from the biblical movement (Danielou 1956), and the historical consciousness was half-implicit in biblical renewal (Ahlstrom 1975:52). In addition, the rediscovery of church and the ecumenical longings also sprang in part from the liturgical, biblical, and social movements.

Yet these minimovements and trends represent more than conceptually distinct tendencies. Each was truly unique, with its own articulators, separate goals, and distinct, developed movement organizations and networks. In addition, these developments were the most notable agents of ferment within the Catholic Church in America during the era before Vatican II. Not until the 1960s did a new movement appear, overarching and superseding the earlier trends.

Legitimation Accompanied by Mobilization

The inner changes described above in stage one were readying the church for Pope John XXIII's revolution (Ahlstrom 1975:525). Hennesey (1981: 306-307) called the 1960s a new turning for the American Catholic Church, a revolutionary moment. Many things happened during that dramatic decade, including Catholic involvement in civil rights, the response to the Vietnam War, and the development of a Catholic Left. Yet the most significant change in the Catholic Church was the Second Vatican Council itself (Brown 1969; Ellis 1969; Hennesey 1981:chap. 21).

Of necessity we turn to the Vatican to examine this period, 1959 to 1962. Although we remain interested in the American expression of the movement for radical change in Catholicism, official American Catholicism was part of a larger worldwide event for Catholicism, namely, the Second Vatican Council. What happened there was also happening to all national hierarchies in the world, because the official teachings of Vatican II would automatically become the official teachings of all segments of Catholicism. We examine the Vatican Council with the awareness that conclusions about it will also apply to the American scene. This period of legitimation and mobilization constitutes stage two of the movement for change.

Legitimation. The Second Vatican Council (1962–1965), along with its preparatory meetings (1959–1962), involved a long series of deliberations over the modernization of the Catholic Church (see Rynne 1968; Fesquet 1967). Major questions of this council focused largely on whether and to what extent the official Church should endorse the minimovements and trends discussed above.

We have already seen that the Second Vatican Council gave its approval to the main ideas of the minimovements and trends preceding the Vatican II. The citations (quoted above from the official council constitutions and other documents) should be sufficient evidence that the individual goals, as represented by these minimovements and trends, were legitimated.

In addition to continuity with stage one, the movement in stage two represented an effort to change the relationship of the Church to modernity. Pope John, in calling the council, said that the Church "no longer needed to confront the world with severity"; it was time to reevaluate the Church's inner structures and update its dealings with humanity. He insisted that the council would refrain totally from condemnations, thereby hoping to negate the approach of narrow-minded clerics who had, in Murphy's words, "induced a reign of terror in the Church" in attempting "to ferret out churchmen whom they suspected of the heresy of Modernism" (Murphy 1981:75–76).

Pope John justified calling the council by stating that the Church's structures and theological expression needed a total turning of the Church upside down or inside out (ibid.:76). During the Roman Synod, held in 1960 as an exemplar of the worldwide council to come, John changed a long-standing practice (ibid.:82). He decreed that priests who had given up their ministry and refused to repent should be treated with consideration and helped, even temporally, rather than being ostracized. This was typical of his revolutionary and pastoral thinking.

In addition, the Council Fathers debated (sometimes hotly) an array of issues (see Brown 1969; Kaiser 1963; Fesquet 1967; Rynne 1968).[1] Many of these, such as tolerance for those of other religious faiths and reforming the Church along biblical lines, were implied by the minimovements and trends discussed above. Many additional topics arose from other sources, such as missionary concerns of Third World bishops and ideas expressed by expert theologians, who instructed the bishops on the sidelines about contemporary theology. Both kinds of issues often touched the most basic orientations of Catholicism; they were potentially revolutionary.

Revolutionary issues included the following (see Abbott 1966; Brown 1969; Fesquet 1967; Rynne 1968): Should the Church define itself in the newly debated corporate language? Should it become more pastorally oriented, more tolerant, and less dogmatic? Should it move closer to the position of the Protestant Reformers in outlining the source (or sources) of revelation? Should it accept freedom of conscience? Should it incorporate aspects of democracy within itself? Should it embrace contemporary psychological understandings of marriage and family life? Should it be more accepting of the modern world in general? Should it attend, more directly and consciously, to issues of social concern?

After a series of dramatic debates, interventions, and exchanges (Brown 1969:165–166; Fesquet 1967:75–78; Rynne 1968), the Council Fathers answered these and other basic questions in the direction of a pastorally oriented, reformed, and modern Church. In the final votes and in the resulting documents, they put their stamp of approval on a radically changed Catholic Church (Cullman 1968). They softened the previous emphasis on papal authority by underscoring the joint authority of bishops with the pope (see "Decree on Bishops' Pastoral Office in the Church," in Abbott 1966). They cast a new spotlight on the whole church, not only on the hierarchy (see "Dogmatic Constitution on the Church," ibid.). They broke from the age-old two-source theory of revelation (scripture and tradition) by emphasizing coordination between scripture and tradition and by presenting a more biblical and less philosophical treatment of revelation (see R. McKenzie 1966; also "Dogmatic Constitution on Divine Revelation" in Abbott 1966). They accepted a radically new description of marriage and family life, placing children in the context of conjugal love rather than calling procreation the primary end of matrimony ("Pastoral Constitution on the Church in the Modern World," #49 and #50, ibid.). As noted above, they accepted many of the Reformers' ideas, including the church as people of God, a return to Scripture, and the centrality of Christ (see Brown 1969; Abbott 1966). Pope Paul VI even gave a public apology for the sins of the Catholic Church—a dramatic turnabout from the long-entrenched official church attitude of Counter-Reformation (see Brown 1969). Finally, the Council Fathers described a more pastoral Church; one of tolerance, of openness, of ecumenical outreach, of social action (Kaiser 1963; Rynne 1968; Novak 1964). As one example of the pastoral orientation, they even reinstated the worker-priest only six years after the movement had been condemned (Fesquet 1967:813). As Fesquet (ibid.:809) remarked, the closing of the Council (1965), with all its promulgations and documents, "will go down in history as the transitional date between two very distinct eras of Christianity."

In addition to the Council Fathers' approval of the major thrust for radical change in the Catholic Church, other indicators demonstrated that this era (1962–1965) included characteristics of the legitimation period mentioned above: (1) that the movement typically passes into the hands of governing officials, who now recognize the worthiness of movement issues for discussion and problem solving, and (2) that interest groups address these legislative officials, attempting to educate them and to lobby in favor of the issues.

The governing body of Catholicism (pope and bishops) took the issues of minimovements, trends, and radical change into its hands simply by placing them on the agenda for the council. Certainly the council may not have begun in that way, as preliminary drafts of documents gave little legitimacy to most of the new ideas (Kaiser 1963; Rynne 1968; Fesquet 1967). Curialists dragged their feet during the preparation period (1959–1962) and tried to undermine Pope John's efforts to bring in fresh air (Rynne 1968; Fesquet 1967; Kaiser 1963).[2] One bishop who arrived early for the first session of the council told a reporter not to expect anything newsworthy or unusual. Yet by October 1962, the world knew that the council was dominated by unexpected, headline-making events (Fesquet 1967; Rynne 1968). Pope John himself set the tone in his opening speech when he said that doctrine should be "studied and expounded through the methods of research and through the literary forms of modern thought" (cited in Fesquet 1967:23). Other early actions by Pope John and some courageous cardinals helped turn the council precisely toward accepting the new issues as legitimate points of discussion.[3] At about this point, ideas from minimovements, trends, and contemporary theology passed into the hands of Church legislators.

This legitimation period included the actions of interest groups, who attempt to educate the legislators and to lobby in favor of the movement ideas. Rynne points out that during the first session of the council (1962) "prelates from the United States held meetings every Monday at the North American College." Rynne continues (1968:62):

> They [the meetings] were at first dominated by blocs under [conservative] Cardinals Spellman and McIntyre, but as Cardinals Ritter and Meyer gained in stature owing to their stand in the conciliar discussions, their leadership made itself felt among the bishops, first from the mid-west and then among a considerable group of the younger men from both the east and the west coasts. Those American bishops who had contact with the prelates and theologians of other lands quickly became aware of the immense educative value of the proceedings.

Clearly, many episcopal legislators were educated to the new ideas both by other bishops and by theologians.

Other educative meetings occurred regularly. Theologians and official non-Catholic Observers gave presentations and instructions to various groups of Council Fathers (see Cullman 1968; Fesquet 1967; Rynne 1968). Prelates were often cited as saying that the education they received during the council was a chance of a lifetime, a crash course in updating themselves (Fesquet 1967; Rynne 1968). Meeting places existed for informal communication; coffee bars set up inside the conciliar meeting area provided the opportunity for reporters, Observers, and Experts to buttonhole the Council Fathers. There, one could observe a good deal of informal lobbying (Rynne 1968).

This period, then, had the marks of a legitimation phase. The officials of the Catholic Church took into their own hands the issues that had been raised by the minimovements and trends noted above. In addition, the Council Fathers discussed for possible approbation the larger issues of more radical change in church structure, ritual, norms, discipline, and orientation toward other religious groups and toward the modern world. By doing so, they and the proponents of change raised the phenomenon to a generalized movement for radical change of the Catholic Church.

Mobilization. This period contained a secondary related leitmotiv—namely, mobilization. This aspect began during the Vatican Council (perhaps more precisely with Pope John's call for the council) and reached its zenith during the late 1960s. Although the legitimation remained the focus, people and resources were being mobilized in support of (or in resistance to) the movement for change.

This sequence of stages differs from the ideal typical sequence presented above. In most reform actions, especially in open democracies, stages follow the order given above, with legitimation following mobilization.

Evidence for mobilization emerged on many fronts. The movement became a public event. In a striking way, the debates of the Second Vatican Council became public through weekly and monthly reports of the attending journalists, published regularly in the press, and through the writings of Official Observers (e.g., Brown 1969; Cullman 1968). In the United States, writings by Xavier Rynne (pseudonym) in the *New Yorker* provided inside information about the weekly workings of the council and brought its activities to a general public. Some writers have noted that this was a dramatic change in Church policy (Goldner, Ritti, and Ference 1977). In any case, multitudes of Catholics and others around the world were stimulated by the frank reporting, which included accounts of episcopal politicking and hot exchanges from the council podium (e.g., Kaiser 1963; Rynne 1968), and became aware of progressive and traditional stances within the Church.

Movement leaders emerged. Those who followed the council soon became aware of theologians who helped formulate the new ideas, as well as the Council Fathers who promoted these ideas in the council drafts and debates. The more articulate of these leaders, whether present at the council or not, included theologians Karl Rahner, Yves Congar, Jean Danielou, Hans Küng, John Courtney Murray, Edward Schillebeeckx, and with them, the ideas of Pierre Teilhard de Chardin. Council Fathers promoting ideas of change included Cardinals Alfrink, Bea, Dopfner, Frings, Koenig, Leger, Lercaro, Lienart, Montini (later Pope Paul VI), and Suenens. Americans who forcefully supported the changes included Cardinals Cushing (in a limited way), Meyer, and Ritter. Archbishop Paul J. Holliman was probably the first American bishop to clearly disassociate himself from the extremely conservative position of Cardinals Spellman and McIntire. Archbishop Helder Camara and other prelates from the Third World were also outspoken proponents of new perspectives. Finally, both popes—John XXIII and Paul VI—acted as leaders of this movement for change in the Church. For evidence, see detailed reports of council proceedings (Fesquet 1967; Kaiser 1963; Rynne 1968).

In addition, these men became known as generally supporting the changing Church during the council. In many cases, they were well known before the council in a local or broader context for promoting specific minimovements of change in a particular Church realm. They had written books or spoken out in public for specific changes. Now they became known more universally; now they were associated with the Vatican Council, with all the media attention and the focus on general leadership. Because of the broad media coverage and widespread interest, Catholics became increasingly aware of the issues of change (Hennesey 1981:312).

A coherent ideology and overarching theme seemed to develop toward the end of the council, as analysts tried to summarize what had happened. For some, the council represented a newly open Church (Novak 1964). For others, it created a pastoral and pilgrim Church (Fesquet 1967; Rynne 1968; Kaiser 1963). Still others regarded the central theme as a radical restructuring of the Church (Fichter 1977; Suenens 1968:4; Kung 1968:4). For all these analysts, the new Church at last was clearly delineated (in theory) to be part of the twentieth century.

This was the vision of Pope John XXIII, who first called for aggiornamento, modernization. His way of reaching that goal during council crises was to opt for the pastoral solution (Fesquet 1981; Rynne 1968; Kaiser 1963). The other central themes, such as the open Church, the restructured Church, and the pilgrim Church, were also necessary ways of achieving a modernized Church —a Church that could abandon the siege mentality and the legalistic approaches (Murphy 1981:84–85). The overarching theme became the new Church, the modernized Church.

These visions of the Church, reflecting the documents of the Second Vatican Council, were not accomplished immediately. They became rallying cries of the progressives, goals to be attained in the long struggle ahead (Murphy 1981;chap. 5). Furthermore, the coherence and the revolutionary nature of the changes probably became clearer toward the end of the council and immediately afterward. Many commentators have suggested that even the

Council Fathers, who ratified all the documents separately, probably did not know the depth of the revolution they had begun (Ahlstrom 1975:526; Brown 1969; Ellis 1969; Fichter 1977; Hennesey 1981).

Slogans, chants, symbols appeared. A change of symbols began during the council years, immediately after the introduction of some new liturgical rites in 1962. Signs of new Catholicism included the new Mass, the use of the vernacular, the reversed altar, the handshake of peace, and the guitar Mass. In the new Mass, vocal congregational participation, both in song and in the spoken word, replaced the silent reading of missals and the telling of rosary beads. A social and communitarian emphasis replaced individualism. The new symbols reflected a new theological understanding of worship as community dialogue with the Almighty.

In this arena, too, implementation was not immediate. Progressive bishops, clergy, and worshipers initiated the new Mass, with its various innovations, but often the new symbols, slogans, and chants were perceived as confrontations with traditional bishops or Catholics. At the same time, they were attractive to college students and other Catholics and became a means of mobilizing people to the progressive wing (see Greeley 1977).

Diagnoses came forth. Among the Council Fathers, the speakers for change articulated the problems in the Church. These problems were found not only in the immediate targets mentioned so often above—the curia, the obstructionist politics, the Holy Office with its Inquisition and Index of Forbidden Books (Fesquet 1967; Rynne 1968; Murphy 1981)—but, more important, in the whole approach of the Church. Council Fathers who lead the progressive assault often criticized the lack of understanding of the world, the doctrinal rigidity, the defensiveness, the legalistic and siege mentality (Fesquet 1967; Rynne 1968; Kaiser 1963; Murphy 1981). The solutions, they decided, required basic change in almost all aspects of ecclesiastical life.

Such solutions were not drawn from the sky. Theologians, influencing the progressive bishops, laid a groundwork of new theology that was heavily biblical, historical, conscious of the church's social dimensions. The rationale for change was an emerging new theology.

Resources could be identified. Mobilization phases, almost by definition, include recruitment of resources to move the new ideas into widespread acceptance (McCarthy and Zald 1977; Tilly 1978; Oberschall 1973; Gamson 1975; Jenkins 1981, 1982). As noted above, these resources include key leaders, affected groups, organization, legitimacy, and other resources.

The Catholic Church was no exception. In preparing for the council, Pope John called to Rome such experts as Karl and Hugo Rahner (Jesuit theologians from Innsbruck), Yves Congar and Marie de Chenu (French Dominicans), Jean Danielou and Henri de Lubac (Jesuits). These were all leading scholars in the realms discussed here under stage one and on the Church, laity, worship, religious freedom, and an array of additional theological topics such as grace, salvation, and Christology (Murphy 1981:80). As the council moved into action, key leaders came to include the broader spectrum of theologians who indoctrinated the bishops, as well as the prelates from around the world who spoke informally in small groups and more formally from the council podium. Not only were they key resources; they helped recruit, intellectually, the council delegates who would form the dominant elements. Later, after the council, the recruitment would broaden its scope.

Certainly, the council was an arena for attempts to recruit key persons, especially bishops, to the cause of change. Both conservatives and progressives applied such pressure, according to Fesquet (1967:199), who noticed "passions and politicking in both camps."

Affected groups (clergy, religious, laity), many of them also key leaders in implementing the new ideas, were crucial resources as well, and many of them followed the council proceedings in the media. Others were recruited and partially socialized in the new ways during the council years, especially in reference to liturgical changes, which were first introduced in 1964. The years after the council saw an increase in the socialization of these affected groups (see below).

Other resources also emerged during the council era, though they blossomed more fully after the council ended (Stewart 1978). In 1964 the *National Catholic Reporter (NCR)* was founded, the first truly independent Catholic newspaper of that period in the United States (Cogley 1973:176–178). It reported all the news about the Church, including liberal-conservative battles, and it became an effective way to keep up with the actions of the council. The *NCR* believed in scrutinizing the Church, and its editorial policy was unequivocally liberal. Read throughout the country, it probably promoted change indirectly by calling attention to the issues and controversies of the council. Additional organizations, networks, and media emerged in larger numbers to facilitate change after the council.

Other powerful resources included the two popes of the council and the council itself. The council obviously gave legitimacy to the ideas of change expressed in the prior minimovements and trends discussed above. Popes John XXIII and Paul VI, in speeches and in guidance of the council, became speakers for and symbols of change. Being highly visible and extremely credible, they lent legitimacy and thus served as a strong resource in the movement for radical change.

Countermovements, another evidence of mobilization, apparently arose or gained strength after this period. The most famous traditionalist movement— one specifically directed against Vatican II—was founded by the French

Archbishop Marcel LeFebvre during the era immediately following the Vatican Council (McSweeney 1980; *Newsweek*: July 16, 1979).

During this phase of the movement (1959–1965), one could note easily the strain between traditionalists and liberal Catholics, both in the council chambers and among those following the council from afar (*National Catholic Reporter* 1964–1965, passim). Perhaps the strain prefigured the coming struggles between the movement for change and the traditionalist countermovements. Perhaps the foundation for the flowering of countermovements was being laid as one would expect, during the height of mobilization.

Confrontations and resistance developed. As noted above, a number of significant confrontations took place during the Second Vatican Council. An early confrontation occured in the call for a recess by Cardinal Lienart of France, who wished the Council Fathers to meet in national groups and develop their own preferred slates of candidates for council committees (Brown 1969:162; Fesquet 1967:21). Cardinal Lienart's move, seconded by Cardinals Frings, Doepfner, and Koenig and adopted by a large majority (Brown 199: 162), effectively blocked the attempt of traditionalists to give overwhelming power to conservatives via committee assignments (Brown 1969:161–162).

A later conflict involved Cardinal Frings of Cologne and Cardinal Ottaviani, head of the Holy Office—the agency in Rome charged with the examination of heresy. Fesquet (1967:215) writing in his diary style, describes the two men, beginning with Frings: "He is open to ecumenism, contemporary exegesis, and all currents of modern thought. The second is a Roman who has never lived outside of Italy . . . [He is] feared for the severity of his judgments." The two men exchanged bitter words during the discussion of the relation of the Roman Curia to bishops. As Rynne (1968:216) says, this topic was bound to produce fireworks because many Council Fathers were very unhappy about the parochial and Italianized outlook of the curia. In addition, the discussion took place after Cardinal Ottaviani's maneuverings to consider the recent and strongly endorsing council vote on the authority of the college of bishops merely as a directive vote and not as binding. Frings went to the podium on November 9, ten days after that turning-point vote (Rynne 1968: 215), which (by a majority of 84 percent) restored to bishops an equivalent share in the authority exercised only by the Pope since Vatican I (Fesquet 1967:201; Rynne 1968:214–215).

Frings strongly criticized the theological commission (committee) for tampering with the wishes of the council on the question of bishops' authority. Then he said that the methods of the Holy Office (headed by Ottaviani) were "out of harmony with modern times and . . . a cause of scandal in the world." After an interruption for applause, he continued, "No one ought to be judged and condemned without having been heard, without knowing what he is accused of, and without the opportunity of correcting his views" (cited in Fesquet 1967:215).

Cardinal Ottaviani replied a few minutes later, "his voice trembling with anger and emotion." He accused his critics of ignorance and stated that "to attack the Holy Office is to insult the Pope" (Fesquet 1967:216). Though several others—cardinals and archbishops—came to Ottaviani's defense, the weight of debate seemed to support Frings. Council Fathers from India, Portugal, and elsewhere spoke in favor of reining in the Roman Curia and underscoring the bishops' power (Fesquet 1967:206ff.).

Resistance to the Pope's sharing of supreme authority came from many sources, including the integralists, who wished to retain all the traditional doctrines of the Church. Fesquet (ibid.: 201–202) remarks that with the new emphasis on episcopal authority, the integralists "fall behind the Council by about a century. Their efforts and their intimidations have been foiled to a degree one could not have imagined." Their concerted efforts could not dissuade the Council Fathers from endorsing the statement that the college of bishops enjoys, with the pope, "plenary and supreme authority over the universal Church" and that it "succeeds the college of apostles in the task of preaching the Gospel, sanctifying and shepherding the flock" (Rynne 1968:214).

Religious liberty—another issue—also triggered resistance from integralists (Fesquet 1967:354). Here, "the fury of the enemies of this text was extraordinary" (ibid.:775). These enemies did almost everything possible to undermine the original text proposed by Cardinal Bea, one of the Church's leaders in ecumenism. They even attempted to change the procedures that had been approved by the council, in order to hand over the writing of the document to those opposed to religious liberty (ibid.:421-423). This step occasioned a letter to Pope Paul VI by seventeen Council Fathers in favor of such liberty. In the letter, they complained of an apparent violation of council regulations and asked for his intervention (ibid.:422). In the end, the original text, approving religious freedom, was basically restored. "The Church of pastors carried the day over certain doctors who are armed with quotations but do not see that all doctrine . . . is subject to organic evolution" (ibid.:775).

Such stories of conflict and resistance, of intrigue and subterfuge, pepper the pages of the council accounts (Fesquet 1967; Rynne 1968). They suggest that the conflicts surrounding mobilization began in Rome in the early 1960s and extended outward from that time and place.

There was also a great deal of opposition to the election of Cardinal Montini as pope (Paul VI), which occurred during the council years (1963). The conflict was based precisely on "the fact that the cardinal of Milan (Montini) would prove a champion of the Johannine line." The opposition to Montini, headed by Cardinal Ottaviani, emanated from the curial bloc—those twenty-nine cardinals who were attached directly to the Vatican (Murphy 1981:99). It also included Cardinal Siri, who was "violently opposed to Montini's candidacy," both as a career competitor of Montini and because of Montini's agreement with Pope John's "opening to the left." Siri feared that Montini would carry through the proposed reform of the curia, and that the Communists would take over the Italian government as a result of Church liberalization (ibid.:105-106).

This protest, of course, was a continuation of opposition to the policies of Pope John XXIII. The curial group had thought that John went too far in many new directions, especially in the encyclical *Pacem in Terris* and in his preparations for the council (ibid.:87-90). He had asserted the human right to freedom and to live in peace, and to exercise freedom of conscience. He had made overtures to the Communist world by distinguishing between the Communist ideology and their actual political system, with which the Church could cooperate in a common effort for human rights. In preparing for the council, he had contacted a number of non-Catholic churches and invited them to send official observers. In the eyes of the curialists, John had begun to undo the work of other venerable popes, including their condemnations of Communism and ecumenism and the age-old axiom that error has no rights (ibid.).

The resistance to Montini took the form of "abrasive Vatican politics." Curial leaders accused him of lacking depth and competence in theology, and they tried to line up the Spanish and Latin American cardinals to vote for their own papal candidate. According to one source, this Vatican politicking continued even into the sacred hall for the election of the pope, where the curial maneuverings were condemned by Cardinal Testa as scandalous intrigue (ibid.:105-107).

Outside the Vatican, controversy abounded concerning the new decrees already being implemented during the council era. Liturgical reform in particular occasioned strong reactions, largely because traditional rituals were so deeply imbedded in Catholics' consciousness (*National Catholic Reporter* 1964–1965). Bishops such as Cardinals Spellman of New York and McIntyre of Los Angeles opposed the changes because they watered down the mysterious element or distracted the people (Hennesey 1981:312). Many lay persons resisted the diminution of practices they considered highly sacred, including the recitation of the rosary, Marian devotions, and Latin hymns. In their place, the guitar Masses, the handshake of peace, and Communion in the hand seemed to profane the most sublime moments of religious experience.

A Foreshadowing of Later Developments

Later periods will be discussed in subsequent chapters, but here is a brief overview.

Stage three (1966–1971), mobilization accompanied by implementation, was a short transitional period, at least in the United States, where a great struggle ensued between those oriented to change and those who opposed it (Neal 1970–1971). It was also a time when the American hierarchy was excessively resistant to change. It was a period of particular crisis (Greeley 1977: 159), when conflicts between priests and bishops seemed to dominate the Catholic scene. Therefore, implementation proceeded at a relatively slow pace, and the struggle for mobilization reached its high-water mark.

Stage four (1971 to the present) was dominated by implementation, at least in the United States. During this time, the Church pursued change in a more robust and extensive way. In 1971 Pope Paul VI decreed that all dioceses should create priests' senates, advisory councils, and other structures of grass-roots input to governance. In the early 1970s, a new apostolic delegate was named to the United States—Archbishop Jean Jadot—who subsequently saw that a whole new cohort of progressive bishops was appointed throughout the country as vacancies occurred (Greeley 1977:159; 1978). These bishops were much more strongly dedicated to reform than the majority of those in office immediately after the council. In addition, as most observant Catholics know, this was an era in which many goals of the council were implemented, including the introduction of modified rituals for confession and marriage, a creative burst in modern liturgical music, the emergence of such programs as the married deaconate, lay ministers of the Eucharist, and ecumenical dialogue. In regard to the last item, one long and serious set of conversations resulted in the famous Catholic-Lutheran Statement by theologians of both faiths (U.S. Lutheran-Roman Catholic Dialogue Group 1983).

Yet, implementation was neither easy nor completely successful. Conflict also riddled this period, because many Catholics resisted implementation. As we shall see, the meaning of aggiornamento was called into question, and the traditionalist countermovement claimed its share of members. It is still not clear to what extent the spirit of the Second Vatican Council will truly be implemented.

The social movement stages of Catholicism described here are especially noteworthy. Early legitimation—which allowed little time for large segments of the Catholic world to digest the new ideas—probably contributed to the crises that occured in stage three during the immediate post–Vatican II era

(Greeley 1977:159). Instead of being introduced gradually to the justifications for radical change through a prior mobilization stage, the majority of Catholics were abruptly required to alter dramatically their rituals and their ways of conceiving the path to salvation. For members of a Church that prided itself on its certainty and its bedrock constancy, this was a difficult medicine, and it probably created additional conflict.

Early legitimation had other consequences. It meant that during stage three, a kind of double mobilization occurred: mobilization of support for the ideas of reformed Catholicism, and mobilization to promote implementation. During that era, of course, this double mobilization had the appearance of a single mobilization: Rome and the bishops of the world had decreed certain changes, and Catholics were expected to follow directions. Local clergy, if they accepted the changes, would not only induce their flocks to change but they also would explain the rationales for change. In retrospect, however, this sudden double mobilization appears to have been too difficult for many lay Catholics and for many clergy, who mobilized their flocks only half-heartedly.

The theoretical implications that will be discussed in later chapters involve important concepts: the extent of early legitimation in a social movement and the transition from a traditional to a more broad-based organization. In this case, the Church apparently thought in a traditional mode when it commanded priests and other key leaders to implement the changes of the council immediately. Apparently, it expected its obedient subjects to follow the new ideas without hitch. Yet the Church probably did not realize the extent to which ordinary Catholics had incorporated the democratic ethos and thus expected change to be voluntary. In addition, Church officials may not have understood the extent to which the new guidelines produced an inconsistency for many Catholics: The new rules appeared to violate some of the deepest Catholic truths.

Chapter Five

Key Features of Church Modernization

The movement for change in the Catholic Church seems to have reached its dramatic height between 1966 and 1971, and the arena of change, with its confrontations and mobilizations, moved from Rome to the local dioceses, parishes, and other local arenas (Hennesey 1981:chap. 21).

The mobilization phase is apparently the ideal typical time of any movement; social analysts give great emphasis to this period. In fact, the currently dominant school of thought—resource mobilization—studies a social movement by examining the marshaling of resources that promote a movement's success or failure (Tilly 1978; Oberschall 1973; McCarthy and Zald 1977; Gamson 1975). Other ingredients of the mobilization stage—emergence of leadership, a coherent ideology, slogans, countermovements, and conflict—also trigger theoretical and empirical discussion (Turner and Killian 1972; Killian 1973; Lang and Lang 1978; Wilson 1973; Mottl 1980; Smelser 1963).

Mobilization is also important from another viewpoint. Specialists in collective behavior give abundant attention to the conflicts and crowd activities of this period (Turner and Killian 1972; Perry and Pugh 1978; Smelser 1963; Meyer and Seidler 1978; Seidler et al, 1977).

Finally, most people seem to recognize a movement during the height of its mobilization stage because at that time the conflict is greatest, the voices most strident, and the publicity most memorable. The mobilization stage incites high levels of public curiosity.

The definition of a social movement—a collective effort, often accompanied by confrontations and conflict, to promote or resist change in some aspect of the social system—implies that the mobilization stage holds the key to understanding any social movement. Truly collective efforts to promote or resist change usually imply ideological refinement, clarity of goals, leadership, and the development of social movement organizations (Freeman 1983; Killian 1973; Smelser 1963; Turner and Killian 1972). The definition suggests that the social movement has reached the mobilization stage.

On the other hand, a movement need not have been legitimated or implemented to be recognized as such. The era of Martin Luther King was one of attempting to get the laws implemented, whereas the contemporary women's movement aims at both legislation and implementation. In both cases, interest in the movements occurred primarily during the stage of mobilization, whether this came before or after legitimation.

As we look at the change of the Catholic Church especially during the height of the mobilization stage, we may find answers to lingering questions about the social movement described within Catholicism.

Implementation is a topic of sociological importance. Struggles over implementation reflect one of the most elemental issues of social change (Veblen 1934, 1948), and treatments of the success and failure of social movements have long peppered the literature (Killian 1973).

Recently, analysts have debated the relative importance for movement success, of such features as centralization of the Social Movement Organization (SMO) (Lawson 1983; Gerlach and Hine 1970; Dwyer 1983), mass defiance (Priven and Cloward 1977; Burstein 1981; Jenkins 1983), movement membership and organization (Snyder and Kelly 1976; Jenkins 1984; West 1981: 292–303), and a context of crisis (Gamson 1975; Goldstone 1980; Jenkins 1983). Within an organization, additional factors presumably also affect movement success. Logically, these include the personal openness of executive officers, the general openness of the membership, the indoctrination program, the opportunity for member updating, and the orientation of new recruits.

In the American Catholic Church, diocesan variation in movement success depended on some of these factors. Lower-level defiance, a crisis context, leadership orientation, and other phenomena of the implementation period will be examined for their effects.

The implementation period of the Catholic movement for change (1971 to the present) is an opportune era for investigation; it constitutes the prime time for studying success or failure. In addition, various characteristics have emerged, which may lead to further theoretical discussion. This period apparently witnessed the height of the battles of interpretation of Vatican II. At the same time, the agony of transformation occurred, as well as a large measure of reality shock.

Our interest in this period, then, is twofold. We will document the unique characteristics of the implementation period and advance the discussion of the causes of movement success within organizations.

The skeptic may ask questions at this point: Was the change in Catholicism pursued with enough coherence and consciousness to justify the term *social movement?* Did the changes originate from below, as in most social movements, or from above, as in leader-initiated change, which requires no social movement? The answers will rely mostly on evidence from the mobilization stage (1966–1971).

Both questions imply that if the Catholic change is to be considered a true social movement, organized efforts at change should have been made from below. We assume with Heberle (1951:8) that social movements are not synonymous with organization; nevertheless, social movements only get off the ground when there is sufficient organization to promote the cause (Abel 1973; Freeman 1983:9; Killian 1973; Turner and Killian 1972). Thus, without some evidence of organized efforts, the Catholic episode may simply have represented a trend or turn of events—a way in which the Church updated itself through its normal, institutionalized channels.

No single model exists to show how all social movements are organized, let alone whether they are organized from below. Some movements are tightly knit and coherent; in others, the parts are only loosely affiliated (Gerlach and Hine 1970). Still others include a combination of coherence and segmentation (Lawson 1983). Each model seems to have advantages and disadvantages for recruitment, movement success, and so forth (Gerlach and Hine 1970; Lawson 1983; Dwyer 1983). Perhaps more important, in each of these three models the movement organization constitutes a conscious effort to achieve the movement goals.

In our view, the Catholic case was characterized by a combination of coherence and segmentation. In the early stages—probably until the end of the Second Vatican Council (1965)—the loose affiliation among movement segments seemed to dominate. After that, however, a more coherent level of movement organization developed, though a variety of uncoordinated avant-garde efforts remained. Regarding coherency, the hierarchical Church structure was mobilized to aid the implementation of council decrees. This process involved a double thrust for change after the council: initiatives came both from the top and from the grass roots.

The grass-roots level included several partially segmented approaches to the movement for change. At the far left of the spectrum was the Underground Church (Boyd 1968; Steeman 1969), which experimented with changes beyond those that were currently approved. Then there were the more visible nonterritorial or floating churches (Hennesey 1981:315), such as the Northern Virginia (NOVA) group, which also experimented with the Sunday liturgy. In addition, many parishes continued a kind of coalition between a progressive priest and change-oriented parishioners, who, in a territorial parish, also moved swiftly to incorporate new structures and rituals. Often they were confronted and disciplined by more traditional and slower-moving bishops. Then, as progressivism became the norm among lower-level clergy during the late sixties (Seidler 1979), the general body of lower clergy became another movement segment, pushing for change and explaining the new ideas to the common Catholic (Greeley 1977; NORC 1972). Finally, a majority of women religious constituted another leading force for change.[1] In the United States, these and a number of other groups (Hennesey 1981:315–316; Stewart 1978) were all fighting against middle-of-the-road leadership by bishops (NORC 1972; Seidler 1972) and in some cases against the conservative policies of traditional bishops. As described by Gerlach and Hine (1970), these forces were segmented, polycephalous, and reticulate rather than hierarchically unified.

On the other hand, a top hierarchical level also promoted change. Pope Paul VI, following John XXIII, had intervened at the council in favor of change. When the council ended, Paul called the worldwide Synod of Bishops (1967) to perpetuate the spirit of the council (Murphy 1981). He also made a number of decrees, including the decree in 1970 requiring parish and diocesan pastoral councils, as well as diocesan priests' senates, to implement shared responsibility (Hennesey 1981:316). He promoted new scholarly and ecumenical Bible translations, and he continued to initiate ecumenical overtures and programs such as the Association for the Ecumenical Institute for Tantur, Israel, and to make other signs of rapproachement with the modern world (Murphy 1981). Finally, during Paul's regime, the mechanisms were set in motion for the complete liturgical, homiletic, biblical, and pastoral renewal at the local level (Murphy 1981).

Such hierarchical actions are considered part of the social movement for change precisely because they constituted a struggle against the long-entrenched Catholic system. Although this system was defeated in the council, it persisted in the curia, which even Paul had trouble changing (Murphy 1981), and in the habits of the hierarchy and of common Catholics throughout the world.

The change in Catholicism was not merely a trend or a simple adjustment by the usual institutional mechanisms. Instead, it seems to have been a true social movement—a loosely coordinated set of collective efforts to modernize the long-entrenched Catholic system.

Bishop and Parish Priests:
Pivotal Figures

Bishops and parish priests are pivotal figures in the implementation of change because they occupy key positions or perform key functions in their respective organizations, the diocese and the parish.

Hawley (1970) defines the key function as the position in an organization through which that organization has most access to the surrounding environment, especially in obtaining needed resources. Therefore, it is the position that exercises most power and sits atop the hierarchical ladder.

In all these senses, the ordinary (the bishop) and the pastor (chief administrator of a parish) fulfill the definition of the key function.[2] Through the ordinary come all the spiritual powers that filter down to the local levels (*Dogmatic Constitution on the Church*, #21ff.). To the bishop come all the guidelines from Rome for diocesan action, and to the bishop come the diocesan funds that are distributed around the diocese. In much the same way, the pastor functions for the parish (*Dogmatic Constitution on the Church*, #28). The pastor represents the parish to the bishop as well as to community leaders and other important contacts. Consequently, bishop and pastor top the hierarchical ladder and exercise the greatest power in their respective organizations.

Ordinaries have exercised great power. Authors have noted the extraordinary independence and almost autocratic power exercised by bishops, especially American bishops (Haughey 1971:518–520; Spencer 1966:100; Valliser 1969:149ff.). Pastors, too, have had the decisive voice in all matters of the parish, as long as the bishop did not intervene.

Bishops and parish priests, then, had the power to promote or to block the movement for change in their respective spheres. They could promote it in a number of ways: by initiating new modes of worship, by establishing new structures of shared governance, by discussing the meaning of the council documents, by becoming involved in ecumenical activities, and by appointing others to move forward in religious education, biblical studies, church music, and so forth. Obviously, they could block it by default—by neglecting to take these initiatives. They could also block it by countermanding the progressive initiatives of clergy associates and others under their supervision, and by minimizing their compliance with council-derived decrees from Rome, which were gradually institutionalized. Such power to promote or block change inheres in key functions and confers on those filling such functions, here clergy, pivotal importance described by Schoenherr (1987) as a linchpin status. Bishops and priests displayed a variety of responses in both promoting and blocking change, including the gamut just mentioned.

Those men who served in the priesthood during the mobilization-implementation period (1965–1971) faced a variety of difficulties and perceived inconsistencies, any of which could produce conflict.

A major problem for priests was dealing with anguishing differences (NORC 1972; Fichter 1968, 1974). These differences might separate priest from bishop, priest from priest, or priest from member of the congregation, whether woman or man, religious or lay person (see Hadden 1969:211ff.; Steeman 1969; Wood 1981; Hoge et al. 1975). The differences arose, it seemed, largely from variations in acceptance of the new Catholicism (Schoenherr and Greeley 1974). Although there were many degrees of acceptance (*Emerging Trends* 1983), the great dividing line seemed to fall between those who wanted rapid implementation of the Vatican spirit and those who proceeded more cautiously (Seidler 1972).

The differences were made most anguishing by the whole historical flow of the movement for change. Before the council, a Catholic could assume a larger degree of unanimity among co-believers (Greeley 1973, 1977, 1981). The priest and the bishop taught basically the same thing, though they expressed different orientations to the Church because of differing administrative/professional perspectives (Hall and Schneider 1973). Now, however, when radically different theologies were superimposed on these differing perspectives, a small divergence became a wider gap (Fichter 1968; Greeley 1977; NORC 1972:chap. 6).

Additional characteristics added to the strain between progressives and traditionalists (or moderates). There was a sense of righteousness on each side (Greeley 1981). Both traditionalists and progressives could call on sources of legitimation and some degree of alliance from the membership. The long traditions of the Church, the endorsement of past councils, and the wonderfully integrated Catholic structure all lent legitimacy to the more traditionally oriented. In their view, the new ideas might be just a fad, a mistaken turn initiated by one senile pope, who was influenced by Communists, and carried through by another, who was seriously misled (Murphy 1981). On the other hand, progressives could point to the new Church documents, agreed upon by a majority of bishops around the world and endorsed by the popes. The latest gathering in Rome was not a charade but a true council of the Church. The feeling of righteousness on each side seemed to sharpen the differences.

The differences were exacerbated in some cases by an overlay of authority (Fichter 1974; Dulles 1974). When the differences involved bishop and priest, or priest and congregation—obvious locations of authority conflicts—the differences were likely to result in sanctions. Further, progressives and traditionalists disagreed quite fundamentally in the appropriateness of certain kinds of sanctions, especially punishments, such as suspensions, relocations, and interdicts.[3] As Pope John had indicated forcefully for the progressive side, stern punishments were inappropriate for men who had committed their lives to the Church (Murphy 1981; see also Etzioni 1961). In addition, a huge gulf separated the theology of authority endorsed by traditional Catholics and those committed to change. The traditionalists espoused a more hierarchical authority, in which all power emanated from the top down and was expressed largely as rulership. Progressives tended to accept a more collaborative authority (Dulles 1974; Küng 1976), such as that proposed at the council and expressed as the authority of service (McKenzie 1966).

When conflicts occurred, especially those involving a major position in the hierarchic line (priest, bishop, or pope), complications increased because of authority views, righteousness, and different theologies. These elements gave a certain explosiveness to the battles.

One should consider that priests did not have the educational advantages of attending the council itself. Most priests probably followed journalistic accounts of proceedings, but these were abbreviated reports, and not everyone took the time to read them. Bishops presumably had read several drafts of each document, witnessed and participated in the debates of all important issues, and received special instructions from expert theologians. Not so the priests, who remained at the parish helm.

Yet the parish priest, along with other men and women religious, was the key person who was asked immediately to indoctrinate a congregation. For many, especially the older priests (Fichter 1968), this was a difficult if not impossible task. How could one teach a new theology—one whose basic principles contradicted the foundation of one's seminary training and lifelong commitment? Especially on short notice and with little time to digest the council's orientations, how could one begin to undermine the liturgical mystery so long protected? How could the priest turn and face the people at Mass, speaking in English and shaking their hands? How could he start to teach that the lay life was basically as good as the religious life?

The first adjustment for priests was to promote a new cause that seemed to contradict their past assumptions. This demanded a corollary adjustment, namely a rapid self-education in the new thinking.

The priest was called upon not only to reeducate others but also to reorient himself. This may have been easy for some priests, especially the young, who had received an updated seminary education. For others, it was anguishing, if possible at all. Their orientation to the world had to be turned upside down, after the mind of Pope John (Murphy 1981). Furthermore, as exemplary Catholics, priests were expected to complete this about-face quickly and gracefully.

The priest constituted a dramatic expression of the new Church. His modifications of ritual were the first noticeable changes: he switched to English, reversed the altar, introduced a new style of church music, and simplified the bows and other liturgical gestures. These actions signified one aim of the council—to portray the meaning of liturgy more vividly and more directly (*Constitution on the Sacred Liturgy* 1963).

The priest, whether pastor, assistant pastor, or occasional parish helper, was also the prime religious educator, as mentioned earlier. If and when he digested the new Catholicism, he funneled it to his congregation. From the pulpit or in other forums, this idealized priest explained the new ecumenical spirit, the call for lay action, new understandings of the Church, priesthood, revelation, worship, marriage, missions, and involvement in the world.

The parish priest was also responsible for the reorganization of the local parish and thus for the structures in which new concepts of authority would be tested. At the insistence of Rome (Murphy 1981), he created parish councils—advisory boards composed largely of laity. In the spirit of Vatican II, he paid close attention to input from his own council.

If he caught the Vatican spirit completely, he also exhibited a greater pastoral concern, (see NORC 1972; Fichter 1974). Parishioners with previously unsolvable religious problems such as remarried divorcees, found a more open priestly ear and often a new solution that would include them more fully in liturgical worship. Instead of condemnation, former isolates received a warm welcome (Murphy 1981).

At the parish level, the priest also was the key to other activities inspired by the Vatican Council. These included ecumenical discussions with those of other faiths and serving on interracial commissions.

For those who wished a slower pace of change or even a return to the Tridentine Church, the change-oriented priest was the most visible target of dissatisfaction. Whether the priest followed the new norms or the old, he was almost assured of standing in the front lines of battle.

Much has been written about priests during this time of transition. Researchers have commented on the new norms embraced by priests (NORC 1972; Greeley 1977; Fichter 1974, Dulles 1974). They have also noted the anguish experienced by clergy in modernization (Schallert and Kelley 1970; Hadden 1969) and the frequently followed option of resigning from the priesthood (Schoenherr and Greeley 1974; Schallert and Kelly 1970; Seidler 1974, 1979). Priests experienced the changes in a profound way, and they expressed their experience in a variety of reactions.

Such reactions seemed dramatically to reflect the breakdown of old structures and the beginning of new ones. Resignations, for example, apparently stemmed from incorporating the new norms and the desire to marry (Shoenherr and Greeley 1974). New norms, one could infer, included greater personal autonomy, new respect for lay life (the priesthood of the laity), and an emphasis on individual rights in the Church. By departing their clerical status, priests symbolized the acceptance of such new norms. They also suggested a partial breakdown of the old compliance structures that minimized the individual and emphasized religious fidelity and obedience (Fichter 1968). This breakdown is seen in the deprivation experienced by priests who resigned the ministry (Schallert and Kelley 1970).

A Focus on Questions
of Structure

Research questions arise from the previous discussions and focus on the mobilization and implementation phases of the movement for change.[1] In part, they emphasize the parish priest and the bishop as those who symbolized and experienced the vortex of change in a special way. They also underscore the themes of conflict, disarticulation, and accommodation.

The following research questions emphasize structural rather than individual issues. Though some discussion concerns the individual—for example, the special difficulties of the priest—our goal is to illuminate structural changes. The research following will draw on these discussions expressly for structural analysis.

The research issues are presented under three headings; then, research questions will be presented by stages in the social movement. These general issues and questions will set a foundation for the specific focuses following in empirical chapters. Obviously, one cannot test the whole theory as presented in previous chapters. Therefore, we will select key topics from a subset of relevant issues.

Conflict has often been linked with social change (e.g., Marx 1964; Veblen 1934, 1948; Lenski 1966) and also has constituted a prominent part of the "contested accommodation" theory, as developed here. The social change occurs through and in conflict.

We have already seen that confrontation with the ecclesiastical status quo laid the groundwork and helped establish the movement for change in Catholicism. In stages one and two, conflict was both initiator and byproduct of the movement for change.

In the chapters to follow, the conflict dimension will be probed from several angles, all related to the social movement aspect of change. For example, was the conflict greater during the mobilization period (stage three) than during the implementation era (stage four), as one would expect from the theory? Did the conflicts concern different aspects of change? Who were the main antagonists? Did the issues or the major characters of conflict change as the movement passed from the mobilization to the implementation phase? These questions also assume that in the mobilization and implementation stages, conflict operated as both initiator and byproduct of change.

Authors have also noted that great social upheavals produce anomia—that is, normlessness (Durkheim 1951; Merton 1968). Almost by definition, social change includes the introduction of new norms, and this normative change often leaves whole segments of society in confusion or uncertainty.

In the case of Catholicism, normative replacement constituted a key element of the changes (O'Malley 1983). Change-oriented Catholics professed new and different norms from those of cautious Catholics (Murphy 1981:125–128; Neal 1970–1971), and this difference caused confusion. Suddenly, the church structure became quite disarticulated, especially if the parties holding contradictory norms performed important ecclesiastical functions (e.g., priests and bishops) which required that other Catholics relate to them regularly (Janowitz 1978).

One would expect that such normative disarticulation and confusion would have been greatest immediately after the Vatican Council (stage three). During this period, according to our delineation, mobilization was at its height; progressive and traditional factions vied intensely for the righteousness of their norms

(Murphy 1981: 125–129). The beginning of implementation, with continous new demands for additional changes, compounded the confusion. Officially required implementation of such elements as new liturgical rites and parish councils compelled people to make behavioral changes that implied new principles of action. At the Mass, for example, the norm of silence in the face of supernatural mystery was largely replaced by the norm of solidarity in worship as greater vocal participation and sociability were introduced.

We address kinds of anomia or disarticulation by examining the early byproducts of social change expected to occur during mobilization. These include the withdrawal syndrome, due to unclarity or weakness of norms, and disarticulation, especially between segments of the social movement and traditionalist authority figures. We investigate the disarticulation expected during implementation, too. This includes a wider spectrum of disarticulation, as the new thinking gradually affects new realms of Catholicism, and the anomia of structure building.

Patterns of accommodation are important. The theory of contested accommodation, sketched earlier, allowed room for local variation in the degree and rapidity of accommodation to the spirit of Vatican II (that is, to modernization). Although accommodations (changes) were decreed and required starting dates were set for some, many aspects of change were left to the discretion of the bishop and the goodwill of other key Catholics. Even in commitment to the Council spirit, dioceses showed great variation.

Dioceses also showed different patterns of acceptance. Some were collectively slow to incorporate the new ideas, whereas others were collectively quick. In some dioceses, a great struggle ensued between forces of modernization and the status quo. These varied patterns occurred across dioceses and across time periods, but we suspect that the conflict pattern occurred more frequently during mobilization than during implementation.

Some research questions cluster around the typical processes experienced by local dioceses on the path to accommodation. What issues of accommodation caused conflict and disarticulation? What were the common modalities of diocesan cohesion during the process of accommodation? Did they include conflict, cooperation, and other attitudes?

Study of the mobilization implementation period (1965–1971) centered on the first three questions below. Questions four and five were addressed to the implementation period (1971 to the present); the last three questions compared mobilization-implementation with implementation.

1. Did the conflict and disarticulation of this period seem to revolve around the key figures (priests and bishops)? Did their dominant collective orientations to change suggest conflict or disarticulation?

2. How much conflict actually occurred, especially between progressive

priests and traditional bishops? Were priests and bishops the predominant antagonists during that era? What other kinds of conflict occurred? What topics engendered the conflict?

3. Did the increase in priest resignations during this period (NORC 1972) coincide with changes in the official compliance structure of the Church? Or did it (as one would expect) precede ecclesiastical policy changes that would reflect the new attitude of Church self-examination, pastoral concern, priestly rights, and so forth? In other words, did the increase in priest resignations reflect a disarticulation problem?

4. What were the special successes of the implementation stage?

5. What were the most common problems of accommodation from diocese to diocese—conflict, the disorientation of symbols, cultural change, or structure building?

6. Was the conflict greater in the mobilization period than in the implementation period, as the stage theory would have us expect?

7. Did the conflicts of the two stages involve different issues and different antagonists, as the stage theory would have us expect?

8. Were the disarticulation and confusion greater (as expected) during the mobilization stage? Was this situation reflected in the nature of conflict issues and/or antagonists across periods? Was it reflected in diocesan cooperation?

Chapter Six

The Spiral of
Conflict

The contested accommodation of American Catholicism remains a central theme of this book. We now turn to that contest—that is, to the conflictual and contending-for-power aspects of the Catholic transformation.

Conflict both initiates and accompanies change. Such conflict constitutes the wisdom of sociology and underpins the social movement theory proposed in previous chapters. It appears to be reflected in each stage of the recent and continuing Catholic experience.

We will now examine empirically the length and breadth of this Catholic conflict. We also will see whether aspects of conflict support the contested accommodation theory, especially as elaborated in the social movement stages.

Conflict in the recent American Catholic Church falls into several pertinent categories. The categories derive in part from reflection on data culled from the *National Catholic Reporter* in the 1960s and 1970s. More important, they reflect the theoretical ideas presented in earlier chapters.

As reflections of the social movement notions, one would expect the issues and location of conflict to differ during mobilization and implementation stages. In mobilization, a movement becomes highly politicized—articulating its basic message, confronting old structures, and reaching out for new constituents. One would expect conflicts of that period to arise over core issues of the movement and to involve the most relevant key functions. During implementation, core notions ideally move into actuality, affecting people in ways probably not considered previously. One might expect affected parties to raise additional issues and to question the meaning of new decrees. Conflicts also involve a wider range of protagonists, as issues move outward from central structures.

Conflicts can be identified by their location inside or outside the Church. Many conflicts, such as battles over church finances or liturgies, were primarily internal. In these cases, all significant aspects of the conflict lay inside the Church, including primary antagonists and matters of contention.

In other cases, a significant aspect of the battle—usually the bone of contention and a major target or antagonist—lay outside the Church. For example, when the Berrigan brothers opposed the war in Vietnam and poured human blood on draft records, they were sharpening a conflict between church figures and federal government. Such conflicts we will label external because of their primary or initial focus. These conflicts also contained subordinate internal battles, such as those between Catholic supporters of the Berrigans and church officials (and Catholic laity) who wished to quash the Berrigan protest.

Internal Conflicts

By core internal conflicts we mean those arising over changes initiated directly by the Second Vatican Council, especially those affecting deep-rooted structures and symbols. Such changes include those affecting the authority structure and central symbolic acts and roles. Central symbolic acts include liturgy, especially the Mass; central symbolic roles include the organization of the life of hierarchs—the duties and life-style of parish priests and other men and women religious.

Such changes brought conflict. Affecting central and long-standing characteristics, they disrupted what many Catholics considered most sacred. One might predict that from these changes would emerge bitter battles of early mobilization.

The following examples highlight only one or two segments of ongoing and dynamic interplays, often among a variety of protagonists. We make no attempt to spell out the complete picture of each conflict. In addition, the categories are not mutually exclusive. Conflicts can fall into more than one category. Finally, note that we make numerous references to the *National Catholic Reporter* (NCR), which provided the data for this chapter.

Authority conflicts were exemplified in public demands by priests for the resignation of their bishop. In Raleigh, North Carolina, this confrontation concerned the legitimacy of Bishop Vincent Waters's traditionalist and punitive style of leadership, as he resisted change and exiled his progressive clergy.[1] Across the country, similar controversies erupted over the top-down, nonaccommodative style of episcopal authority. Cardinals Patrick O'Boyle of Washington, D.C., and James Francis McIntyre of Los Angeles, along with many other prelates of the late 1960s, met the storm in dramatic confrontations. Two of the most celebrated battles involving O'Boyle and McIntyre concerned Pope Paul's birth control encyclical and the renewal of the Sisters of the Immaculate Heart of Mary (see following). In expressing authority conflicts, American Catholics picketed chancery offices, refused to comply with bishops' directives, and protested their treatment of progressive clergy.

Some authority struggles touched directly the issue of consultation. By 1970, for example, many dioceses contained priest councils, nonapproved associations of local priests that had sprung up since Vatican II (Hennesey 1981). Where bishops resisted the authorized initiation of priest senates, councils surfaced as an alternative—an act of defiance in the new spirit. Father William DuBay even tried to form a labor union for priests, but was suspended from his priestly functions by Cardinal McIntyre (*NCR:* March 9, 1966).

Other authority fights involved subsidiarity, as when bishops delegated a task but scrutinized its performance, redirecting the process and changing the final product. Priests commonly complained that bishops looked too closely over their shoulders, undermining their autonomy and showing no respect for their professional competence.[2] Perhaps this strong episcopal supervision derived from the enormous concentration of authority enjoyed by bishops before Vatican II (Spencer 1966). In Chicago the Archdiocesan School Board criticized Cardinal John Cody for closing four schools without consulting the board first. Consequently, Cardinal Cody suppressed the school board and the priests' senate, rescinding their consultative powers (*NCR:* July 18, 1975).

Authority conflicts also occurred at the parish level. In Alexandria, Virginia, a five-month public battle raged over the role of the parish council; the council desired a shared ministry with the pastor, Father John Hannon, who allowed it only an advisory role. During this struggle, which divided the parish, the pastor disbanded the parish council. In turn the council appealed for due process and was finally reinstated (*NCR:* October 11, 1974 to February 7, 1975).

Battles raged over freedom, the obverse of authority. A new set of freedoms seemed to be legitimated by Vatican II documents, including freedom of conscience, academic freedom, professional freedom, personal freedom, and freedom of the press. Such freedoms became frequent battlegrounds after the Vatican Council. A booklet on human sexuality, prepared by medical students at Georgetown University in 1972, occasioned a conflict over academic freedom. Jesuit Father Edmund G. Ryan, executive vice-president for educational affairs, defended the students' right of expression; Cardinal Patrick O'Boyle and his officials criticized students and Father Ryan (*NCR:* December 15, 1972). In 1965, the restraints applied to such priests as Daniel Berrigan and Bonaventure O'Brien sparked a number of fasts, vigils, and advertisements—all in protest over the silencing of church members. These protests occurred on campuses such as Notre Dame and Iowa State, at the cathedrals in Chicago and Manchester, New Hampshire, and statements appeared in the *New York Times* (*NCR:* December 22, 1965). In addition, a number of diocesan newspapers were censured and their editors were fired (*NCR:* January 30, 1976).

Change itself was an issue, especially liturgical change. For many Catholics, a bedrock symbol of the church's validity was its very stability. Its presumed unchangeable nature, like the gospel, underscored its truth. Particularly subject to this traditional thinking was the Mass, which was virtually identical throughout the world. Many people wondered whether liturgical changes, even if introduced gradually and authoritatively were desirable. Furthermore, did those who jumped the gun to introduce new practices violate church law?

Catholics of different viewpoints often locked horns on these issues. In Beeville, Texas, Bishop Thomas Drury ordered Father Robert O'Hara out of the diocese after O'Hara allowed dances of celebration by Mexican-American children during an ordination liturgy (*NCR:* March 5, 1976). In Philadelphia, when Jesuit Father John Burton said an unauthorized experimental Mass in a private home, Cardinal Krol expelled him from the diocese and told him never to return for priestly work. The Mass had been said in English, without liturgical vestments, and with communion under both species (bread and wine) (*NCR:* January 4, 1966). In South Winston, Connecticut, Archbishop John Whealon ordered the priests of St. Margaret Mary Church not to give communion in the hand. When copastors and parishioners refused to comply, Wheaton threatened to transfer the copastors (*NCR:* September 26, 1975). Fights also occurred over altars facing the people, English translations of the scripture, folk or guitar masses, and other issues of liturgical change.

The Church experienced conflict over the new theology. Archbishop Lucey of Texas attacked Jesuit scripture scholar John McKenzie, labeling his book *Authority in the Church* heresy. Lucey took issue especially with the concept that authority belongs to the whole church and not just to the hierarchy (*NCR:* November 29, 1968).

The application of new theological ideas also brought conflict. Two religious education teachers in Alexandria, Virginia, resigned when Bishop Welch decreed that confession had to precede first communion (*NCR:* January 23, 1976).

Conflict arose over the symbolic role of especially focal Catholics—priests, men and women religious. The more experimentally-minded men and women religious met resistance as they adopted lay clothing or followed other secular patterns in housing or in political action.

Social and political action occasioned a great deal of conflict. When Father Eugene Boyle, a San Francisco priest, announced his candidacy for a legislative seat, Archbishop Joseph McGucken suspended him from preaching (*NCR:* February 22, 1974). When Father James E. Groppi, along with other priests and women religious, helped lead the boycott for public school desegregation in Milwaukee, Bishop Atkielski banned them from futher participation in such activities (*NCR:* December 15, 1965). In Albany twelve hundred students at St. Bernardine of Sienna College protested a similar diocesan ban on the civil rights activities of Reverend Bonaventure O'Brien (*NCR:* November 17, 1965). In New York, after Father Daniel Berrigan was exiled to Latin America to curtail his antiwar activities, Fordham University students picketed the house of his Jesuit Provincial Superior; Father Jogues Epple said he would fast in protest (*NCR:* December 1, 1965 and December 8. 1965).

The life-style issue also triggered strong reactions. Bishop Fury of San Diego suspended a pastor, Father Talmage Glazier, and ordered him to leave the rectory within forty-eight hours for penance in a monastery, after Glazier allowed a nuptial mass of a nonlaicized priest to take place. Father William Leahy of

Philadelphia, who performed the nuptial celebration for his brother John—married earlier in a civil ceremony—was suspended by Cardinal Krol. John Leahy was excommunicated.

Many Catholics protested the treatment of these priests. Protestors included the National Association of Pastoral Renewal and 250 signers of a petition to Cardinal Krol (*NCR:* December 6, 1967 to December 20, 1967). Controversy also boiled whenever women religious decided to eliminate their traditional uniform and identifying dress.

These issues (authority, freedom, change, new theology, and symbolic roles) appeared to match the characteristics of mobilization outlined in chapter 4. These characteristics included ideological battles, conflict over change itself, struggles of the most strongly affected groups (priests, women religious), and the targeting of pope, bishop, and pastor for blame.

These issues also seemed especially indicative of early mobilization efforts. They derived directly from the debates and documents of the Vatican Council. Though other issues were also discussed in Rome, the core of initiated change seemed to regard authority, freedom, symbolic updating, and direct work in the secular world (Fichter 1977; Murphy 1981; Fesquet 1967; Rynne 1968). Most of these root issues automatically involved the performers of key functions (bishop, priest, and other men and women religious). These issues had sharply divided the council itself, as progressive and traditional bishops struggled for the dominance of their respective positions (Fesquet 1967; Rynne 1968).

These conflicts appeared to be central. They touched what many conservative Catholics regarded as the main arteries of Catholicism—its authority structure, its stability, and its basic symbolism of liturgy, episcopacy, priesthood, and religious life. For progressive Catholics on the other hand, the conflicts also entailed a continued struggle for the rights that had been newly acquired at the Second Vatican Council.

Other conflicts involved age-old debates and secondary issues of accommodation. Age-old debates may have gained new popularity because so many other things were being questioned, but we have no way of making comparisons with the past. By secondary issues, we mean those issues that arose in the spirit of the Vatican Council but were not immediately a major focus. One would assume that such issues would be later causes of conflict, as proponents of change realized the full extent of implementation.

There were perennial issues of conflict, including money problems, clergy retirement, Christian burial, and boundary disputes. When Bishop Sullivan of Richmond, Virginia, denied a Catholic funeral service to a woman who had been cremated because of the decomposed condition of her body, he was deluged with protesting phone calls (*NCR:* January 5, 1973).

Then there were women's issues and issues regarding marriage and sexual norms. Women's issues focused on abortion, women's rights, the role of women in the Church, and the ordination of women. In 1975, for example, Bishop Maher of San Diego ordered his priests not to administer the Sacraments to any members of the National Organization for Women or to others who believed in abortion (*NCR:* April 18, 1975). In Chicago a young woman who was killed in a sky-diving accident was refused a requiem mass because she had administered an abortion clinic (*NCR:* May 24, 1974). Charity Ann Sack took her plea to become an altar girl, which was refused at the local level, all the way to the pope (*NCR:* February 1, 1974). The National Coalition of American Nuns denounced a study, issued by the U.S. Bishops' Committee on Pastoral Research and Practices, which failed to endorse the ordination of women (*NCR:* May 30, 1973)

Matters of marriage and sexual norms included birth control, marriage interpretations, divorce, remarriage of Catholics, changes in the marriage tribunal, and sexuality. In Murfreesboro, Tennessee, a group of women from St. Rose of Lima parish protested the Church's understanding of marriage after attending a church-sponsored workshop on natural family planning. They sent a letter to all United States bishops stating that this method of family planning was unacceptable as the only Church-approved method of birth control (*NCR:* July 2, 1976).

A series of social issues brought conflict. In San Francisco the Catholic Interracial Council of Mid-peninsula protested the construction of the San Francisco Cathedral on the grounds that it would increase the gap between the affluent institutional Church and its poverty-stricken members, especially those in the neighborhood of the new cathedral (*NCR:* November 24, 1965). In Sacramento four hundred people kept an around-the-clock vigil at the Cathedral of the Blessed Sacrament to protest Bishop Alden Bell's restrictions on Father Eugene Lucas. Lucas had participated in protest activities against the DiGiorgio grape growers in the Monterey-Fresno area, and Bell curtailed those activities (*NCR:* July 6, 1966).

Then, there was the issue of married clergy and the role of former religious. Father Anthony Girandola, a married priest, said Mass in a public school cafeteria in St. Petersburg, Florida, in order "to restore his own dignity," he said. Officials of the Bridgeport, Connecticut, diocese to which he belonged, stated that he was excommunicated (*NCR:* April 27, 1966). Another married priest, Father John Czaplewski, said Mass and preached a renewal service in Orrin, N.D., in the parish of Father Richard Sinner. The bishop demanded the immediate removal of Sinner from his parish for allowing the event (*NCR:* January 5, 1973). The National Conference of Diocesan Directors of Religious Education voted to oppose the Vatican regulation prohibiting them from hiring former priests and women religious as teachers (*NCR:* May 25, 1973).

Conflict arose over educational policies, including school closings and unionization of teachers. When Bishop Helmsing of Kansas City backed the diocesan school board's decision to close an inner-city school, parishioners marched and picketed a new school while a priest member of the school board resigned in protest (*NCR*: April 13, 1966). In Los Angeles, Catholic school lay teachers voted almost three to one to unionize, but the archdiocese refused to recognize the union despite threats of strikes and boycotts (*NCR*: April 30, 1976 and June 4, 1976).

Ecumenical policies occasioned conflict. In Detroit, twenty-five members of a Catholic traditionalist movement walked out of the Most Blessed Sacrament Cathedral and knelt in the vestibule saying the rosary when Rabbi Richard C. Hertz started speaking. The rabbi's talk was part of a ninety-minute observation of the Week of Prayer for Christian Unity (*NCR*: January 25, 1967).

A final set of secondary issues involved experimentation and new styles of worship, such as the Catholic Charismatic Movement and experimental parishes. Reports of factionalism and abuses of personal rights within the charismatic community at South Bend, Indiana, triggered a defense of the Charismatic Movement of Cardinal Suenens and a call by a former member of the True House Community for a thorough investigation of charismatic practices (*NCR*: August 15, 1975). A schism occurred between the official Catholic Church and an experimental parish—the Community of Pope John XXIII in Oklahoma City—over sharing communion with non-Catholics, accepting divorced Catholics, and congregational selection of the pastor (*NCR*: March 14, 1975).

As implied above, many of these conflicts were multilayered: they often included protagonists at several authority levels, such as pope, bishop, pastor, and congregation. In addition, the conflicts often could be described more precisely as a set of interrelated conflicts. The two following examples will illuminate these points.

In 1968, the conflict over the renewal efforts of the Los Angeles Sisters of the Immaculate Heart of Mary (IHM) reached a boiling point. Cardinal James F. McIntyre opposed the IHM renewal package, which included eliminating religious garb, searching out apostolic work, relaxing regulations within their convent community, and not being subject to the local bishop (*NCR*: March 13, 1968). Then the conflict extended to Rome. In the second week of March, the Vatican Congregation of Religious ruled against the IHM changes. In turn, several top-ranked IHM sisters petitioned the case in Rome; later, Rome appointed a four-person team to investigate (*NCR*: April 24, 1968).

The conflict simmered inside and outside the IHM community. Inside, the Vatican ruling was followed by a forty-hour meeting, in which the IHM sisters decided to appeal the order and to postpone obeying it. Given an individual option, the sisters voted ten to one to join the renewal group (*NCR*: June 16, 1968). Eventually a split occurred; the loyalists retained their traditional work and diocesan ties.

On the outside, laity and other women religious took up the battle. Many considered this case a test of whether women religious would have the right to decide their own internal reform in light of Vatican II (*NCR:* March 20, 1968). According to the *National Catholic Reporter,* three thousand sisters around the country supported the IHM renewal (*NCR:* March 27, 1968); by April 10, Los Angeles lay people had obtained over twenty-five thousand signatures on their petition to Pope Paul in support of the IHM sisters (*NCR:* April 10, 1968).

The IHM conflict was multilayered; it included protagonists at congregational, diocesan, national, and international levels. In addition, central issues varied from religious autonomy to appropriate renewal.

Other conflicts were also multilayered. The much-publicized conflict over Pope Paul VI's encyclical on birth control included protagonists at local, national, and international levels. The famous confrontations surrounding the Berrigan brothers centered on several related conflict issues, including peace, justice, authority, and appropriate religious behavior. The conflict occasioned by the Berrigans involved a range of antagonists from the U.S. government to Jesuit superiors to local bishops.

The Substance of Conflicts

Contested accommodation seems an apt description of the processes underlying these conflicts. The conflict issues seemed concerned largely with how the Church would adapt to the modern world in authority structure, religious dress, religious ceremonies, and other areas.

Yet was accommodation the dominant focus of these conflicts? Was accommodation the major stimulus to these conflicts in intensity or quantity? In order to analyze the conflicts, the extent to which they evidenced accommodation, and their correspondence to social movement stages, we gathered data from the *National Catholic Reporter* from 1966 to 1968 and from 1973 to 1976. (See Appendix 1 for methods used). Our expectations dealt with accommodation and with the stage theory of social movements developed above. Recall that the application to Catholicism stages overlapped. Yet, the late 1960s were a time of both mobilization and implementation, though the former overshadowed the latter. In the 1970s, implementation was dominant.

In a study of conflict issues of these two periods, we expected a substratum of identical issues, along with noteworthy differences. The overlap of stages suggested continuity, as did the closeness of the sample time periods from 1966 to 1968 and 1972 to 1976, with only a four-year break between them. In a longer period, one might predict less continuity of issues and more dramatic differences.

Specifically, we expected the Church to experience during both periods a high percentage of conflicts that focused on issues most resistant to change. In this case, we expected resistant issues to include the basic thrust of the movement because of its revolutionary character. As mentioned above, this thrust involved changes in core structures and symbols. Operationally, it included structural issues of authority and freedom, symbolic issues of liturgy and the role of key functions, and the ideological issue of the new theology. In short, during the 1960s and 1970s, a strong component of conflict issues should have concerned authority, freedom, liturgy, key functions, and new theology.

At the same time, the sixties and seventies should have reflected the distinctive features of their dominant social movement phases. During mobilization (late 1960s), we expected the core issues to be involved in conflicts even more dominantly than during the implementation phase (1970s). As noted above, core issues included changes of deep-seated structures, symbols, and ideology. Conflicts of the 1960s should have reflected the characteristics of mobilization detailed earlier. Though these characteristics overlap the core items just mentioned, they also elaborate them and include the types of protagonists. Mobilization issues would include change itself (e.g., the liturgy) and ideology (e.g., new theology, freedom, authority). They also would include conflicts targeting key people for blame (e.g., bishop and priest) and conflicts involving those most affected by the changes—that is, those with newly delegated roles and those initiating changes most prominently (e.g., priests, brothers, and women religious).

During the 1960s even more than during the 1970s, Church conflicts should have involved the core issues—authority, freedom, liturgy, change, ideology, and roles of key functions (bishop, priest, men and women religious). During the 1960s even more than during the 1970s, Church conflicts should have involved the following protagonists: bishops, parish priests, other men religious (priests and brothers) and women religious (sisters).

We expected to find during the later implementation period, the 1970s, other issues and protagonists to become more prominent than they were during the late 1960s. These included women's issues, marriage and family concerns, social issues, married clergy, educational policies, charismatic movement, ecumenism, and sexuality. In addition, the expansion of conflict should have been reflected in targets outside the Church itself. Thus, the 1970s should have witnessed greater degrees of external conflict.

Conflict issues and protagonists of the seventies should have followed the features of implementation. These include conflict over the meaning of changes, controversy surrounding public acceptance and legitimacy of new decrees, and mass enthusiasm or mass refusals. One would expect increased conflict over groups representing new interpretations, such as the charismatics or the traditionalists. One might also notice increased involvement in the conflicts by laity and by various organizations, both Catholic and non-Catholic.

During the 1970s more than the 1960s, Church conflicts should have concerned such subjects as women's issues, marriage and family concerns, social issues, married clergy, educational policies, sexuality, ecumenism, the Charismatic movement, and experimental communities. During the 1970s there should have been a higher percentage of external conflicts than during the 1960s. During the 1970s more than the 1960s, Church conflicts should have involved a wider variety of issues and protagonists. During the 1970s more than the 1960s, Church conflicts should have involved the following protagonists: laity, Catholic organizations, non-Catholic organizations, and other members of the hierarchy (beyond bishops and priests) such as the pope, the National Conference of Catholic Bishops, and regional associations of bishops.

To test these expectations, research centered on each relatively independent incident of conflict in the United States involving a Catholic side and described by the *National Catholic Reporter* for 1966–1968 and 1973–1976.[3] Two research assistants who were unacquainted with the hypotheses coded all pertinent conflicts after reading all pages of all issues of the *NCR* for the two periods. The Catholic protagonist was frequently but not always a member of the hierarchy or the clergy. Often laity and Catholic organizations constituted the Catholic side (or one of the Catholic sides).

The *NCR* was chosen for several reasons. It was the only paper to cover national Catholic news, including such conflicts. It came into being during the Second Vatican Council and represented an attempt to deal with changing Catholicism; this attempt increased its reliability for our purposes. Its somewhat liberal outlook made it more likely than a more traditional publication to print stories about conflict (Seidler 1974c). During those years it maintained a continuity of editor, publisher, and basic policy.

Conflicts in a Pattern

Research findings about the issues attracting most conflict during both 1960s and 1970s are in Table 6.1. Issues were indeed issues of accommodation, as expected. Struggles over authority and freedom indicated conflicts of updating—conflicts over the degree to which contemporary structures, such as consultation, subsidiarity, and personal autonomy, should be incorporated. Battles over liturgical change reflected the struggle to modify ritual according to recent scholarly advances in biblical and religious studies. Often, they also suggested a tug-of-war between those who approved and those who disapproved of expressing religious feeling through popular culture, as in the folk or guitar mass.

Social justice issues (n), too, reflected accommodation. As in the examples given above, conflicts of social justice often reflected two opposing viewpoints. One advanced the involvement of key persons, especially religious personnel, in social or political action to relieve suffering and aid the disadvantaged. The other position restricted priests and men and women religious from such

Table 6.1. Frequency Distribution of Issues

	Percentage involved in conflicts	
	1960s	1970s
Core Issues (internal conflicts only)		
a. Authority structure or style subsidiarity, consultation	78	66[a]
b. Freedom: professional, personal, academic, press, conscience	65	45[b]
c. Change: new liturgy, old liturgy, experimentation against norms	34	26
d. New theology	9	7
e. Bishops' life-style (or that of official church)	1.5	3
f. Clergy life-style, dual roles	8	2[c]
g. Women religious, life-style	5	2
Secondary Issues (internal conflicts only)		
h. Abortion	1.5	3
i. Equal Rights Amendment, National Organization for Women	0	3
j. Ordination of women	0	3
k. Women's role in the church	5	6
l. Marriage interpretation, divorce, remarriage of Catholics, changes in marriage tribunal	0	9[b]
m. Birth control, sexual norms	6	6
n. Social issues	23	30
o. Married clergy, role of ex-religious, ex-clergy	6	6
p. Educational policies, closing of schools, unionization of teachers	3	16[b]
q. Ecumenical cooperation	1.5	3
r. Charismatic movement, cults	0	6[a]
s. Experimental parishes, communities	5	6
Perennial Problems (internal conflicts only)		
t. Money problems, handling of finances	11	8
u. Clergy retirement	0	1
v. Christian burial	0	2
w. Boundary disputes	3	6
Totals (internal conflicts only: i.e., a-w)	[d]	[d]
(*N*)	(65)	(88)
Additional and Aggregated Issues		
x. External issues (all conflicts)	39	50[a]
(*N*)	(100)	(145)
y. Women's issues (h + i + j + k above; most salient issues only)	0	8[b]
(*N*)	(68)	(96)
z. Laity issues (h + l + m + p + v above; most salient issues only)	3	16[b]
(*N*)	(68)	(96)

Note: For calculation of differences involving most salient issues (see y and z), *N*s were slightly greater than the *N*s for calculation of differences involving internal issues. This discrepancy was due to the inclusion of complex conflict incidents (those with both internal and external aspects).

[a] Difference of proportions is significant at $p < .05$, one-tailed test.

[b] Difference of proportions is significant at $p < .01$, one-tailed test.

[c] Difference of proportions is significant at $p < .10$, one-tailed test.

[d] Total percentages for internal conflicts of the 1960s and 1970s are higher than 100%, because of the inclusive nature of responses.

secular action. Thus the contention often revolved around the extent to which religious functionaries should use secular action to solve social problems.

Many other issues listed in Table 6.1 also implied accommodation. Ecumenism, marriage, birth control, abortion, women's concerns, experimental parishes, new theology, ordination of women, and the life-style of bishop, clergy, and men and women religious all stemmed from the incorporation of contemporary thought. Our expectation that conflicts of accommodation would dominate during both decades seems to be supported.

The data also showed continuity between conflicts of the 1960s and those of the 1970s. In both periods, authority issues dominated the scene. Two items in Table 6.1 reveal this situation: authority (a) and freedom (b), which were closely interrelated. In addition, both periods experienced repeated conflict over change, especially liturgical change (c) and social justice (n). In both periods, conflicts also frequently involved priests and bishops (see Table 6.2), though they entailed some shifting, which will be explained later. Finally, both periods show a preponderance of internal conflict: 65 percent of the conflicts studied in the 1960s and 88 percent of those in the 1970s.

Other things we expected about conflict during the 1960s and 1970s received only implicit support. New theology (Table 6.1, issue d) and the role of key

Table 6.2. Frequency Distributions of Protagonists (internal conflicts only)

		Percentage involved in conflicts	
		1960s	1970s
a.	The ordinary—bishop, chancery official, spokesperson for diocese	74	66
b.	Priest clergy	72	65
c.	Other male religious (brothers)	14	7
d.	Women religious (nuns and sisters)	17	13
e.	Lay Catholics	52	72[a]
f.	Other hierarchy, at diocesan, regional, national, or international levels (e.g., pope, regional association of bishops, National Conference of Catholic Bishops)	32	44[a]
g.	Catholic organizations, institutions, schools, parishes, official organs (newspapers)	57	70[b]
h.	Non-Catholic organizations	14	19
i.	Non-Catholics, or individuals of unspecified religion	18	8[b]
	(*N*)	(65)	(88)

Note: Percentages total more than 100%, because of the inclusion of several protagonists in each conflict incident.

[a] Difference of proportions is significant at *p* < .01, one-tailed test.

[b] Difference of proportions is significant at *p* < .10, one-tailed test.

functions (e,f,g,j,k,o) were not numerically dominant. Even so, conflict over new theology and key functions lurked beneath the issues that predominated most visibly. For example, battles over liturgical change (c), freedom of conscience (b), consultation and subsidiarity (a) all arose because of the new theology, which legitimated them. Many issues of authority and freedom (a, b) pitted a traditional bishop against a priest who wished to exercise his newly understood professional activities. In addition, conflict over the civil rights activism of priests (n) often reflected opposing viewpoints of the role of clergy.

The implicit nature of this support requires an additional explanation. Because the coders recorded only explicit and specific issues in the conflicts, certain general and basic issues, such as new theology and role of clergy, were not always recorded. Thus, conflicts involving basic, resistant, and explosive issues predominated during both decades.

At the same time, findings indicate a differentiation between decades along the lines expected. The reported conflicts of the 1960s included higher proportions of the core issues than did those of the 1970s (see Table 6.1). Thus issues of authority (a), freedom (b), liturgical and related change (c), ideology (d), and roles of key functions, especially those of clergy (f) and of women religious (g), all triggered significantly more conflict in the 1960s. In other cases, such as conflicts over new theology and life-style of women religious, the reported cases were so few that significance was difficult to reach. In any case, all items except bishops' life-style produced the expected trends. Further, the late 1960s produced greater proportions of conflict involving the ordinary (bishop), priests, brothers, and women religious (see Table 6.2, items a-d). Though no difference was statistically significant, all differences were in the predicted direction.

We now turn to the 1970s. The 1970s saw increased proportions of conflict over other issues. Statistically significant increases occurred in conflicts over marriage and family concerns (Table 6.1, issue 1), education policies (p), the charismatic movement (r), and women's issues in the aggregate, combining abortion, ERA, ordination of women, and women's role in the Church (see issue y). Expected increases, though not statistically significant, also arose over ecumenism (q) and social justice (n). Three issues—birth control (m), experimental communities (s), and married clergy (o)—did not produce the expected differences; but the birth control issue quickly became an authority issue of the late 1960s (Greeley 1977) and deserves separate treatment. The findings generally suggest that other issues emerged more strongly during the seventies.

External conflicts occurred more frequently in the 1970s than in the 1960s as expected (in 50 percent of incidents in the 1970s, versus 39 percent in the 1960s) (see Table 6.1, item x).

There was an increased variety of issues during the 1970s. In Table 6.1, column 2 (1970s), all twenty-four cells were occupied, in contrast to eighteen cells in the 1960s. Conflict apparently extended outward to include more frequently such issues as women's concerns, social justice, new religious movements, and lay issues.

Lay issues provided an interesting indicator of this extension thesis because conflicts in the 1960s tended to focus so heavily on priests and other religious personnel. Lay issues included at least the following: educational matters, marriage issues, sex norms, abortion, and Christian burial. Aggregating these issues (if they were the most salient in any incident) produced the significant differences reported in item z (Table 6.1). At the minimum, then, conflicts seemed to extend outward by embracing lay issues. At the same time, the new issues of the 1970s did not completely replace the dominant issues of the 1960s. Instead, the new issues seemed to present additional arenas of conflict.

Our expectation that there would be a greater variety of protagonists in the 1970s was not supported by these data (see Table 6.2). Both decades saw a great variety of protagonists, though the 1970s probably saw a greater balance between the involvement of traditional authority figures (bishop, priest, women and men religious) and others, such as laity and organizations.

Finally, the data show a shift in type of protagonist, as expected. During the 1970s, we note increases in involvement by laity and organizations, both Catholic and non-Catholic (see Table 6.2: e,g,h). Two of the three predicted cross-decade trends were statistically significant.

Interpreting the Pattern of Conflict

The data supported a variety of predictions based on the proposed theory, including the concept of contested accommodation. The Catholic structure was riddled with conflict and even with schism, as in the case of the experimental congregation mentioned earlier and the case of the traditionalist movement led by Gomar DePauw.[4] In addition, the conflicts centered overwhelmingly on issues of accommodation, a continuation of the nearly century-old battle to update the Catholic Church.

Findings also supported the framework of social movement stages, at least as applied to the perids of mobilization-implementation (1965–1970) and implementation (1970–1980s). We saw this pattern in a variety of continuities and differences between the conflicts of the 1960s and those of the 1970s.

In particular, continuities included the dominance of basic and resistant issues such as authority, freedom, and change, especially in liturgy. Differences included a greater emphasis on authority structure and clergy life-style in the 1960s, and increased variety and extension of issues during the 1970s. A shift in type of protagonist also occurred; lay Catholics, organizations, and other hierarchy were involved more frequently during the 1970s.

The continuities imply an overlap of movement stages. They also suggest that the controversy over fundamental changes—in structure, key functions, and symbolic activities—was prolonged and bitter. As noted above, the strong presence of continuities probably also reflects the small time span (four years) between the two periods under consideration.

The differences lend solid support to the other aspect of the proposed theory—namely, the domination of mobilization in the 1960s and of implementation in the 1970s. Mobilization was indicated by the conflicts over changes in deep-rooted structures and symbols, as well as by the underlying ideological struggle over authority, freedom, and role of clergy. Mobilization efforts were also typified by battles involving key targets for blame (priest and bishop) and by the struggles of those initiating changes most prominently (priests, women and men religious). Such conflicts reflected the early battle to win or retain special resources in the Church. These resources included legitimacy for new or old structures or activities, visibility (see Bromley and Shupe 1979), and de facto power through organizational strength or support by other Catholics.

A few examples from the 1960s may suggest the flavor of mobilization. The famous birth control controversy of 1968 triggered innumerable petitions, sanctions, demonstrations, speeches, and editorials, all aimed at winning supporters and obtaining organizational clout. In addition, survey data show that many American Catholics formulated modern attitudes toward birth control at the time of this controversy (Greeley 1977). Thus the conflicts over authority and birth control signaled a time of intense mobilization.

The late 1960s saw a range of conflicts surrounding attempts to organize the middle and lower echelons within the Church. For example, Father William DuBay was at the vortex of dramatic Church confrontations in California when he began a priests' union and announced officers (*NCR:* March 9, 1966). Conflicts also arose over the formation of many other new groups—black clergy, lay associations, priests' councils and senates—all battling to win their rights as interest groups and thus struggling toward wider participation (Kiely 1968; Stewart 1978:14–15). At the other extreme, the traditionalist movement suddenly surged forward, causing additional tension (Dinges 1983). There was a special air of excitement and drama during these years,[5] and much of it focused on winning constituents or marshaling strength for a particular Church orientation.

The skeptic may attribute this high Church drama of the 1960s to spillover from the larger society, which experienced so much confrontation and violence in those years. The skeptic may also think that the apparently quieter 1970s corresponded to the cooling of greater America. These data show more than mere drama and quiescence. Furthermore, the 1970s may have shown fewer signs of the mobilization/ politicization drama, but they were anything but quiet: on the average, the *NCR* reported more conflicts per year in the seventies (36) than in the sixties (33).

The 1970s witnessed fuller implementation, as indicated by the extension and permeation of conflict. These conflicts involved a greater variety of issues and higher percentages of laity and organizations; this trend suggested in turn that the United States Church at large was gradually turning its attention toward the manner and desirability of applying the principles of Vatican II to a whole set of new situations. It did not turn its back on the basic issues of radical change, but by the 1970s it seemed to have moved beyond the constant focus on key persons and symbols. Apparently, in the 1970s, Catholics at large accepted basic change more generally. Now they fought more frequently over change at other organizational junctures, involving more secondary issues. They struggled over the extension of change to additional nooks and crannies within Catholicism.

A few examples may be useful here. Conflict in the 1970s included laity and other hierarchy besides the local ordinary. At times, protest groups confronted the Vatican; at other times, they attacked the National Conference of Catholic Bishops. Religious people fought administrators of Catholic hospitals, schools, and other institutions. The local parish also saw increased conflict during the 1970s; laity often demanded greater input, and fought over the dismissal of parish councils and religious educators. The laity also battled among themselves, as in attacks and counterattacks regarding charismatic communities. This increased involvement of lay, organizational, and other hierarchical protagonists indicated an extended implementation during the 1970s.

One serendipitous finding also supported the hypothesis of extended implementation. Internal conflicts of the 1970s were apparently more complex in greater proportions. That is, they increasingly involved subordinate extraorganizational conflicts; the percentage jumped from 6 percent to 17 percent (15 of 88). In 1976, for example, the Archdiocese of Los Angeles refused to allow its Catholic school teachers to unionize, even though the vote to unionize was ordered by the National Labor Relations Board. Like many dioceses in that year, Los Angeles was in conflict with its own teachers and the supporting labor arm of the federal government.

Another conflict involving a subsidiary battle grew out of plans by St. John's High School in Washington, D.C., to give Governor George Wallace a President's Medal at a school banquet. The major conflict pitted members of the Christian Brothers, who teach at the school, against the school administration, but an additional implied conflict existed between the brothers and Governor Wallace. A final example is the 1974 demonstration of Catholic Women for ERA, aimed at the National Conference of Catholic Bishops and the National Conference of Catholic Laity and challenging them to support the Equal Rights

Amendment. The Catholic Women for ERA challenged both the Catholic leadership and wider social structures.

Many of these complex battles were fought over social and political issues, especially those concerning justice. Such battles reflect the diffusion of change, as many within the Church worked toward renewed responsiveness to contemporary society.

The shifting issues also imply that change was actually occurring. Let us recall the change in importance of authority conflicts.

Conflicts in the 1960s seemed largely to reflect a progressive or radical challenge to traditional episcopal authority. Many bishops (and pastors) apparently were not ready at that time to accept as legitimate a variety of steps toward aggiornamento. Though the Church, through its council, had officially approved the progressive agenda, many of its leaders could not tolerate the speed and innovativeness of progressive advances. The crisis of official or constitutional legitimacy during the council years gave way in the later 1960s to the crisis of local legitimacy, or legitimacy among Church members at large.

The decrease in importance of authority conflicts in the 1970s probably reflected the hierarchy's growing acceptance of the progressive thrust. Apparently, this growing acceptance brought the American episcopacy closer to the thinking of mainline Catholics and the bulk of the clergy (NORC 1972; Seidler 1972, 1974b, 1979). Along this line, Greeley (1977) notes that those appointed to the episcopacy in the United States during the 1970s tended to be more in tune with the spirit of the Second Vatican Council.

Additional aspects of the contested accommodation theory also received support here, including the long struggle and the role of key functions.

The data remind us once again that the progress of this movement was not automatic. True enough, they suggest a steadily advancing permeation of change from central to peripheral organizational points, but the continuation of conflict over both radical change and secondary issues suggests a long battle over restructuring and renewal. In fact, the data point to important battlegrounds, such as authority, where change was anything but automatic.

Key functionaires both advanced and slowed the movement, especially in priest-bishop conflicts. In addition, a variety of subgroups played important roles; these included the organizations mobilizing resources for change as well as subgroups that resisted change. Lay boards, school administrators, parishioners, and traditionalists all lent their power and support to one side or the other in the battle for determining the direction of the Church. The speed of change and its direction were often determined by a host of key functionaries and other subgroups.

These findings support the stage theory almost exactly as proposed above, with overlap of stages and gradual permeation of movement ideas to new arenas. These notions provide a dynamic view of movement stages that apparently reflects reality.

We would now go even further in proposing the continuity of basic processes such as legitimation. In this case, the legitimation struggle has extended from stage one to stage four, though the focus has changed from constitutional legitimation to local legitimation and from legitimation of core issues to legitimation of secondary issues. Mobilization, too, continued throughout the movement, though its high points apparently occurred during the late 1960s as predicted. Implementation began during stage two and has continued ever since.

Chapter Seven

The Battle over
Birth Control

At this point, the reader may desire a longer look at a single salient conflict. To supplement the wide-angled view of the whole group of conflicts, this chapter presents a series of closeups from many angles, all focused on a famous battle.

Here we will describe and interpret from newspaper accounts the conflict over the birth control encyclical, issued by Pope Paul VI in 1968. This controversy was chosen because it represents preeminently the root issues of church transformation. It touched on contested aspects of authority and other key topics, including papal power, freedom of conscience, control over laity, and the roles of expert commissions, professional theologians, and priest-confessors.

The method will be a looser kind of content analysis than employed in the previous chapter. This approach includes reading and sociological reflection on documents and news accounts of the pertinent actions. The documents include the encyclical itself *(Humanae Vitae)* and a supporting statement issued by the American Catholic bishops. Newspapers and magazines include the *National Catholic Reporter*, the *Washington Post*, the *New York Times*, *Time* magazine, and others.

The goal is to increase our sociological understanding of the conflict and of the change process itself by studying a major battle of that era. In particular we will ask, "How can we understand this conflict in its organizational context?" and "Can the details of this conflict help us understand the meaning of the larger process of change?" These questions will lead us to investigate various aspects of the conflict, including its issues, protagonists, and resolution.

In July 1968, Pope Paul VI published his seventh encyclical, *Humanae Vitae*, which condemned abortion, sterilization, and artificial birth control. A storm of criticism broke, especially over the condemnation of artificial birth control. The criticism was especially strong, in part because the pope himself set aside the majority opinion of a special theological commission he had convoked to study the issue.

In effect, the encyclical dashed the rising expectations of many Catholics; thus the controversy was intense. In the words of Pope Paul VI himself, speaking a decade later (Foy 1978:64), "there was a certain climate of expectancy" that the encyclical would relax traditional church teaching on birth control. A number of developments had contributed to such expectations.

The Vatican II document on marriage had formulated a new working principle for understanding sex within marriage. It stated a more personalist under-standing of the marriage relationship, underscoring the love between partners as the context in which children emerge (*Pastoral Constitution on the Church in the Modern World*, #48–52, in Abbott 1966:250–258). This principle re-placed the old terminology of the primary and secondary ends of marriage (chil-dren and personal fulfillment, respectively). The new personalist understanding gave theologians and others a rationale to support the use of artificial birth control.

Other factors too, although not always recognized consciously, contributed to a climate of expectancy among Catholics. These included recent increases in life expectancy for women, greater percentages of women in the work force, and newly developing norms of smaller family size, even among Catholics.

The climate of expectancy about the official norms was accompanied by a real shift in the everyday norms of lay Catholics. As Greeley (1977:129) reports, the changes can be seen by comparing survey results of the mid-sixties with those of the mid-seventies. The percentage of Catholics who agreed strongly with the notion that husband and wife may have sexual intercourse for pleasure alone al-most doubled, from 29 percent to 50 percent. The percentage of Catholics ap-proving artificial contraception rose from 45 percent to 83 percent in a decade. In 1963, 41 percent thought "a family should have as many children as possible and God will provide for them"; only 18 percent agreed with that statement in the mid-seventies.

This was also the period of new expectations about the papacy. No longer did Catholics generally expect autocratic utterances such as those from Pius XII, the pre–Vatican II pope who represented a monarchical papacy. Their expecta-tions were indeed supported by the documents of Vatican II, which worked out a compromise between papacy and collegial church (*Dogmatic Constitution on the Church*, in Abbott 1966:14–101). Accordingly, post-Vatican II popes were to reflect the entire church (*Newsweek:* August 26, 1968).

Greeley's data reflect this change. In 1963, 70 percent of Catholics thought it was "certainly true" that Jesus handed over leadership of his church to Peter and the popes; ten years later, that figure had dropped to 42 percent. Further-more, in the later period only 32 percent thought it was "certainly true" that the pope was infallible when speaking on faith or morals (Greeley 1977:128).

Pope Paul chose to ignore the consultative leadership style legitimated at the Council, at least for the birth control issue. Some say he was unduly influenced by ultraconservative curial officials. In *Humanae Vitae,* Paul spoke only for a limited viewpoint (Woodward 1968).

In this new papal role, Paul VI was especially vulnerable. He himself encour-aged and required the institutionalization of more consultative and representa-tive structures. Church leaders at lower levels were expected to consult with a greater range of people and to delegate responsibilities increasingly. Ironically, however, Paul seemed to countermand his own requirements when he refused to listen to the advice of his special commission. No wonder, then, that he heard such an outcry when he reaffirmed the traditional ban on artificial birth control. In effect, he had promoted increased consultation and then had reverted to the old monarchical papal style.

Throughout this country—indeed, throughout the whole Western world—Catholics disagreed publicly with the pope. In Washington, D.C., the site of the most celebrated conflict on the topic in this country, forty-four members of the Association of Washington Priests, led by Reverend John E. Corrigan, stated their position, which the *Washington Post* (September 23, 1968) reported as follows: "They say they believe the encyclical must be respected. But they say that they respect the right of the individual to differ, in conscience, with the encyclical, and to practice contraception in accordance with their *(sic)* conscience."

In Washington, as in many other places, the bishop acted as a second catalyst in the conflict. Patrick Cardinal O'Boyle, in a continued dispute with the dissenting priests, maintained that the papal encyclical banning contraception must be obeyed strictly. After the forty-four priests publicly reaffirmed their position on September 14, 1968, O'Boyle began to interview them individually. By September 23 he had suspended two from public ministry and had imposed lesser penalties on eleven more, including Father Corrigan.

On Sunday, September 22, 1968, Cardinal O'Boyle—called the harshest of papal defenders (Hoyt 1968)—pursued his attack on dissenters from his pulpit in St. Matthew's Cathedral. At both the 10:00 A.M. and 12:30 P.M. masses he read his own pastoral letter, in which he warned against "false ideas of freedom of conscience" (*WP*: September 23, 1968). He also ordered this letter to be read in all churches of the archdiocese, in place of any other sermon and without any commentary. In the letter, according to the *Washington Post* (ibid.):

> the Cardinal said "false prophets" led many couples to practice contraception. He said he felt compassion for those who "were misled for a time, but who listened to the teaching reaffirmed by Pope Paul." But he cited a stern Old Testament curse visited on those who instead follow "a false idea of freedom of conscience." " . . . 'the Lord will blot out his name from under Heaven'," the Cardinal quoted, telling worshippers that he felt he had to act because he could not "stand by and let you be misled by an idea of freedom of conscience that could bring down on you so horrible a curse."

Reactions to the cardinal's letter were swift and varied. Some parishioners walked out of Mass as the cardinal began to read his pastoral letter, but most of the 800 to 1000 people who remained for the reading of the letter at St. Matthew's at the 10:00 A.M. and 12:30 P.M. masses gave the cardinal a standing ovation when he concluded. About 150 persons walked out during the 12:30 P.M. mass, and about 30 or 40 at the 10:00 A.M. mass. Most of these protesters filed out of church silently, but one woman hurried to the communion rail and began to shout statements, apparently in support of the dissenting priests, until the ushers led her away.

Among some, reactions and emotions ran high. Outside the church after the 10:00 A.M. mass, impromptu debates erupted between supporters of the cardinal's position and those backing the priests. Three or four women shouted, "Communists . . . hippies . . . " at some dissenters.

Later that day, Father Corrigan issued a statement saying "he was 'hurt and embarrassed' that the cardinal implied he and the other dissenters would be subject to the curse." He then counterattacked by stating that he believed the cardinal had isolated himself from the rest of the Church by claiming that "conscience is formed exclusively by an encyclical" (*WP:* ibid.).

Similar walkouts occurred at other churches in the Washington metropolitan area as the cardinal's letter was read. In most cases, as planned by the walkout organizers, parishioners returned when the letter ended (*WP:* September 22, 1968; September 23, 1968).

Other kinds of protest actions also took place. One member of the clergy renounced his monsignorship (*Newsweek:* August 26, 1968), and John Cogley, the distinguished Catholic author, stopped writing his column for diocesan journals, at least until his doubts were cleared. Cogley took this action to express his personal anguish at the dissent over the birth control encyclical. He struggled to reconcile his view that the papal ruling was a disaster with the notion that the church speaks with divine credentials (Dotey 1968).

Pope Paul was not the only focal point of conflict. His episcopal colleagues (bishops), especially those who attempted to force compliance with the papal decree in their local jurisdictions, also received flak. Therefore we will analyze the conflict in its two organizational forums—the local diocesan scene and the wider international (or at least Western) Catholic Church.

One may categorize this conflict—that is, this congeries of related conflicts—in a number of ways. We will organize initial analysis around the following subtopics: the ideology of the conflict, its organizational setting, and its resolution. Later reflections will concern the political side and the larger meaning for the Church.

Conflict Ideology and
Organizational Setting

Ideologically, the conflict revolved around three intertwined but separable issues: birth control, freedom of conscience, and authority. For each issue a variety of understandings prevailed, but the meanings generally boiled down to a new and an old understanding.

The new understanding of birth control derived from a number of sources: historical exegesis of Church positions on sexual behavior (Noonan 1965), inductive theologies (Küng 1976), personalist and existentialist philosophies, and contemporary sociocultural facts about life expectancy, population problems, and the role of women (Greeley 1973). So the Vatican carefully chose statements about the marital context of childbearing.

The old understanding derived from opposite sources: firm loyalty to traditional church doctrine on sexual behavior, deductive theologies, Thomistic philosophy, and a nostalgia for the sociocultural facts of a bygone era. So there were traditional norms of many children, birth control only by sexual abstention, and children as the main goal of marriage.

In the realm of authority, a number of related topics apparently magnified the controversy. In addition to the monarchical versus consultative style of leadership and the different theologies of service and governance, sharp differences existed on the meaning and use of sanctions, the place of lay expertise, and the role of the priest as professional.

In the case of Cardinal O'Boyle, these authority factors converged. He acted as the completely traditional leader in portraying monarchical leadership and a governance mentality, in using negative and exclusionary sanctions, in minimizing the professional autonomy of clergy, and in neglecting lay expertise in the birth control issue. A more progressive leader would have embraced at least some of the opposites.

One organizational setting of the conflict was the diocese. In Washington the conflict was largely vertical. It pitted Cardinal O'Boyle against the dissenters, who were mostly curates engaged in parish work. In fact, the Washington dissenters consisted of fifty-two priests, of whom only two were pastors.[1] They were his subjects, with little recourse to outside appeal. Given the independence and power of American bishops, this vertical conflict—between subject and superior—was real. The cardinal possessed tremendous authority and the dissenters had little, at least in setting diocesan policy.

Even in other places where the context was different but the topic was the same, conflict was vertical. In Buffalo, Bishop McNulty dismissed six priests from the faculty of St. John Vianney Seminary for publicly dissenting from the papal encyclical (*Time:* September 6, 1968). The major relevant power became that of the bishop over his subjects.

Subsidiary conflicts in Washington were also largely vertical. Supporters of the dissenters, such as those who walked out of church during the pastoral letter, clearly targeted the cardinal as their problem. O'Boyle was the sole authority, and he expected dissenters and supporters alike to obey.

These vertical conflicts, however, involved more than the usual subject-superior problem. Other overtones emerge if one considers the whole range of supporters. In the Washington area, supporters of the dissenters included thirteen staff members of elementary schools, twenty-four Jesuits from Gonzaga High School and Georgetown University (*NCR:* October 16, 1968), twenty-one faculty members of the Catholic University of America (*NCR:* January 8, 1969), four hundred members of the Committee on Freedom in the Church, and seven hundred members of the Washington Lay Association (*WP:* September 22, 1968). Many of these supporting groups reflected staff or professional reactions, stemming in part from their expertise.

In addition, the historical context modified the simple vertical relation. During this period of change, many groups, such as the Washington supporters, represented a challenge to traditional line authority. The groups listed above included professional theologians representing the new theology, members of religious orders (such as Jesuits) who were likely to initiate change, and lay groups who were conscious of their recently affirmed participation in church authority. All of them had a reason to believe that the bishops did not have, or should not have, all diocesan power.

The vertical conflict was also complicated by the involvement of groups from other substructures within Catholicism. The dissenters received support, implicitly or explicitly, from groups that publicly championed freedom of conscience regarding birth control. They included the Detroit priests' association, 170 Brooklyn priests (*NCR:* October 16, 1968), 72 Baltimore priests, 150 Boston priests (*NCR:* October 2, 1968), 55 British priests, 76 London laity (*National Register:* October 13, 1968), 317 priests from throughout the U.S., and 3,000 laity (*NCR:* September 18, 1968).[2] In addition, 650 American Catholic theologians agreed that spouses may decide whether to practice birth control (*NCR:* January 8, 1969). In Europe 20 theologians took a similar stand at a professional meeting in Amsterdam (*WP:* September 22, 1968).

On the other side, Cardinal O'Boyle also received support. At his request, two prominent priests, one a moral theologian and the other a professor of ethics, spoke in support of the encyclical to the priests and the Catholic school teachers of the diocese (*NCR:* September 18, 1968; October 2, 1968). In addition, Catholics United for the Faith and ninety lay men and women of Washington gave the cardinal public support.

The Washington conflict moved quickly into the wider public sphere. Groups from other American dioceses and from other countries—priests, women and men religious, laity, theologians—all applied pressure or gave support to the antagonists in the local conflict. All parties were aware of the general debate within Catholic—and non-Catholic—public opinion.

The vertical conflict became one catalyst of a wider debate within Catholicism about the birth control norm and the legitimate uses of authority and freedom of conscience. The Washington conflict seemed to sharpen the issues and magnify their importance.

Yet even with these added conditions, the Washington conflict remained dominantly vertical. One reason for this was the rather decisive segmental differentiation within Catholicism. Dioceses remained basically separate entities; bishops retained immense power and independence.[3] Especially in this case, where the cardinal sided with Rome, his position bent to no pressure. On the other hand, the dissenting priests, although supported psychologically and in the public realm, had to face the cardinal on their own.

Lateral conflicts also occurred, though they were apparently of lesser importance. For example, when parishioners engaged in disputes and name calling among themselves, both sides occupied positions at the bottom of the organizational chart. Their fights simply involved two moderately powerless groups.

In the wider, international forum—indeed, even in the national American setting—the conflict appeared to be largely diagonal. That is, it was a clash between lower-ranking people in one unit (theologians) and higher-ranking people in another unit (bishops), the units being distinguished roughly on the same basis as professional and administrative segments of a university.

The wider conflict appeared to set theologians against bishops. Of course, not all theologians took the progressive stand, and neither were bishops unanimously traditional. Yet by and large, the originators and spokespersons of the new and the old positions were theologians and bishops, respectively. Theologians, such as Karl Rahner and Bernard Haring, developed the counterdoctrine regarding both conscience and birth control. Theologians, such as the 650 Americans and the 20 Europeans noted above, then led the fight for public acceptance. On the other hand, bishops—including the pope—articulated the traditional birth control doctrine.

In addition, theologians and bishops reflected different units or substructures within Catholicism. These were loosely structured units of specialization; bishops and theologians each functioned with their own unique tasks and orientations. The functional differentiation between hierarchy and professionals resulted in nonterritorial substructures that cut across dioceses.

Evidence for these different substructures appears in the Washington conflict. There, Cardinal O'Boyle was slower in disciplining the professionals than the other dissenters. During the autumn months of 1968, he punished the parish priests by removing their right to perform public priestly functions, but he did not touch the dissenting professionals. One explanation for this is that these professionals usually belong to another substructure, such as a university or a religious order, through which the cardinal may have been attempting to work his sanctions. In addition, theologians and Catholic scholars had gained a degree of unofficial autonomy in recent years, and the cardinal may have decided to deal with them cautiously. In sum, theologians and scholars, although subject to the local bishop in certain regards, could take partial refuge in another sub-structure of authority.

As suggested above, the conflict occurred basically between professionals and administrators. The papal commission on birth control, which recommended relaxation of the Church's traditional stand, consisted of professionals—phys-icians, scientists, bishops, theologians, sociologists, psychologists, and marriage counselors. It was theologians who elaborated the personalist moral philosophy of liberal Catholicism.

Bishops, on the other hand, are top administrators of their diocese, as well as top administrators, jointly, of worldwide Catholicism. True, they are also ex-pected to be doctrinal leaders, but the requirements of office leave little time for professional theologizing, and, indeed, few were trained to be professional theologians (Reese 1983). In their statement of November 1968, the American bishops recognized this role-related source of conflict when they set down norms for fruitful dialogue between bishops and theologians (1968:4).

Four aspects of the conflict flowed from professional-administrative differ-ences: expertise versus discipline, staff-line problems, traditional versus charis-matic authority, and distinctive basic concerns. Progressive theologians and others who joined their side argued in a typically professional way, whereas the traditionalist bishops, Pope Paul, and others who defended papal authority and the encyclical took a typically administrative approach. We emphasize the American scene, with some citations of European reactions.

Blau and Scott (1962:247) stated the difference between expertise and disci-pline: "Professional expertness and bureaucratic discipline may be viewed as al-ternative methods of coping with areas of uncertainty. Discipline does so by reducing the scope of uncertainty; expertness, by providing the knowledge and social support that enable individuals to cope with uncertainty and thus to as-sume more responsibility."

As if to echo Blau and Scott, Cardinal Charles Journet, a Swiss theologian and a staunch defender of Pope Paul, said, "The teaching of the encyclical . . . brings certainty. It does not make sense for a son of the church to oppose the authority of the church" (*NCR:* October 16, 1968). Apparently, then, Pope Paul and the defenders of the encyclical expected the pope's statement to reduce uncertainty via bureaucratic discipline.

Professionals who supported the opposite viewpoint approached uncertainty quite differently. They used the expertise of a number of disciplines—scripture studies, theology, philosophy, biology, and the social sciences. Placing the in-formation together, they brought new input to moral conclusions, changing the understanding of the actions and circumstances under consideration. The result was the new understanding of the marriage act, as reflected in the documents of Vatican II, and a new emphasis on personal decision making and responsibility. Reflecting Blau and Soctt's statement above, they provided the knowledge and support that would allow the laity to cope with uncertainty and assume more responsibility.

Major articulators of the opposition were those in staff positions, such as professional theologians, teachers of philosophy, and canon lawyers (*NCR:* January 8, 1969). The main defendants of the status quo were the line officers, especially pope and bishops.

Their conflict seemed typical of staff-line problems. As Dalton (1964) stated, "To the thinking of many line officers, the staff functioned as an agent on trial." In this case, too, Catholic theologians were on trial. The staff of the Buffalo seminary were called in to the bishop and questioned about their views on the pope's and the bishop's authority, then dismissed if they gave the wrong answer (*Time:* October 4, 1968). In Mobile, Archbishop Thomas Toolen demanded that the forty-five theologians and scholars on the faculty of a forum to discuss post-Vatican II theology take a loyalty oath, pledging that they would uphold the Catholic Church's teaching on birth control (*NCR:* September 8, 1968). Consequently, the forum, scheduled to open on September 16, 1968, was canceled. In Sioux City, the bishop demanded a loyalty oath unto death regarding the birth control encyclical (*NCR:* October 16, 1968).

The conflict also reflected a struggle over professional autonomy (Pondy 1967; Etzioni 1964:76); specialists wish to be treated as responsible adults. As one representative of the Washington dissenters put it, "We are all children of God—but we are not children" (*WP:* September 22, 1968). The birth control conflict reflected the status of Catholic professionals, who were frequently scrutinized with suspicion. To counteract this tendency, forty European theologians petitioned for a reform of the Roman congregation that investigates doctrinal matters, so that there would be open, public hearings (*New York Times:* December 18, 1968; *NCR:* January 8, 1969). In addition, a group of Protestant and Catholic scholars drafted a bill of rights for the Christian community, which they forwarded to the U.S. Conference of Catholic Bishops (*NCR:* October 16, 1968).

Whereas bishops based their stand on traditional authority, theologians based theirs on the more diffuse charismatic authority of expertise (Etzioni 1961:203). As if to reinforce their traditionalist view, bishops and pope took recourse in typical traditionalist orientations (see Blau and Scott 1962:30). They legitimated the birth control position in terms of long-standing church traditions. In the encyclical, Paul said he could not follow the recommendation of the commission "because certain criteria of solutions had emerged which departed from the moral teaching on marriage proposed with constant firmness by the teaching authority of the church" (Pope Paul 1968:6). And the American bishops said that Paul's decision was "an obligatory statement consistent with moral convictions rooted in the traditions of Eastern and Western Christian faith" (American Catholic Bishops 1968:2).

In addition, defenders of the pope referred to the sanctity of the item in question—family life and human sexuality—and the fact that the pope spoke "in the name of Christ" (American Catholic Bishops 1968:2). Such references to the sanctity of the status quo and its legitimation by supernatural powers are also typical of those using traditional authority.

The defenders expected personal loyalty from their subjects regarding birth control. As seen above, Bishops McNulty and Toolen demanded loyalty, as did Pope Paul. This demand stood in stark contrast with the sentiment expressed by Theodore Hesburgh of Notre Dame, that "theology must be free" (*NCR:* September 18, 1968).

Apparently, the traditionalists feared a groundswell of acceptance of another kind of authority—that based on knowledge and new interpretation. As John Cogley (ibid.) said, "There is more trust in the dissident theologians as authentic teachers of the gospel than there is in the ecclesiastical authorities." The conflict, then, appeared to be largely over the locus of authority.

Professional theologians vied with church administrators in a typical conflict over basic concerns. As Blau and Scott (1962:244) put it: "The professional is bound by a norm of service and a code of ethics to represent the welfare and intersts of his *(sic)* clients, whereas the bureaucrat's foremost responsibility is to represent and promote the interests of his *(sic)* organization."

Here the dissenters manifested the professional concerns. In a two-day emergency session on the birth control crisis, the National Federation of Priests' Councils met in Washington and made the following statement: "Our immediate specific concern is with justice and human rights. The present code of canon law is inadequate to safeguard human rights. The law of the Church must serve persons" (*WP:* September 24, 1968).

As George Tavard interpreted the work of the pope's special commission on birth control, "the majority conclusion [leniency regarding usage of birth control] . . . started from a philosophy of the human person and responsibility" (*NCR:* October 2, 1968). The pope rejected this majority opinion because it departed from traditional teaching. Rather than argue against the reasoning of the commission, he simply opposed it by stating organizational concerns.

The diagonal conflict seemed to be moving toward a lateral conflict at the top: a number of national episcopal conferences, as well as individual bishops, appeared to have incorporated the more liberal thinking of the dissenting theologians. Thus a top-level conflict arose among the bishops themselves.

On one side were the majority of bishops around the world who apparently supported the papal encyclical in every detail (Callahan 1968). These included the bishops of Australia, Colombia, East Germany, the Philippines, Scotland, and the United States—all of whom made public statements in support (see *NCR:* September 18, 1968; October 2, 1968; October 16, 1968; November 13, 1968; *Catholic Standard:* November 21, 1984).

On the other side, several national bishops' conferences proclaimed in formal statements essentially the same position as that of the dissenters. These groups included the bishops of Holland, Canada, England, Austria, West Germany, and Belgium (*NCR:* October 2, 1968; *Time*, October 4, 1968; Haughey 1968). The German bishops seemed to chide the pope for not asking enough input from bishops and for not giving enough weight to conscience. The Canadian and Austrian hierarchies dealt positively with couples who, having done all in their power to respond affirmatively to the papal teaching, still found themselves committed to behavior at odds with that teaching. They said that such people are to be considered of good conscience and in good standing within the Church. The Italian bishops seemed to waver between strict loyalty to the encyclical and using other criteria to form one's conscience. Most national episcopates, if they interpreted the encyclical, modified the pope's decree that "each and every marriage act must remain open to the transmission of life" (*Time:* October 4, 1968).

Individual bishops also espoused the theologians' viewpoint. In a pastoral letter, Archbishop Louis Jean Guyot of Toulouse said that married couples have the right, after careful consideration, to decide whether they will use contraceptives (*NCR:* October 16, 1968).

Cardinal O'Boyle did not miss the growing disharmony among bishops. He questioned publicly the liberal positions taken by Dutch, Belgian, and West German bishops:

> If their teaching or any part of it amounts to, implies, or supports the position I here condemn, to that precise extent I should be compelled to disagree with them. The reason is that I intend to teach in unison with the Catholic teaching of Vatican II and Paul VI, and I must reject whatever is incompatible with this teaching.
>
> If there is any disagreement between me and my brother bishops, I submit it to the judgment of the Supreme Pontiff, to which I am always prepared to defer. In the meantime, I counsel my own faithful people that they should ignore any voices that sound discordant from my expression of Catholic teaching (*NCR:* September 18, 1968).

Further, in the pastoral letter read from the pulpits, O'Boyle complained of a "few of [his] brother bishops in other lands" who "seemed to have adopted 'the new morality'" (*Time:* October 4, 1968).

Sharp disagreement seemed to exist at the very top level of church administration. Some bishops incorporated more of the professional orientation; others adhered more firmly to administrative concerns.

Conflict Resolution

By mid-October, Cardinal O'Boyle had penalized thirty-nine of the forty-seven priests who had clashed with him over the birth control encyclical. All thirty-nine were ordered not to hear confessions. In addition, some were told they could not preach or teach. Five also were removed from their rectories. The cardinal said he would remove all of them if they continued in their public dissent (*NCR:* October 16, 1968), and he enacted additional sanctions in subsequent months.

In the meantime, both sides were attempting to guide the outcome in various ways. Cardinal O'Boyle lectured all the pastors of his diocese (*WP:* September 24, 1968). Leaders of the forty-seven dissenters asked for Cardinal O'Boyle's retirement to end the impasse (*WP:* October 3, 1968). The National Federation of Priests' Councils requested mediation in the dispute (*NCR:* October 2, 1968). The National Association for Pastoral Renewal (priests, former priests, and laity) called for Vatican Council III to settle the birth control issue and other disputes. The NAPR statement said that suspension and intimidation of theologians, priests, and laity "who have followed the dictates of conscience in dissenting from *Humanae Vitae* is unseemly, unchristian, and absolutely untenable" (*NCR:* September 18, 1968).

In November, Cardinal O'Boyle, who had rejected the earlier request for mediation, asked Bishop Joseph L. Bernardin, general secretary of the National Conference of Catholic Bishops, to try to settle his dispute with fifty-four priests (*NCR:* November 13, 1968).

> The cardinal acted in the face of a major rally backing the priests, an appeal by priests from around the country to the U.S. bishops asking for "due process" in the church, and as word came from Canada that Pope Paul had received "with satisfaction" the statement of the Canadian bishops concerning the encyclical. . . . The Washington priests . . . say they fully accept the Canadian bishops' statement and "feel that it accurately defines our position."

The dissenters accepted Bishop Bernardin's role with guarded optimism, though they feared this action might prevent mediation at a higher and more appropriate level—namely, the bishops' committee on arbitration and mediation. In fact, Cardinal O'Boyle insisted that mediation itself was inappropriate, as the dispute involved a matter of doctrine.

Ultimately, the dispute went to Rome. In early 1971, the Vatican Congregation of the Clergy set up a hearing procedure for the Washington 19—those dissenters who still remained at odds with Cardinal O'Boyle. Facilitating this appeal were the American Canon Law Society and the National Federation of Priests' Councils (*NCR:* February 12, 1971). Yet by this time, the cards seemed already to be in place, and a new process was not able to accomplish much.

In the long run, there appeared to be several outcomes. The slow process cooled out many dissenters. Some retracted their opposition to O'Boyle. Others resigned the priesthood altogether, going into government and other executive positions (*WP:* November 13, 1978). They even celebrated a ten-year reunion in 1978, where most declared that their dissent had been important, though it did not seem to change the hierarchy to any significant degree.

Each side seemed to stand firm in its position. Theologians asserted their expertise, but the Vatican deplored the freedom of theologians (*NCR:* January 8, 1969). Dissenters remained in dissent; loyalists remained loyal. Years later, Pope John Paul II reasserted the position of Paul VI.

The whole affair seemed to signal the need for a fuller discussion of papal authority and its proper use. Biologists, theologians, and many others questioned the logic of the papal document on birth control. They also questioned the lack of consultation with all levels of church membership (O'Connor 1968:31–35). Was it not time, they mused, to reinstate Vatican II, or to call for a Vatican Council III?

As Greeley (1977) has suggested, the birth control edict was a watershed event. In its wake, large numbers of Catholics apparently decided to make their own judgments and to abide by them.

A Changed Catholicism

The birth control affair symbolized a new era for the Catholic Church in the United States. Before the Second Vatican Council, a majority of American Catholics did not think of their church as an arena for open political conflicts— for battles over church policy, moral principles, different kinds of theologies, and even constituents. Yet by the late 1960s, such battles were commonplace and well known. The struggle par excellence over birth control brought this reality to public view.

The Catholic Church has always been a highly political institution, especially in other countries and other ages. Yet in the United States, during the pre–Vatican II years of the twentieth century, the Church seemed to be apolitical.

Now, however, the American Catholic Church demonstrated just how political it could be. Theologians themselves lined up in different philosophical schools with different moral conclusions, and they presented different moral norms for the bishops to choose. Like supporters of different political philosophies struggling by way of political parties, they battled for acceptance. Theologians attempted to gain additional autonomy by obtaining support from church members (constituencies) and from bishops. This attempt became a struggle for power. Bishops and theologians worked for the same end, like political leaders who try to be accepted as charismatic. Change-oriented theologians struggled for the legitimation of new locations of charisma. Bishops and theologians differed in emphasis; bishops were more oriented than theologians to preserving the organization.

The process of conflict, too, was quite political. The birth control conflict grew to such proportions largely because of support and pressure groups, as well as resistance to policy by subordinates (Simpson 1969:1, 34). In the above description of the conflict, we have seen the development of rival philosophies, the growth of support and pressure groups and their alliances, and even the simple refusal of Church members to believe and obey the official teaching. Such support created constituencies for theologians espousing the new norms on birth control. In turn, these constituencies—both internal and external— triggered the conflict, making the new norms competitors. Both sets of norms vied for acceptance by the top executives (pope and bishops). Foreign relations also came into play, as indicated by the indirect support given the dissenters by the twenty-six hundred scientists of the American Association for the Advancement of Science, who said the encyclical was immoral (*NCR:* January 8, 1969).

The birth control conflict appeared to coincide with a new recognition of pluralism within the Church. The Catholic Church had always contained pluralistic tendencies, but in more recent decades, especially at the end of the nineteenth century and well into the twentieth, the Church had become more rigidly single-minded.

Here we see strong contradictory positions, each with many staunch supporters, and neither side willing to budge. We also note the new majority of Catholics who were willing to endorse birth control, despite the official position of the Church.

These positions seemed to represent relatively fixed subgroups within Catholicism. Although many of the Washington priest dissenters were forced from their leadership roles, most others, who espoused essentially the same position, remained. The Jesuit professors of theology of Alma College, California, wrote that the Holy Spirit speaks through many channels *(magisteria)* and not solely through the official *magisterium*—the hierarchy of bishops and pope (Hill 1968). Yet they were never sanctioned.

John Cogley (1968:10) wrote that many Catholics were putting more trust in the dissident theologians than in the ecclesiastical authorities. This trend represented a shift in the locus of legitimacy for the Church, or perhaps the emergence of competing legitimacies.

The era of advanced industrialized society may have hastened this event. The greater education of Catholics (Greeley 1977) may have increased the likelihood that they would express their independence. Perhaps, too, theologians were proclaiming a new sense of self-sufficiency, given the new insights from a range of ancillary disciplines and their reflections on the contemporary world. Certainly, they seemed to reflect a strong feeling of professional competence in the face of papal pronouncements.

In any case, a change in Catholicism had occurred, for which the great shifts in Catholic belief and practice give strong evidence. The intensity and perseverance of the conflict, examined here, also suggest such a change. Monolithic Catholicism no longer reigned; at least a period of multiple legitimacies arose in its place. For some these included the traditional authority of the official Church (pope, bishops, and so forth). Others give legitimacy to those exercising diffuse charismatic authority, especially if they combined expertise with a thorough understanding of the human condition. Historically, support for the pope has always been diffuse and erratic, as it ebbed and flowed over time (Callahan 1968). The papacy has survived other, greater challenges, such as the Protestant Reformation.

The birth control conflict seemed also to reflect a new mode of thinking for many Catholics. Instead of simply accepting moral principles that church leaders had inferred deductively, many Catholics now seemed more attuned to moral norms justified in an empirical way. For example, theologians and bishops who disagreed with the pope often referred to the experience of Catholic couples, those who felt in good conscience, after reflecting on traditional church teaching, that they must practice birth control. They seemed to be saying that morality needs to be based not solely on Scripture and traditions but also on the contemporary experience of those living the Christian life.

Such thinking was quite consistent with the newly reigning theologies. These included existential or situationist theology, or theology from the ground up (Küng 1976).

The birth control battle reflects the basic theoretical themes; obviously, it occurred over what traditionalists thought was an accommodation to worldly norms. As suggested in the early part of this book, the Church indeed was accommodating—perhaps not officially, but in a real way. Among many theologians and lay members, birth control was now acknowledged as an acceptable practice.

The birth control controversy also demonstrated the depth of the power struggle that emerged. Bishops disagreed among themselves; perhaps more important, dissident theologians flexed their muscles and showed that they possessed formidable power with support from around the world. Did this controversy prefigure a new age of Catholicism, when theologians would have more control over the thinking of Catholics than did the official hierarchy?

The movement for change continued amid deep-seated conflict. Despite the success of the hierarchy in holding the official line, change continued to occur at the levels of staff and membership.

Cardinal O'Boyle and other members of the hierarchy tended to use coercive sanctions to bring dissidents into line. Their threats, transfers, retraction of responsibilities, suspensions, and excommunications were all intended to force straying members into conformity. One might expect this pattern, as traditional authority tends to use coercion when threatened by a rival norm.

Still, the use of coercive sanctions triggered a problem for the Church. Coercion in general tends to weaken the normative characteristic of the organization. To use coercive means to insure unanimity in the nonpractice of birth control—or in any other norm—is to admit that that norm is not accepted by all the members. By using such sanctions, the hierarchy was confessing implicitly that the complex normative system, of which birth control guidelines were a part, was becoming unglued—or worse, that the nature of the organization was changing.

How then can normative organizations, such as the Catholic Church, prevent this corrosion of their normative trait? How can they prevent coercive tactics regarding norms? The official hierarchy could prevent rival norms from emerging or from receiving support. To do so, the administrative line (pope, bishops, and so forth) would need to preempt all expertise, or else norms would have to be derived only from a sacred source. (Indeed, the official Church seems to have attempted this action during the decades following the 1968 crisis.) To prevent alternative norms from arising, the official Church would need to halt or minimize contact with the outside world, including science and new philosophies.

Realistically, this option seems impossible. Aggiornamento and communication are entrenched too firmly to be displaced. In this scenario, norm-authority conflicts should arise frequently, and the hierarchy would react with coercive sanctions. We might also expect members to continue dropping out of the official Church.

Yet a second option exists. Top executives (pope and bishops) might take a more patient and tolerant viewpoint toward conflicting opinions, letting them battle it out and allowing the better ideas to rise to the top. Of course, if pope and bishops were to do this successfully, they would need to develop a new attitude about their church. They would have to minimize the number of norms that one must accept to be a normative member, and they would have to allow many different opinions to exist at any one time.

This conflict also represents a particular point in the change process. During the late 1960s, the Catholic hierarchy in the United States was far more conservative than the bulk of Catholic clergy (NORC 1972; Seidler 1972). Many of the bishops, including those leading the fight against change, seemed to be carry-overs from the pre–Vatican era. Only in the 1970s did a turnaround occur, when more change-oriented and more progressive bishops came into power (Greeley 1977).

The conflict was especially acute in 1968, because of the leadership of a few crucial pre–Vatican bishops. With time and with a continuation of more moderate or more progressive bishops, one would expect a quieting of such conflict, a lessening of coercive sanctions, and the emergence of a more tolerant official church, at least in the United States.

Chapter Eight

Battleground for Clerical Rebellion

Questions remain about the conflict of mobilization. Though we have already studied national trends and a single dramatic conflict, we have yet to investigate the diocesan context of such conflicts.

The diocesan setting often gave special meaning to the conflict. In Washington, for example, the conflict arose from a particular authority situation and triggered reactions that could be understood only in the diocesan context. In addition, large percentages of conflict of the 1960s seemed to focus on bishops and on authority relationships—in other words, on diocesan relationships.

How extensive was the bishop-related diocesan conflict during the period of mobilization? Which contextual and leadership factors within the diocese produced the most conflict—or the most harmony? And which of the bishop's reactive options—sanctioning or tolerating rebellion—was more effective?

The focus on diocesan authority conflicts may increase our understanding of collective efforts for structural changes at the local level. As many have noted (e.g., Fichter 1977), the impetus for such structural changes represented the core outcome of the Second Vatican Council. In addition, such conflicts seemed to highlight the mobilization era.

Because the diocese often constituted the battle arena, almost by definition it became the appropriate place to conduct a study of conflict. Other researchers have reached the same conclusion. In Gibson Winter's words (1968:47), the diocese "is the central fact in this organization." Ivan Vallier (1969:140–153), in view of his own empirical research, strongly recommended the diocese as the unit of analysis in research on Catholicism.

Both researchers considered the diocese as a complex organization, also a theme of this book. When Winter (1968:47–65) pointed to the diocese as the central fact of Catholicism, he referred to the wide empirical variation across dioceses. They differed substantially in such features as size of bureaucracy, number of parishes, and average number of priests per parish. Vallier (1969: 147–184) noted, in addition, the large variation in two clusters of diocesan elements. One he called the relational infrastructure (communal and associational groups and activities); the other he named the diocesan adaptive strategy (ideological position, normative stance, and preferred rate of change). Many of these features came from episcopal authority, but the variations suggest that we should look further than authority relations and focus on the diocese.[1]

The diocese provides the items of interest for this chapter: authority, priest-bishop relations, and attempts to realign the power structure. It also serves as an arena where related things happen: disarticulation and confusion, priest resignations, a withdrawal syndrome, differing modes of accommodation, and so forth.

The diocese also has other advantages for study: it sets clear boundaries for one important aspect of the birth control controversy and the challenge to authority during the late 1960s, which centered largely on the diocesan authority of the local bishop.

Such authority conflicts in the diocese occurred for two reasons: local ordinaries exercised great independence and power, and the Second Vatican Council encouraged lower-level participants (laity and clergy) to participate more strongly.

What evidence shows that local ordinaries exercised great power in recent centuries? One telling indicator is the size of episcopal spans of control, which in recent decades have numbered in the hundreds and thousands. According to Spencer (1966:100), such a circumstance was unique in the history of hierarchical structure. At least until the time of the Second Vatican Council, the position of intermediaries between bishop and parish priests was very weak. Bishops exercised authority without much delegation.

Historical developments help to explain such large spans of control. Catholicism underwent a transformation after the Renaissance, as the hierarchical structure, formerly more widely delegated, was partially dismantled. Population and geographic increases also resulted in larger spans. Consequently, as Spencer notes (1966:98): "It is no exaggeration to say that, up to Vatican II, the (Catholic) Church had only three effective levels of authority: parish, diocese, and papacy. The Church is structurally much less hierarchic than it was in the Middle Ages."

On the American scene, authors have noted the bishops' power and independence (e.g., Vallier 1969; Haughey 1971). Haughey (1971:518–520) explains the almost autocratic power exercised by American bishops by referring to special circumstances in this country such as the pioneering context and the relative isolation from Rome of the early American Church. Consequently, bishops developed a tradition of making decisions with little consultation or limitation.

During the period of transition studied here, American bishops retained immense de facto authority. Such has been the majority view of the consultants and informants for this study. Despite the realignment of authority mandated by Vatican II, including the establishment of new structures for consultation and delegation, old traditions died slowly. By the early 1970s, some ordinaries were still listed as chair of each staff department. In some dioceses, the ordinary appointed the president of the priests' senate and controlled the agenda for discussion. The obverse—the tradition of acceptance—also continued, as large numbers of subjects deferred to the ordinary's authority.

Such immense episcopal power could hardly avoid an attack. The Vatican Council itself proposed a more collegial authority structure, thus encouraging the intradiocesan attacks that occurred so soon after the close of the council. Bishops, trained and governing in the old school, often could not chart a new course soon enough, and so the diocese became a natural arena for the battles of authority.

The diocesan authority structure was typified in the organizational chart (see Figure 8.1). Medium-sized and large dioceses contained a vicar general and regional vicars, or deans, who administered the ordinary's (bishop's) policies, though the ordinary usually ruled personally and immediately. The staff side contained various diocesan departments such as liturgy, ecumenism, education, information, and recruitment. Each of these was headed by a director, or superintendent, or chair.

The ordinary could retain immense power simply by not delegating much responsibility, and the organizational diagram was very flat, again an indication of minimal delegation of authority. The diocesan structure contained the huge spans of control mentioned earlier.

Bishop-Clergy Relations
(1966–1971)

To assess bishop and clergy relations in U.S. dioceses, Seidler (1972) surveyed 1,279 diocesan priests in all 137 Latin rite dioceses that had ten or more diocesan priests from 1966 to 1970. The ordinary's leadership policies were generally perceived as moderate or middle-of-the-road in matters of religious change. Bishops also received much higher ratings on the desire to maintain order (an administrative orientation) than on the desire to serve all people (a professional bent). They were also perceived as more willing to listen to problems than to share their power.

Informants generally regarded the pace of change as moderate, but they also seemed to indicate a national pattern of ecclesiastical renewal. The first and fastest item to change was liturgy, followed in order by ecumenical activities, changes in theology, teaching, and decision making. The slowest to change was religious life-style. Structural reordering seemed to be the hardest area to tackle.

High percentages of diocesan priests were perceived to be at ideological loggerheads with the ordinary. Approximately two-thirds of diocesan priests disagreed with the ordinary by being either more traditional or more progressive (see Table 8.1). These data were consistent with those of Greeley and his associates, reported in *Study on Priestly Life and Ministry* (National Conference of

Fig. 8.1. Organizational chart

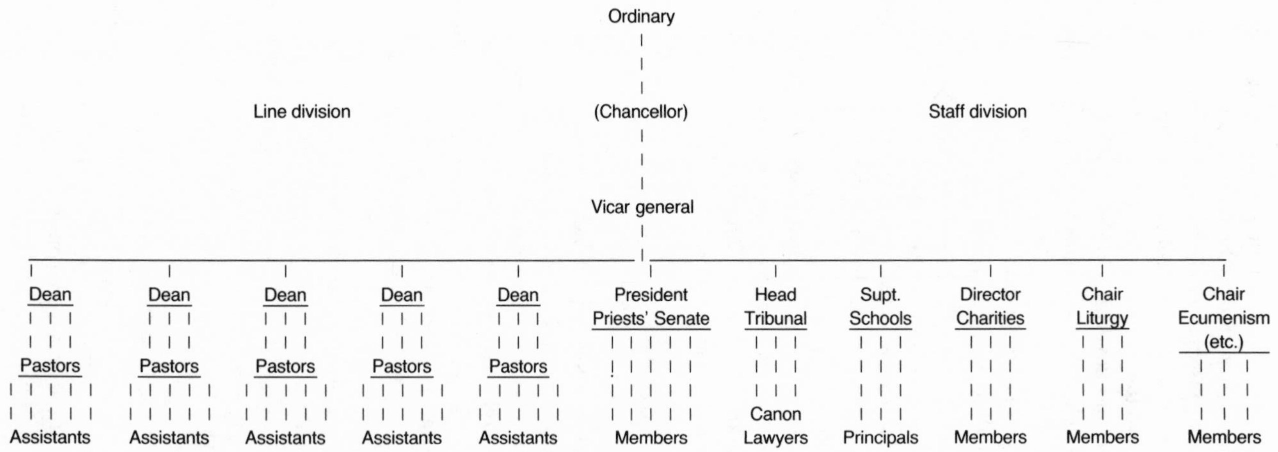

Ordinary
│
(Chancellor)
│
Vicar general

Line division

Dean	Dean	Dean	Dean	Dean
Pastors	Pastors	Pastors	Pastors	Pastors
Assistants	Assistants	Assistants	Assistants	Assistants

Staff division

President Priests' Senate	Head Tribunal	Supt. Schools	Director Charities	Chair Liturgy	Chair Ecumenism (etc.)
Members	Canon Lawyers	Principals	Members	Members	Members

Table 8.1. Attitudes Toward Progressiveness of Clergy and Ordinaries

Image	Priests (%)	Ordinaries (%)	Rated attitude[a]
Very progressive	18.37	8.8	Very progressive
Somewhat progressive	54.8	24.3	Somewhat progressive
Middle of the road	21.4	34.6	Somewhat traditional
Very traditional	0.5	11.8	Very traditional
Total	100.0	100.17[b]	
N	935	136	

[a] The categories for rated attitudes of ordinaries are created by making five cutting points of equal intervals among the mean scores for ordinaries in each diocese. For example, scores between 1.000 and 1.800 = very progressive, between 1.801 and 2.600 = somewhat progressive, and so forth.
[b] Total differs from 100% because of rounding.

Catholic Bishops 1971:50–55). In Greeley's sample, diocesan clergy were much more progressive than bishops regarding reform in the church, though they were more conservative regarding certain social issues. Ironically, then, the clergy at large seem to have incorporated the norm of renewal more quickly than the bishops who were involved in the Vatican Council that legitimated it.

As leaders, bishops faced policy dilemmas. They needed to decide how much and how quickly they should take up the spirit of the Second Vatican Council. If they moved too fast, they might water down doctrine and lose the monocratic style of leadership that had fared so well, and thus alienate people. If they moved too slowly, they might be perceived as failing to incorporate Vatican II, and alienate people in that way. Different factions within most dioceses made sure that bishops felt this tug of war. Which policy generally seemed better?

Bishops frequently needed to react to the protest by clergy and others. If a bishop compromised, apparently condoning the attacks on authority, he would undermine his own authority. If he punished the deviant priests, he might lose them, along with others who agreed with criticisms.

The Study of Rebellion

Our aim was study rebellion in context. (See Appendix B for model and operationalization of variables.) Several data sources were used. The questionnaires mentioned earlier elicited information about clergy relations and events of the immediately preceding five-year period, which began with the completion of the Second Vatican Council (December 1965). Return rate was 74 percent (941 usable questionnaires).

Another data source was a directory of basically demographic traits of American clergy (Luzbetak 1967).[2] Because these data referred to relatively stable structural conditions as they existed in 1966, the first year of the observation period, they were used as antecedent conditions in the analysis.

In each diocese, the questionnaires were sent to ten priest-informants who were chosen after a detailed preliminary investigation (see Appendix C for methodological information). For comparability of judgment, the priest occupants of ten different structural positions in each diocese were chosen, including one member of the priests' senate or council, a Newman chaplain, a member of the liturgy commission, a member of the information staff, and a dean or vicar. All informants were priests below the rank of bishop and below the position of chancellor. This selection of a range of positions (excluding extremes) was intended to reduce reporting bias. (Reliability and validity of survey information is presented in Appendix C.)

Fixed-answer questions focused on clergy relations, especially the authority climate. Informants were asked, for example, to rate the religious progressivism of the ordinary and the degree of camaraderie among various groups of clergy. They also were asked to recall the amount of conflict between priests and bishop in their own dioceses—a phenomenon discussed off and on in the priestly grapevine during those days. (See Appendix C for scoring of conflict, sampling of dioceses, and analysis of data.)

The measurement of all variables, along with reliability and validity scores (where appropriate) is given in Appendix C, but we present here the measurement of the main variable of interest: priest rebellion. Informants reported several indicators of such rebellion. They estimated the degree of dissent or opposition expressed by diocesan priests in reference to their chief bishop. They enumerated the number of kinds of acts of individual rebellion which they remembered as having occurred in their diocese during the five-year period. Such acts included writing of protest letters to bishops, personal confrontations with bishops, and refusals to obey orders. To report social rebellion, respondents gave the number of kinds of acts they remembered as occurring in their diocese. These acts were performed by groups of priests rather than by individuals. (A checklist of twelve kinds of rebellious acts was given to informants, who then checked them if they had occurred at least once during the pertinent period.)

In analyzing conflict, we used all three measures. For the regression analysis, however, only the global measure of estimated rebellion was used.

Extent and Meaning of Clergy Rebellion. During the five-year period from December 1965 through March 1971, diocesan clergy demonstrated that they had entered the age of protest, the extent of which may be judged after a consideration of the details of Table 8.2.

Table 8.2. Frequency of Occurrence of Dissent Events

	Actor	Dioceses in which dissent occurred (%)
1. Private letter writing to ordinary, in opposition	Individual	95
2. Private letter writing to ordinary, in opposition	Group	55
3. Lending support to fellow priest in conflict	Individual	43
4. Refusing to change manner of administering sacraments and of preaching	Individual	38
5. Encouraging support from laity in opposition	Individual	30
6. Appearing at chancery office to confront ordinary	Individual	28
6. Publicly refusing to implement general directives of ordinary	Individual	28
8. Lending support to fellow priest in conflict	Group	26
9. Publicized letter writing in opposition to ordinary	Individual	22
10. Publicized letter writing in opposition to ordinary	Group	18
11. Appearing at chancery office to confront ordinary	Group	16
12. Holding a news conference in which ordinary is opposed	Individual	12
13. Engaging in demonstrations aimed at ordinary	Individual	8
14. Holding a news conference in which ordinary is opposed	Group	7
14. Encouraging support from laity in opposition	Group	7
16. Engaging in demonstrations aimed at ordinary	Group	4
16. Making appeals to other ordinaries or members of the Church's hierarchy	Individual	4
16. Making appeals to other ordinaries or members of the Church's hierarchy	Group	4
16. Encouraging support from other religious in opposition to ordinary	Individual	4
16. Encouraging support from other religious in opposition to ordinary	Group	4
21. Publicly refusing to implement general directives of ordinary	Individual	1
22. Refusing to change manner of administering sacraments and of preaching	Group	4
22. Engaging in destruction of diocesan property	Individual	0
22. Engaging in destruction of diocesan property	Group	0

Note: If 50 percent or more of the priest-respondents in each diocese said that the dissenting event had occurred, it was considered to have occurred for that diocese. The percentages, if anything, are underestimates because of difficulty of remembering, lack of awareness, and geographic spread within dioceses. Not every possible type of protest is represented, but only those that a preliminary search revealed to be salient. At the same time, we know of no other important type of protest by clergy of that period that has come to light since then.

Diocesan priests dissented in many direct ways. The most common was the private letter written in opposition to the ordinary, although public refusals to change ministerial methods or to implement directives also occurred in many dioceses. Such refusals suggest that a common source of conflict involved control over diocesan priests' major area of competence and responsibility. Personal confrontations with the ordinary were also known to have occurred in over a quarter of (the) dioceses—more frequently, it appears, than the highly publicized news conferences of protest.

Diocesan priests also protested in indirect ways, especially by lending support to those in conflict with the ordinary and by encouraging support from others. Some indirect tactics, however, were employed only very infrequently. For example, making group appeals to other ordinaries or members of the hierarchy for support was estimated to have occurred in only 4 percent of American dioceses.

Such protests were found to be the activities of individuals far more frequently than of groups. The protesting activity had the appearance of being organized only sporadically. At the same time, the two kinds of dissent—individual and group—should not be confused. This study showed (with data reported elsewhere) that individual and group protest were different phenomena with partially different roots.

How widespread was priest protest? Some kind of dissent occurred, according to informants in 93 percent of the 136 dioceses, but most dioceses experienced only a few types of protest. In fact, 48.5 percent of the dioceses reported only one or two different types of protest, and only 25 percent reported four or more kinds. Apparently, only 3 percent of dioceses experienced ten or more types of protest. Acts of dissent, then, appeared to be widespread but undeveloped: protest existed in a limited way in almost all dioceses, but it occurred in full bloom in only a tiny proportion of dioceses. (These data do not report intensity of protest, nor strictly degree.) Extent of priest protest, considered in a single global measure, appeared to be greater than normal, at least for almost 40 percent of dioceses (see Table 8.3, column 1). This measure includes extent and intensity and so represents a good summary, though the information is less specific than previous figures.

Degree of protest can also be measured by other yardsticks. In comparison with acts of political protest of that era—looting, burning, and occupation of buildings—such protest activity was relatively tame. Most of the more prevalent acts of dissent, like letter writing and confrontations, appeared to be an attempt to stay within existing channels of communication. The protesting activity that exemplified a break with the system—calling news conferences, demonstrations, and public refusals to follow directives—were less frequent, yet not

Table 8.3. Comparative Distributions of Measures of Rebellion

Perceived friction (priest protest)		Individual rebellion		Social rebellion		Total rebellion	
Degree of friction	Percentages of dioceses	Number of acts of rebellion	Percentages of dioceses	Number of acts of rebellion	Percentages of dioceses	Number of acts of rebellion	Percentages of dioceses
Extremely small amount	0.7	0	11.0	0	56.6	0	7.4
Small amount	7.4	1	34.6	1	26.5	1	25.0
Less than normal	19.1	2	27.2	2	8.8	2	23.5
Normal amount	33.8	3	11.8	3	0.7	3	19.1
More than normal	28.7	4	7.4	4	0.7	4–6	14.0
Great amount	8.8	5–6	4.4	5–6	3.7	7–9	8.1
Extremely great amount	1.5	7–8	2.9	10–15	2.9	10–15	2.9
Total	100.0		100.1[a]		99.9[a]		100.0
N	136		136		136		136

[a] Totals differ from 100 percent because of rounding.

so infrequent as to cause complacency. The most extreme kind of protest—destruction of diocesan property—was never reported to have occurred.

In comparing this era to the long decades of relatively pacific clergy subordination, one might agree that recent patterns of priest protest were even more striking than contemporary racial rioting and generational conflict, which had more frequent historical models. Who would have predicted even a modest clergy dissent, arising without recent precedent? Further, who would have expected the incorporation of political tactics from outside the Church to within its sacred precincts?

The larger significance of such protest was the emergence of a new social awareness among clergy, an awareness that typified the mobilization stage of the aggiornamento movement. The social movement toward change within Catholicism, which received its legitimation at Vatican II, was in a mobilization stage. Among diocesan clergy, that stage took the form of a mobilization for social power. Having been denied power for so long, diocesan clergy began to seek social support to counteract the lopsided and occasionally devastating

power at the top. We see such mobilization in action during this period immediately following Vatican II.

Mobilization was apparently effective. Later in 1970, all dioceses were ordered by Rome to create structures of decentralization. In particular, priests'
senates, preceded in many dioceses by unofficial priests' councils, became the
official representative voice of lower clergy in each diocese. Such decentralization represented a major thrust of Vatican II renewal.

At this point we may ask which dioceses had the most and which the least
conflict (see Table 8.4).

The last column, total estimated conflict, includes intensity and frequency,
but column three (total acts of rebellion) reports only the total number of different kinds of acts of rebellion experienced in a diocese at least once in this five-
year period.

Dioceses scoring high in both columns three and four included Yakima,
Belleville, Raleigh, Crookston, Charleston, Chicago, and San Antonio. Other
dioceses with high conflict scores (appearing in the top half of either column
three or column four) were San Francisco, LaCrosse, Buffalo, Lincoln, Santa
Fe, Corpus Christi, Detroit, Lansing, Owensboro, and Newark.

Many of these dioceses received local and national publicity for the conflict.
Other highly publicized conflict areas, such as Los Angeles and Washington,
appeared only in column one or two of this table. Washington was reported to
have had four kinds of acts of individual rebellion, and Los Angeles eight kinds
of acts of social rebellion.

Dioceses scoring lowest on conflict appear in the lower half of the table. Dioceses showing up in both columns three and four (lower half) were Amarillo,
Cheyenne, Louisville, and Norwich. Others, which appear in at least one of
those two columns, included Portland, Manchester, Bridgeport, Springfield
Cape, Rapid City, Baker, Duluth, Spokane, Worcester, Brownsville, Syracuse,
Altoona-Johnstown, Allentown, Rockford, Davenport, Austin, Helena, Evans-
ville, and Baltimore. These dioceses at least appeared to weather the stormy
period in relative tranquility.

The data also showed regional variation. Regions undergoing the greatest
conflict during that era included the East North Central, South Atlantic, Pacific, and Mid-Atlantic. Those with least conflict were New England and the
West North Central region. Regional boundaries were those employed in cen-
sus and population studies.

The Nonrebellious Climate. The context of clergy conflict is summarized in Figure 8.2, confirmed by the regression analysis shown in Table 8.5. Cross-status
friendships between bishops and clergy was the single most powerful deterrent
to clergy conflict. It reflected the authority relations and leadership policies

Table 8.4. Dioceses with Most and Least Conflict Aimed at Bishop

Act(s) of individual rebellion		Act(s) of social rebellion		Total act(s) of rebellion (individual + social)		Total estimated conflict	
Diocese	No. of acts	Diocese	No. of acts	Diocese	No. of Acts	Diocese	Average score (1 = highest, 7 = lowest)
aSan Antonio	8	Buffalo	8	aBelleville	15	aYakima	1.500
Newark	7	aBelleville	8	aRaleigh	11	aCrookston	1.600
aChicago	7	Los Angeles	8	aCrookston	11	LaCrosse	2.000
aBelleville	7	Lansing	7	aSan Francisco	10	aCharleston	2.000
aRaleigh	6	Sante Fe	7	Buffalo	9	aSan Antonio	2.000
aYakima	6	aCrookston	6	aChicago	9	Lincoln	2.143
Detroit	5	aRaleigh	5	aSan Antonio	9	aRaleigh	2.200
aCrookston	5	aCharleston	5	Sante Fe	9	aChicago	2.250
aSan Francisco	5	LaCrosse	5	aYakima	9	Corpus Christi	2.429
Washington	4	Owensboro	5	Detroit	8	aBelleville	2.600
aCharleston	3	aSan Francisco	5	Lansing	8		
				aCharleston	8		
				Owensboro	7		
				Newark	7		

Act(s) of individual rebellion		Act(s) of social rebellion		Total act(s) of rebellion (individual + social)		Total estimated conflict	
aPortland	0	aPortland	0	aPortland	0	Duluth	6.222
aManchester	0	aManchester	0	aManchester	0	Spokane	6.125
aBridgeport	0	aBridgeport	0	aBridgeport	0	aAmarillo	6.000
aNorwich	0	aNorwich	0	aNorwich	0	aCheyenne	5.780
aLouisville	0	aLouisville	0	aLouisville	0	Worcester	5.714
aSpringfield-Cape	0	aSpringfield-Cape	0	aSpringfield-Cape	0	aLouisville	5.571
aRapid City	0	aRapid City	0	aRapid City	0	Brownsville	5.500
aAmarillo	0	aAmarillo	0	aAmarillo	0	Syracuse	5.400
aCheyenne	0	aCheyenne	0	aCheyenne	0	Altoona-Johnstown	5.375
aBaker	0	aBaker	0	aBaker	0	Allentown	5.333
		Boston	0			Rockford	5.286
		Newark	0			Davenport	5.200
		Cincinnati	0			Austin	5.167
		St. Louis	0			Helena	5.167
		El Paso	0			Evansville	5.143
						aNorwich	5.125
						Baltimore	5.000

[a] Diocese appears in three or more columns.

Fig. 8.2. Empirically supported model of clergy conflict. Solid arrows represent significant relationships. Broken lines signify that $p < .05$ and added $R^2 \leq .02$.

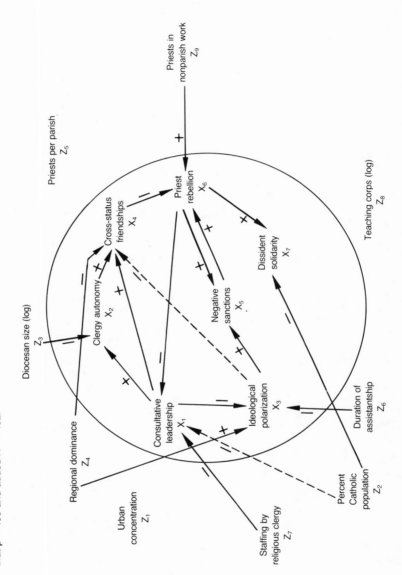

because bishops set the tone for clergy solidarity. Democratic leadership, clergy autonomy—clear indicators of episcopal policy and authority relations—affected priest rebellion in direct ways. Democratic leadership influenced cross-status friendships and in turn decreased clergy rebellion (added $R^2 = .487$). Consultative episcopal policies enchanced clergy autonomy, cut down on ideological polarization, and ultimately minimized rebellion.

By contrast, the environmental factors and structural development and complexity ($Z_1 – Z_9$) exerted less influence. This difference was partly because having many priests in nonparish work only weakly contributed to conflict ($R^2 = .019$) and partly because the environmental and organizational variables had direct and watered down influence on rebellion.

Our expectations were supported. Variables of leadership climate were the most salient determinants of clergy conflict. Factors of environment, organizational development, and complexity contributed remote influences and a small direct influence (from priests in nonparish work).

These results differ markedly from those on student and racial rebellions of the same period (Scot and El-Assal 1969; Spilerman 1970). In those cases, unit size and structural differentiation had relatively more causal impact. We will return to this difference later.

The model of progressive leadership was clearly the effective one in preventing clergy rebellion. It promoted a climate of autonomy and friendship among clergy and cut down on negative disciplinary measures. By implication, in a positive climate dissidents did not present a solid front opposed to the ordinary.

The Besieged Bishops. Our expectations about bishops' reactions to clergy conflict were supported. Conflict apparently led to a tightening of the reins at least in the short run, as shown by the direct negative path from rebellion to democratic leadership (added $R^2 = .29$). This single path meant that clergy rebellion slowed the speed of adaptation and turned the bishop in a more traditional direction, as well as restricting consultative leadership.

Clergy conflict apparently triggered increased negative sanctions. The greater the conflict initiated by lower clergy, the more frequently did the bishop become a harsh disciplinarian.

The disciplinarian approach led back to increased conflict. (The path coefficient from negative sanctions to conflict refers technically only to one phase of the conflict dynamics, but we can assume that it also reflects the continuation of conflict—the reaction to the bishop's reaction.) Similarly, we would expect that a progressively more monocratic leadership further restricted autonomy and cross-status friendships and thus inflated the conflict again.

One clear outcome was a widened gap between progressive clergy and

Table 8.5. Regression Coefficients and Explained Variance for Nonrecursive Model

Dependent variable	Explanatory variable	Regression coefficient	b/sd of regression coefficient	Significance level $(p < \chi)$	Added R^{2*}	Total R^2
Consultative	Control variables					.130
leadership	Percent Catholic population	− .023	1.433	.10	.017	
	Staffing by religious clergy	− .035	1.959	.05	.030	
	Priest rebellion	− .193	3.078	.001	.288	.464
Clergy	Control variables					.082
autonomy	Diocesan size (log)	− .284	1.958	.05	.034	
	Consultative leadership	.795	1.583	.10	.215	.331
Ideological	Control variables**					
polarization	Regional dominance	1.491	2.486	.01	.039	.075
	Duration of assistantship	− .091	2.369	.01	.031	
	Consultative leadership	− .494	2.539	.01	.238	.382
Cross-status	Control variables					.135
friendships	Regional dominance	− .748	2.270	.025	.058	
	Consultative leadership	.368	2.886	.005	.487	
	Clergy autonomy	.135	3.168	.005	.034	
	Ideological polarization	− .176	1.464	.10	.010	.724
Negative	Control variables					.149
sanctions	Ideological polarization	1.035	1.179	.12	.034	
	Priest rebellion	.631	1.971	.05	.164	.347
Priest	Control variables					.084
rebellion	Priests in nonparish work	.127	2.222	.025	.019	
	Cross-status friendships	− 1.575	2.693	.005	.433	
	Negative sanctions	.271	2.155	.025	.014	.550
Dissident	Control variables					.058
solidarity	Percent Catholic population	− .067	1.714	.05	.009	
	Priest rebellion	.378	2.536	.01	.186	.253

* Added R^2 was not given for each variable in the two-stage least-squares program. Therefore, added R^2 was determined by running the model several times, beginning with only control variables in each equation and successively adding explanatory variables. R^2 for a particular explanatory variable was the total R^2 of the equation in which this variable was first inserted minus R^2 of the previous equation.

**Control variables ordinarily included five assumed sources of measurement error: summary diocesan scores for position bias, religious liberalism bias, absence bias, age bias, and between-informant disagreement. They also included a five-category measure of the number of years the main bishop was in power (four dummy variables). In the equation to explain ideological polarization an added control variable was introduced to screen out the possible effects of the fact that informants occasionally did not answer that relatively complex item. This variable was percent reduction in number of informants for that item in that diocese.

traditionalist bishops, which can also be seen in the path from conflict to dissi-dent solidarity. The more severe the confrontations, the greater the social bond among those who disagreed with the bishop.

In sum, the findings regarding bishops' reactions revealed the following: Where conflict was extensive or severe, bishops tended to react traditionally, sternly, in a disciplinarian manner. By contrast, where conflict was less extreme, they tended to react in a more open way. In the more harmonious dioceses, they could afford to include greater consultation and freedom. The disciplinarian reaction was a failure, at least in the short run. Effectiveness of governing the diocese to peace and unity among all levels of clergy accompanied an open, progressive attitude and a consultative leadership style. By contrast, the disciplinarian approach appeared to be a failure.

Implications of this Study

This research agrees with theoretical and empirical studies of other organizations. The central findings here support the axiomatic theory of Hage (1980:40) on consultative leadership, centralization, stratification, and morale. The data here—especially the paths from regional dominance to cross-status friendships and ideological polarization—are also consistent with the findings of those who note the dysfunctions of bureaucracy (e.g., Gouldner 1954; Barnard 1946). We also note here the problem of organizational size (see Blau 1970), especially in the negative path from diocesan size to clergy autonomy. The data in the path from priests in nonparish work to clergy rebellion also portray the often-noted conflict between staff and line (Dalton 1964). Finally, we note a professional socialization to conformity (Hall and Schneider 1973) in the negative path from duration of assistantship to ideological polarization.

At the same time, these findings are unique. They indicate a higher salience of leadership than is often the case. They show a thrust by lower clergy toward a new conception of organization for the future. This thrust implies the movement for change discussed earlier. The principle of synergy did not operate in the short run, but probably did in the longer run. That is, when traditionalist bishops received negative feedback, such as the protest or rebellion from lower clergy, they did not readjust their policies. Within five to ten years, however, the American episcopal scene changed dramatically with the appointment of a number of more progressive bishops (Greeley 1977). Indirectly, at least, the negative feedback seemed to propel the Vatican into a reconsideration of the American episcopate (Greeley 1977).

Progressive Leadership and Norms. Progressive leadership was a powerful indirect determinant of harmony, according to this analysis, as shown by the four causal chains from consultative leadership to rebellion. Most of the indeterminate factors in the causal chains to rebellion, such as clergy autonomy and ideological polarization, were aspects of the clergy climate set largely by the bishop. The powerful impact of clergy climate strongly indicates the influence of episcopal leadership. Apparently, consultative-minded bishops set a tone of respect for clergy and equality in social relations that resulted in tranquility.

Relative to other types of factors, including environmental and demographic characteristics, episcopal leadership, and the resultant clergy climate, were more salient influences on conflict or tranquility. This relationship was reflected in the dominant statistical role of the endogenous variables explaining conflict and other dependent variables. Added R^2 from variables of leadership and clergy climate frequently rose above .20, whereas that from exogenous (e.g., demographic) variables ranged from .01 to .06.

Leadership and clergy climate dominated the analysis, but why should leadership climate be a more dominating influence on rebellion in this context than in other contexts, such as student and racial rebellions? Part of the answer lies in the nature of the rebellion, which may have concentrated the attack more fully on a single individual. Yet this factor suggests further pertinent characteristics of the organization. The Catholic diocese afforded the bishop great power and huge spans of control; authority and leadership were focused on a single individual. In addition, mobility to other dioceses was extremely limited. From Seidler's data, an estimated average (median) of only one percent of priests per diocese moved to work actively as priests in other dioceses during the whole five-year period. This organization, then, was one of focused leadership and a virtually stable location of priests within a diocese.[3] Such conditions evidently concentrated attention on the leadership climate.

Another, perhaps idiosyncratic, characteristic of Catholic leadership concerns the way it was perceived. Good leadership was perceived to be progressive leadership, as reflected in the high correlations among leadership, consultative style, and progressivism. Apparently, a *norm of* progressiveness was built into clerical expectations during this time of rapid change within the church. The data suggest strongly that rebellion was the outcome of nonprogressive leadership, which produced the strained authority relations. Such a norm of progressiveness probably also concentrated attention on the bishop.

The findings reported indicate clearly that the progressive model of priesthood was incorporated widely among diocesan clergy throughout the country. Protestors disliked traditional authority, and the majority of silent clergy must have endorsed the renewal thrust, as suggested by the positive relations between progressive leadership and harmony and the self-classification of informants in this study.

Several aspects of that progressivism can be highlighted. The newly emerging model of priesthood was apparently that of modern professionalism. In their harmonious or rebelling actions, the clergy showed resoundingly an incorporation of professional autonomy, openness to new theological ideas, new forms of social analysis, and new techniques of communicating the Gospel and presenting the rituals. Such values corresponded to professional characteristics of autonomy, expertise, and service.

The emphasis on social leveling and participation in decision making suggests a new ideal: an organic model of organization (Burns and Stalker 1961). In such a model, by contrast with hierarchies, control originates in a network whose center shifts depending on the task. Communication flows in several directions, not simply downward from superiors. In the data available, apparently the professional and organic models went hand in hand (see also Hage 1980:85).

The new values included the right of appeal in the form of a grievance mechanism—a right that had been denied clergy for some time. A view that this was a basic human right was apparently a part of living in the modern world.

A high value seemed to be placed on the speed of movement toward incorporation of these models. Rapid changes produced the greatest diocesan harmony.

The evidence supports all theoretical models of conflict mentioned at the outset. We have already noted the clash of professional and administrative orientations. Conflicts over priestly role and theological interpretation are also clearly implied. An authority conflict can be seen partly in the extent of rebellion itself—a rebellion that in all quarters appeared as a protest against the bishops' uses of authority. Most of the explanatory variables could be labeled authority relations, especially consultative leadership, autonomy, sanctions, and polarization (based on the bishops' ideological stances). Even cross-status friendships apparently derived from the bishops' authority styles.

A social movement model was also suggested. The clash between forces of progressivism and the episcopal establishment suggests a progressive movement, especially because lower clergy endorsed modern values more quickly than did the bishops. A progressive movement was also indicated by the fact that the progressive side initiated the conflict.

Conflict was at least implicitly a strategy. The message of rebellion aimed at traditionalist bishops was clearly that they should become more progressive. As mentioned earlier, the negative feedback (conflict) appears to have failed in the short run. Bishops reacted by moving in a more traditionalist direction and by increasing punishments. Social and ideological cleavages within dioceses increased. Conditions of clergy apparently worsened after rebellion.

In the long run, however, the strategy probably worked. As Greeley notes (1977:159), a new apostolic delegate, Archbishop Jean Jadot, appointed in the mid-1970s, suddenly began to facilitate the appointment of progressive bishops in major dioceses in the United States. This is not to say that Pope Paul or other

Roman members of the hierarchy were persuaded directly by the clergy protest. Greeley says that a representative of Pope Paul noticed the lack of leadership in the United States in 1971, and the pope decided to rectify the situation. No doubt, however, the clergy turmoil helped spark the pope's interest.

Bishops' Resistance. Why did many bishops remain traditional in the face of general progressivism and in the face of rebellion? The answer is complex, though it may be formulated simply as the natural entrenchment of administrative leaders. The gap created between the change orientation of lower clergy and their leaders became difficult to overcome.

The persistence of episcopal traditionalism also admits of a more detailed answer. Why, after an intensive Vatican education in progressive theology and after participating in the Vatican debates and voting and watching the progressive side win over and over again, did bishops not become more progressive?

The data indicate that a progressive approach by bishops would have been nonnormative. Despite Vatican II, an authoritarian emphasis remained. Priest aberrations from traditional religious procedures, unless approved explicitly, were met with episcopal punishment. Despite the increased cycle of conflict, bishops retained a business-as-usual strategy. The difficulty remained, however, and business was not as usual.

Bishops may have misjudged the speed whereby lower clergy embraced religious progressivism. Bishops who maintained their traditional march apparently reasoned that a majority, or at least the most sensible clergy were in step. Only a few marginal priests had got out of hand. Data that appeared in the late 1960s or early 1970s—probably too late to change the perceptions of such bishops—showed that a huge majority of clergy had quickly endorsed the Vatican thrust.

Bishops probably did not realize the depth of the clergy revolution. The progressive trend, the insubordination, and the ineffectiveness of the old strength techniques of discipline all indicated a radical shift in clergy culture. The data implied a new constellation of situational characteristics expected by contemporary clergy, whose ideal priestly life included professional autonomy, positive reinforcement, status equalization, and consultation. The old disciplinary style of leadership no longer worked in such a climate. Bishops may have expected increased costs (sanctions) to spur the priest to increased commitment, but apparently that relationship was completely reversed as priests accepted a more rational model of commitment (Schoenherr and Greeley 1974). In the past, professional identity had often been described largely in terms of loyalty to the ecclesiastical center of power, and traditional bishops no doubt thought that contemporary priests still looked primarily for orders from the top or wished to advance by moving closer to the chancery. Yet the data here suggested that contemporary priests preferred decentralization—consultative leadership and clergy autonomy. One of the greatest complaints was the lack of grievance procedures, peer review, or personnel committees, all of which would have helped decentralize diocesan authority. Such reversals expected of basic relationships—cost/commitment and professionalism/centralization—surely were difficult for many bishops to grasp.

A fear of secularization may also have contributed to the bishops' position. Traditional bishops who recognized the depth of revolution probably chose to retain a purist theological position in the face of change. The purist tradition, implying the separation of priests from the world and devotion to the Sanctuary, stood against the rational model of commitment and the contemporary model of professionalism, which seemed to undermine the religious character of the church.

At least until the 1970s, the system of nomination for bishops within the United States favored the appointment of traditional or middle-of-the-road bishops (Greeley 1977:159). This tendency was due partly to the dominance of entrenched traditional dioceses in American church politics and partly to a conservative influence by the contemporary apostolic delegate to the United States.

These factors, and perhaps others, should help to explain the intransigence of traditional bishops. Such explanations boil down to the leadership lag mentioned above, a lag the analysts should have expected. After all, the diocese had been a structure in which leaders did not need to consider the culture of lower clergy as a hint of the future, in which they could avoid concrete reality (such as priest protest) by embracing a pure spirituality. In the face of deep change, such routine policies lead to a lag in leadership.

Chapter Nine

Priest Resignations in a Lazy Monopoly

The Catholic transformation was bound to bring other problems beside overt conflict. Change often creates maladjustment, or, as Janowitz (1978) put it, disarticulation. That is, one part or function does not communicate or co-operate well with other parts or functions, or even with the whole system.

What causes disarticulation? One obvious reason is that change has introduced new ideas and new norms. Some segments of the organization have absorbed new goals, new styles of action, or new assumptions about what is important. Consequently, those segments are on a different wave length from that of the unchanging segments.

Disarticulation in the Church displays itself in normative replacement, in differing progressive and traditional orientations, in confusion, in a withdrawal syndrome, and so forth. Priest resignations seem to embody several of these aspects.

Disarticulation should be most anguishing and perhaps most common during the mobilization phase, the period immediately following the council. By examining resignations during that time we should achieve some understanding of that disarticulation.

Resignations in the Mobilization Phase

Resignations of clergy became a new problem for the Catholic Church in the late 1960s. Resignation rates rose gradually among diocesan priests in the United States from about .1 percent annually in the 1940s and 1950s to about .5 percent in 1965 and 2 percent in 1969 (NORC 1972:277; Schoenherr and Greeley 1974:408).

Net losses to the active clergy have become apparent more recently. Though an estimated 10 percent of clergy resigned the active ministry between 1966 and 1972 (Schoenherr and Sorensen 1982), net losses appeared to be smaller, probably because of replacement by new ordinands, postponed retirements, and other factors. Fichter (1974:22), for example, notes a net loss of only 2.5 percent, from 59,892 American Catholic priests in 1967 (the peak year) to 57,421 in 1972. Yet, with the numbers of diocesan seminary students reduced drastically from 26,200 in 1966 to 13,600 in 1972 (Schoenherr and Sorensen 1982), the problem of priest replacement became increasingly acute. A recent estimate of net losses among active American clergy was 14 percent, from about

59,000 in 1966 to about 51,000 in 1978; these figures obviously reflect the combination of high resignation rates and low replacement rates.

Even in the early 1970s the problem was noticeable. According to Seidler's data, twenty-four dioceses lost 10 percent or more of their priests to resignations between 1966 and 1970; one diocese lost almost 19 percent in this way. The problem also existed in the larger context: religious professionals, including women religious, were not as abundant as before. Resignation rates for priests belonging to religious orders (those not directly subject to a bishop) were even higher (Fichter 1974:22; NORC 1972:277), and the decrease in total church professionals from 1966 to 1972 was 15.3 percent, according to official church statistics (Fichter 1974:21).

Priest resignations have been an object of scrutiny by sociologists. Several authors, studying resignations in a social psychological framework, analyzed attitudes preceding resignation (e.g., Schallert and Kelley 1970; Schoenherr and Greeley 1974). Such investigations have organizational implications. Cyrns (1970) implied that the clergy climate was too dogmatic; Schallert and Kelley (1970) suggested that the institutional rate of change was too slow for progressive clergy; Schoenherr and Greeley (1974) implied that Vatican absolutism on priestly celibacy resulted in a burdensome structure of clergy life. All these studies suggested that the structure of ecclesiastical Catholicism constituted a stumbling block to the continued commitment of many American clergy, at least during the late 1960s and early 1970s.

Other authors investigated more directly the organizational environment of priestly life and commitment. Hall and Schneider (1973) portrayed a dismal work structure for assistant pastors in one diocese during the same period.[1] Goldner et al. (1977) suggested that the Catholic Church's recent open communication system, although aligning Catholicism with contemporary democracy, had indirect negative consequences for the organization. Open communications produced cynical knowledge and lessened the commitment among lower clergy and other constituents. According to Goldner et al. (1977:540), cynical knowledge is the understanding that presumably altruistic organizational activity actually serves to maintain the institution.

These studies suggest possible ways in which ecclesiastical structures may influence priest resignations. These structures may cause resignations directly, because they are organized contrary to professional norms; they may facilitate resignations indirectly, though they are organized in accordance with professional norms; or they may be irrelevant to resignations. Other possible relationships surely exist, but these give focus to the current investigation.

Other researchers considered the consequences of priest resignations. Fichter (1974), NORC (1972), and McClory (1978) all pointed to the institutional crisis induced by recent resignations combined with seminary losses. Fichter, however, conveyed a tone of optimism about future church structures, partly because he noted and promoted the direction of renewal toward increased clergy professionalism and greater consultativeness. At the same time, many of these writers (e.g., Greeley 1977:chap. 8) depicted a rather conservative set of American bishops who overlooked the institutional crisis and continued to act in a traditional manner.

These and similar studies suggest possible consequences of priest resignations: they may create a conservative backlash by bishops; they may promote modernization; or they may be irrelevant to diocesan structures.

Church Structure
and Resignations

The possible relationship between church structure and priest resignations is worth a closer look. The period of analysis is 1966 to 1970. According to Schallert and Kelley (1970), the decision to resign the ministry arose from an atmosphere in which change-oriented priests were frustrated with ecclesiastical structures. Resignees, over three hundred of whom were interviewed in depth, embraced the values of individual freedom, less rigid authority, personalism, evolution of dogma, a pastoral orientation, and a dynamic view of structures. Frustrated in attempting to live by these values, and alienated, they decided to resign when a crucial other, symbolizing the ministry, let them down.

Most church structure was determined largely by the ordinary of a diocese. We used four categories of structural conditions to investigate causes of resignations:

- Episcopal policies—consultative leadership by the ordinary, clergy autonomy, and negative sanctions.
- Clergy climate—ideological polarization between bishop and lower-level clergy, cross-status friendships among clergy, friction initiated by lower-level clergy and aimed at the bishop, solidarity among dissident priests, and priest passivity and disillusionment.
- Nonbishop-related conditions—urban concentration of a diocese, relative size of the Catholic population of the area, diocesan size, and regional dominance (whether the diocese was a regional bureaucratic center for ecclesiastical matters).
- Formal structure—average number of priests per parish, average length of service before becoming pastor, task specialization (percentage of priests in nonparish work), size of the priest teaching corps, and percentage of parishes run by religious clergy (priests whose main allegiance is to a religious order and not to the episcopal structure, such as Dominicans, Franciscans, or Jesuits).

Although all these categories were possible causes of priest resignations, some explanations seem more likely than others. Episcopal policies and clergy climate were expected to be the major determinants of priest resignations, partly because of Schallert and Kelley's (1970) findings and Fichter's (1974) findings and partly because of a similar pattern found to explain priest protest aimed at bishops (Seidler 1972). In addition, the bishops seemed quite a salient group in the late 1960s; conditions set rather directly by the ordinary seemed crucial. Authority problems were paramount; clergy discussed constantly how bishops treated their subjects, how frequently sanctions were administered, and whether they consisted of nondesirable transfers and other punishments. Priests compared dioceses to discover whether bishops ran them on fear or whether they aimed at consensus governing. Certainly, leadership policies, whether consultative, punitive, or respectful of clergy autonomy, would be crucial in holding clergy to their priestly commitment. Compliance structures that underscored normative consensus and the use of rewards rather than punishments would increase priestly satisfaction. A socially integrated dio-cese—in which lower-level priests shared friendship with the bishop and his staff—would prevent resignations. Such structural conditions, deriving largely from the bishop's leadership policies, seemed the best deterrent to priest resignations.

Resignations obviously could have a variety of structural consequences. Soli-darity might increase with the loss of troublemakers, or disillusionment might grow as those who remained felt that leaders did not make concessions to justifiable demands of potential resignees. Policies might tighten in the hopes of denying freedom and temptation to other clergy, or they might relax as a sign of increased trust in the faithful remnant.

One could argue that bishops who suffered the greatest loss of resigned priests would hear the message and set up a more consultative, progressive clergy climate. Such an outcome is implied by Hirschman (1970), who empha-sizes the symbolic nature of resigning. In this case, however, we expected something different. Judging by the feedback from priest protest in chapter 8, we thought that any change triggered by resignations would be toward less con-sultative leadership, less clergy autonomy, and perhaps increased use of nega-tive sanctions by the bishop, rather than toward a more consultative policy. The bishop probably would assume that too much freedom resulted in the tempta-tion to withdraw commitment. Also, bishops were generally rated as strikingly more conservative than lower-level clergy (NORC 1972), and so such restrictive policies would reflect the natural tendency of traditionalists trying to curb liber-als. In addition, the long-run impact of seminary and clergy shortages was not yet apparent.

As a secondary consideration, however, priest resignations were expected to improve the informal clergy climate because presumably the marginal and divi-sive priests would have resigned, thus allowing for greater overall solidarity among the remaining clergy.

Models of the Church and the Study of Resignations. Models of the church also were implied in the expectations for causes or consequences of resignations. Each diocese had relative autonomy with the ordinary able to lead in an autocratic or consultative way, as he chose. In this view of the international Church, it is not a completely monophasic system centered in Rome, but is at least partly polyphasic (Fichter 1974:61–63; Greeley 1977). Subsidiarity, or home rule meant that clergy commitment and climate depended upon what happened in that diocese, which was viewed as a major center of action.

A transition from a monocratic to a consultative leadership style at the diocesan level was occurring as Küng (1976) and Dulles (1974) hoped. Because new consultative principles were emphasized at the Vatican Council, priests' hopes for changes in that direction would influence the clergy climate. In dioceses where consultative leadership and informal solidarity existed, clergy commitment would be firm; where autocratic authority and hierarchic divisions continued, clergy commitment would slip.

These models also implied a relatively closed social system. Internal influences, such as authority style and informal clergy climate, exerted salient influence, but environment or other relatively stable aspects had only a minor impact. In addition, critical problems, such as clergy protest or resignations, would be handled functionally by the authority structure.

The Church was pluriform as there were substantial local variations in leadership style and interpretations. Each diocese seemed to be its own unique minichurch.

These expectations implied that dioceses in which priests remained strongly committed were headed by administrators (bishops) who minimized the production of cynical knowledge (Greeley 1976 and 1977). Presumably they accomplished this by modernizing local structures and infusing them with the spirit of Vatican II, thereby defusing clergy criticism of ecclesiastical self-interest.

Specific predictions are summarized in Table 9.1, which relates structural conditions to resignations in both antecedent and consequent directions. Operationalization of all variables is in Appendix 3.

Data to study priest resignations came from Seidler's survey of 1,279 diocesan priests discussed in chapter 8. Luzbetak's (1984) data were again used for demographic traits of American clergy.

In Seidler's survey, fixed-answer questions focused on clergy relations, especially the authority climate. For example, informants were asked to rate the religious progressivism of the ordinary and the degree of camaraderie among various groups of clergy. They also were asked to recall the number of priests who had resigned the priesthood during the previous five years—occurrences which were much discussed in the priestly grapevine during those days.

Table 9.1. Predicted Impact of Structural Variables on Resignations and Vice Versa

Structural variables	Predicted relation to resignations	
	Antecedent	Consequent
Episcopal policies		
Consultative leadership	−	−
Clergy autonomy	−	−
Negative sanctions	+	+
Clergy climate		
Ideological polarization	+	−
Cross-status friendships	−	+
Priest protest	+	
Dissident solidarity	+	−
Clergy passivity	+	
Environment and diocesan salience		
Urban concentration	+	
Percent Catholic population	−	
Diocesan size	+	
Regional dominance	+	
Stable formal structure		
Priests per parish	+	
Duration of assistantship	+	
Staffing by religious clergy	+	
Teaching corps	+	
Priests in nonparish work	+	

Agreement within diocese on resignation rates was high, as measured by a reliability score of .97. Agreement was also high between these resignation scores and those obtained through official channels by Schoenherr and Greeley (1974). (The Pearsonian *r*, comparing the two data sets in 55 dioceses, was .91.)

To calculate the diocesan score, we divided the average number of priest resignees, as reported by informants, by the total number of diocesan priests in that diocese for 1966. Thus we created a percentage of diocesan clergy who had resigned the ministry during the previous five years.

The major technique of analysis was regression. The strategy was to trim the number of important variables by regressing resignations on all possible independent variables. Then we developed statistically testable networks of variables, based on the information from the strategy of trimming variables and following the restrictions of causal modeling. The networks were not simplified to one-directional causation, however, so that tests could be made for consequences of resignations. We tested plausible nonrecursive models, allowing for feedback from resignations, and using two-stage least-squares (TSLS) procedures to estimate coefficients.

The Antecedents and Consequences of Resignation. As predicted, many structural conditions appeared to influence diocesan resignation rates (see Table 9.2). Episcopal policies made some difference: negative sanctions and clergy autonomy appeared to promote resignations. The informal clergy climate was apparently influential: priest passivity and dissident solidarity seemed to trigger resignations. Environment and formal structure were quite important. Resignations seemed to be promoted by the percentage of parishes staffed by religious clergy, regional supremacy, duration of assistantship, and priests in nonparish work. Size of Catholic population appeared to prevent resignations. Only one of these relations—clergy autonomy—was in the direction opposite to what we expected. We thought autonomy would lessen resignation rates.

The pattern of relationships, however, was not as we expected. The greatest portion of the variance (23 percent) was explained by environment and formal

Table 9.2. Stepwise Regression of Priest Resignations on All Possible Structural Influences

Explanatory variable	Beta	Significance of regression coefficient	Added R^2	Total R^2
Control variables[a]			.135	.135
Staffing by religious clergy	.365	.001	.119	.254
Clergy passivity	.327	.001	.103	.357
Percent Catholic population	−.240	.001	.051	.407
Regional dominance	.183	.01	.029	.436
Dissident solidarity	.139	.01	.017	.453
Duration of assistantship	.156	.01	.014	.467
Negative sanctions	.111	.025	.0009	.476
Clergy autonomy	.159	.01	.016	.492
Priests in nonparish work	.097	.05	.008	.500
Cross-status friendships	.094	NS	.003	.503
Priest protest	.140	NS	.006	.509
Diocesan size	.136	NS	.005	.514
Urban concentration	−.107	NS	.005	.518
Ideological polarization	.054	NS	.002	.520
Democratic leadership	.095	NS	.002	.522
Teaching corps	−.047	NS	.001	.523
Priests per parish	.062	NS	.001	.524

Notes: N = 131.

[a] Control variables included summary diocesan scores for possible bias due to position, age, religious liberalism, absence, and disagreement among informants.

structure; episcopal policies explained only a small fraction (3 percent) and clergy climate explained a modest amount (13 percent). These findings are especially remarkable in contrast to the model explaining priest protest presented earlier. There, episcopal policies and clergy climate were foremost. Environmental and structural conditions were weak sources of rebellion.

Consequences of resignations could not be tested in such a straightforward way because of the strictures of feedback models, so we organized the variables into a network of endogenous variables (episcopal policies and clergy climate) influenced by exogenous variables (all others).[2]

Then we tested the theoretical model mentioned earlier, incorporating the findings displayed in Table 9.2 and examining plausible consequences of priest resignations on all other endogenous variables. Eventually we found the best-fitting and more parsimonious empirical model, which is displayed in Table 9.3.

Priest resignations had no discernible feedback effect. In fact, the only feedback that appeared in the findings was a negative one from ideological polarization (X_3) to consultative leadership of the bishop (X_1). (See Figure 9.1.) This finding is consistent with conservative tendencies of bishops when clergy become too liberal for them, because the polarization was between bishops and more progressive clergy. The data, however, do not support a retrenchment caused by resignations themselves; nor do they support the other expected result of resignations, namely a betterment of the informal clergy climate.

We examined the differences between models of priest rebellion and resignations[3] (see Table 9.4). Authority relations and the climate among bishop and clergy were more important in triggering protest than in causing resignations. On the other hand, environment and formal structure were more salient in triggering priest resignations. Episcopal policy and clergy climate accounted for 49 percent of the explained variance of priest protest but only 7 percent of the explained variance of resignation rates. Variables of environment and formal bureaucratic structure accounted for only 5 percent of the variance of priest protest but 25 percent of the variance of resignation rates.

We did another companion analysis of feedback effects from rebellion and from resignations to antecedent variables. As noted above, feedback from resignations was negligible. By contrast, episcopal policies turned conservative in reaction to priest-initiated conflict aimed at bishops. Priest rebellion affected episcopal leadership style and use of sanctions, both of which showed a tightening of the reins of leadership—restricting consultativeness and employing more negative sanctions. In addition, priest protest seemed directly to enhance solidarity among dissident clergy. Indirectly, other aspects of the clergy climate were influenced by priest-initiated conflict, reduction of clergy autonomy and cross-status friendships, and increase in ideological polarization.

These findings reflect the operation of models of the church along the lines

Fig. 9.1. Empirically supported model of priest resignations. Solid arrows represent significant relationships. Broken lines reflect marginally significant relationships, with p > .05 and added R^2 < .02.

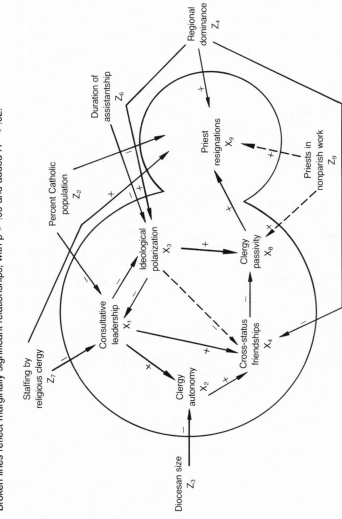

Table 9.3. Regression Coefficients and Explained Variance for Nonrecursive Model

Dependent variable	Explanatory variable	Regression coefficient	b/sd of regression coefficient	Significance level	Added R^2*	Total R^2
Consultative leadership	Control variables[a]					.130
	Percent Catholic population	−.030	1.818	.05	.017	
	Staffing by religious clergy	−.037	1.921	.05	.030	
	Ideological polarization	−.445	2.473	.01	.223	.399
Clergy autonomy	Control variables					.082
	Diocesan size	−.284	1.958	.05	.034	
	Consultative leadership	.795	1.583	.10	.215	.331
Ideological polarization	Control variables					.075
	Regional dominance	1.491	2.486	.01	.039	
	Duration of assistantship	−.091	2.369	.01	.031	
	Consultative leadership	−.494	2.539	.01	.238	.382
Cross-status friendships	Control variables					.135
	Regional dominance	−.748	2.270	.025	.058	
	Consultative leadership	.368	2.886	.005	.487	
	Clergy autonomy	.135	3.168	.005	.034	
	Ideological polarization	−.176	1.464	.10	.010	.724
Clergy passivity	Control variables					.041
	Priests in nonparish work	.101	1.398	.10	.016	
	Ideological polarization	1.231	1.686	.05	.134	
	Cross-status friendships	−1.419	1.650	.05	.107	.298
Priest resignations	Control variables					.135
	Percent Catholic population	−.569	3.291	.001	.042	
	Regional dominance	13.80	2.184	.025	.067	
	Staffing by religious clergy	.907	5.115	.001	.103	
	Priests in nonparish work	.344	1.404	.10	.019	
	Clergy passivity	1.071	1.466	.10	.080	.446

Note: This represents a trimmed model, with nonsignificant variables omitted. $N = 131$.

[a] Control variables included summary diocesan scores for position bias, age bias, religious liberalism bias, absence bias, and residual disagreement among informants.

* Because the nonrecursive program did not print added R^2 for each variable, added R^2 was computed by running several equations starting with control variables and adding one significant explanatory variable to the equation in each subsequent run. R^2 was the R^2 for the equation which had that variable minus the R^2 for the preceding equation.

Table 9.4. A Comparison of the Impact of Priest Protest and Resignations on Episcopal Policies and Clergy Climate

Dependent variable	Independent variable			
	Protest		Resignation	
	Relationship	Added R^2	Relationship	Added R^2
Consultative leadership	−	.29	NS	.00
Clergy autonomy	−*	.00	NS	.00
Ideological polarization	+*	.00	NS	.00
Cross-status friendships	−*	.00	NS	.00
Negative sanctions	+	.16	NS	.00
Dissident solidarity	+	.19	NS	.00

* Asterisk indicates significant indirect impact through other variables.

expected, but with major modifications. As expected, there was a degree of local episcopal autonomy, reflected in substantial variation in consultative leadership, progressivism of bishop, negative sanctions, and clergy autonomy.[4] If we judge by informal comments at the end of questionnaires, dioceses ranged from extremely progressive to extremely reactionary; the position on this continuum was understood by the local clergy as a reflection of the particular bishop. In this sense, then, the Catholic church of that era was not completely monophasic, but somewhat pluralistic or polyphasic.

In addition, the transition from an autocratic to a more consultative style of leadership at the local level seemed to have become an idealized norm. Clergy who acted as informants for this survey—all of whom occupied a position of responsibility in the diocese—judged themselves as substantially more progressive than bishops. The most common written complaint was that the bishop acted in an arbitrary and nonconsultative style.

Yet several modifications must be made, and all of them rest on a distinction between two issues: diocesan harmony and clergy commitment. In general, the expected models applied when the issue was harmony but not when the issue was clergy commitment.

Style of home rule was only partially important. Although episcopal leadership was an important determinant and consequence of priest protest, it appeared to be neither a strong antecedent nor a strong consequence of clergy resignations. More important than local pluralism or home rule were local environment, staffing, and bureaucratic structures.

Consultative structures seemed only partially important. Although clergy harmony seemed to depend heavily on the degree to which the local diocese incorporated emerging ideals of consultativeness, service orientation, and informal solidarity, these elements seemed less important for clergy commitment than structural facilitators or opportunity.

The diocese operated only partially as a closed system. When the same issue was harmony, authority relations and clergy climate operated as a rather complete system, impervious to outside influences. In the case of resignations, however, this system was not able to contain important influences; resignations were triggered by outside factors.

The lack of feedback from resignations, combined with the conservative reaction to protest, apparently indicated a lack of sensitivity by authority figures to professionals and their grievances. We can surmise that such lack of sensitivity may have produced a cynicism about church authority. In addition, bishops and their advisors showed a lack of interest in competition. They reacted negatively where priest protest was in high gear, but they simply let priests with decreasing commitment move to another occupation or market.

The Church as Lazy Monopoly

The lazy monopoly may serve as a useful concept in understanding American Catholic dioceses of the sixties and seventies. The criteria for applying this concept (Hirschman 1970:57–75) can be generalized as follows: If an organization is a virtual monopoly, it has singular control over a resource or product. Executives are slow to improve the quality of product, the policies, or the structure of the organization. Rather than improving quality, executives prefer to lose clients or personnel who criticize. Executives welcome opportunities for critics to exit, often via limited competition. These opportunities allow the continuation of status quo policies or mediocre leadership, because a loss of critics reduces the pressure for change and usually leaves the remnant on the conservative or uninvolved side.

In the late 1960s, Catholic dioceses were monopolies. They maintained unique control over the opportunities of priestly ministry and the organization of life for those ordained as diocesan priests. Dioceses effectively offered the sole opportunity for diocesan priests to continue serving, unless they wished (as extremely few did) to return to a noviceship and a new training in a religious order. Even if the priests decided to change authority structures by joining a religious order, they would remain ultimately under the same bishop's jurisdiction if they wished to continue working in that locale. Furthermore, the opportunity to relocate to another diocese was not given freely. Finally, a very few priests, often in well publicized episodes, chose to change denominations and continue as ministers in a Protestant church. Yet such an alternative was psychologically unlikely for those in a church that remained rather exclusive despite recent ecumenical gestures.

In addition, Catholic bishops of the late 1960s were slow to improve the quality of structure or to address fundamental issues seriously. Increased resignation rates—a sign of a basic problem in clergy life—did not trigger changes in episcopal policy or clergy relations, at least for that period. Even vocal and other direct criticisms did not produce policy changes, except in the more conservative direction. Because these criticisms came from a more liberal clergy and were aimed at an overwhelmingly moderate set of bishops (NORC 1972; Seidler 1972), such reaction to the right could not be considered an improvement in basic issues. At that time, lower clergy still complained in large proportions about the lack of administrative procedures such as due process, grievance mechanisms, and personnel assignments (Fichter 1968; Seidler 1974a; 1974b). It was not until about 1970 that each diocese, by decree from Rome, set up a priests' senate, giving at least formal representation to lower clergy in the diocesan decision-making process, though these senates lacked real legislative power. Overall, then, bishops did not deal with fundamental clergy problems, because they dealt with neither explicit conflict nor resignations as legitimate feedback.

Bishops maintained a status-quo policy—no change—as an outcome of resignations. In addition, they moved in a conservative direction in reaction to the simultaneous problem of clergy conflict, as noted above. Again, because conflict was initiated mainly by more liberal clergy, this tactic, combined with the lack of reaction to priest resignations, shows that bishops considered neither protest nor departure a legitimate form of criticism. Rather, exiting was no doubt a release from the need to move ahead.

Therefore, American dioceses during that era can be described as lazy monopolies; their actions were parallel to those of officers of nonreligious lazy monopolies, who allow disgruntled clients to retreat from their own product to something else rather than dealing with basic issues. Variations existed in the degree to which each diocesan monopoly was lazy, but the general pattern seems to have fit this model.

International Catholicism also could be labeled a lazy monopoly. It was a monopoly because all Western Catholic clergy remained under the jurisdiction of Rome. Though within limits bishops could set local conditions for clergy, the Vatican still controlled basic rules of priestly life. In addition, the worldwide Catholic monopoly became exceptionally salient for clergy during that era. The Vatican Council drew great attention to the new spirit initiated in Rome, which depended not only upon council documents but also on follow-up actions by the Vatican. Indeed, the pope's appeals to prudence and gradualism set a restraint on diocesan progress, and the rising and frustrated expectations of diocesan clergy were associated with Vatican impulses.

International Catholicism hesitated to come to grips with fundamental issues, even while undergoing modifications introduced at the Vatican Council. For example, the Vatican held firm to its celibacy ruling for priests, though the desire to marry was a crucial element in the decision of American priests to resign (Schoenherr and Greeley 1974) and though recent research has shown the arbitrariness of the celibacy law. In addition, the Vatican bureaucracy tempered its structure only slightly, though a basic overhaul was considered of utmost importance. Most decrees of universal change concerned matters of style or presentation rather than basic normative or structural matters (Davis 1967:13–14).

International Catholicism was happy to be rid of troublemakers. The process of official resignation is enlightening: clergy who desired to resign made written application by using a few officially acceptable reasons for asking for release from vows. These reasons effectively defined the appplicant as deviant. Others, electing to marry first without official approval, were released quickly from the clergy ranks. [5] The purity of hierarchy officially was preserved.

The Vatican allowed opportunities for deviants to exit. Deviant definitions were broadened to cope with the increased volume of requests for resignations, and therefore to allow greater opportunity for exiting. The Vatican readily granted permission for those defined as deviant to depart.

International Catholicism essentially maintained the status quo and apparently appeased the loyal conservatives. Pope Paul is generally thought to have catered to the conservative Vatican bureaucracy in doctrine and discipline, even while promoting the spirit of Vatican II in symbolic ways. In addition, his reign brought a slowing of the council thrust, which was perceived by many as a turn to the right.

Roman Catholicism changed its form of monopoly. In earlier decades, when it disallowed clergy resignations and criticism, it might have been named a totalitarian monopoly, but the winds of change legitimated at the Vatican Council apparently initiated a new organizational strategy. Church officials, enmeshed in the ecclesiastical establishment, could maintain conservative policies and a slow pace of change in the face of strong progressive trends by taking the form of a lazy monopoly. Such a strategy, which may have lasted only a few years, seems worthy of note.

Other denominations also can be considered monopolies, whether lazy, totalitarian, or profit-maximizing. In many nations, including Europe and Latin America, religious denominations long have monopolized a geographic region. Even today, despite the influx of American-based sects and increasing religious competition, many European countries (or specific regions within countries) maintain essentially monopolistic religions that allow minimal competition. Similarly, in the United States, indications of Mormon territory, Baptist country, or Jewish neighborhoods may reflect local monopolies within a broader context of religious pluralism.

Monopolies also can develop out of competitive situations. Though Protestantism apparently maintains a tradition of competition and religious freedom as reflected in current denominational switching (Roof and McKinney 1987), regionally monopolistic denominations thrived in early American colonies. More contemporary groups, too, have attempted to establish themselves as monopolies, though they began in a competitive setting. Reverend James Jones apparently sought through the People's Temple in Guyana to create a tyrannical monopoly over his segment of the population—a tyranny in which both voice and exit were stifled. Other groups, such as the Unification Church, also curtail the development of voice and exit while creating an ideology that would support a future monopolistic role in society.

Relationship to Other Research. The research reported here is related intricately to past studies of priest resignations, clergy climate, and other pertinent events of the same time period. New elements of this research include the lazy monopoly model, the test of short-run feedback, and significant structural effects on priest resignations. The last item requires further elaboration.

Other researchers have not discovered the statistical impact of structural factors on priest resignations, despite research on other occupations that shows the effects of such contextual influence as routinization and promotional opportunity (Price 1977). Hall and Schneider (1973) found contextual sources of work dissatisfaction and tension among priests, but they did not examine resignations explicitly. More to the point, Schoenherr and Greeley (1974), investigating aggregate and contextual sources of resignations, found practically no structural effects. They noted only a slight effect from the average resignation rate itself, namely the "cumulative impact of many priests in the diocese planning to resign" (Schoenherr and Greeley 1974:421). They concluded that "aside from important but rare exceptions, higher level social influences are too remote and too dispersed to affect strongly a priest's personal decision to continue" (ibid.: 421–422).

Several factors may explain the discrepancies between their findings and these. Schoenherr and Greeley omitted the five structural variables that in this study produced a significant impact on resignations. Perhaps their inclusion of organizational variables producing psychological inducement or cost (ibid.: 418–419) led them to overlook apparently nonpertinent sources of resignations. They tested a battery of variables and their theory was broad, but the significant structural sources of resignations in this study are unique.

Schoenherr and Greeley (1974:420–421) attempted to find structural effects, largely in addition to individual (or social psychological) effects, whereas we attempted to obtain structural effects only. Granted that in their study the zero-order correlations between group-level and individual-level variables, including resignations, were very low (ibid.:420), the impact of group-level factors might have been masked in the attempt to explain additional influences on individual-level outcomes. Individual-level variables may usurp partially the explanatory power of contextual variables, especially when the contextual variables (such as average resignation rate) consist of the same items aggregated to the group level. If this is the case, it may account for the generally disappointing results of contextual variables in regression analysis (Blalock 1969).

Schoenherr and Greeley's path model implies structural influences, even though the variables are framed at the individual level. In their model, for example, modern values induce work dissatisfaction and a desire to resign, regardless of the motivation to marry (Schoenherr and Greeley 1974:415). Such sequences make sense, however, only if the work climate or structure is regulated by traditional values. Modern values obviously imply new desires for the exercise of authority, job specifications, rules, and other matters, which go against prevailing structures, thus causing dissatisfaction.

The most distinctive element of structural findings presented here is the impact of facilitating variables on resignations. The element considered most theoretically pertinent—the route through passivity—finds continuity with Schoenherr and Greeley (1974) and with Schallert and Kelley (1970), even though both their studies are primarily social-psychological.

A general theme of deprivation runs through the research on priest resignations. Schallert and Kelley (1970) stated in their qualitative study that change-oriented clergy resigned because of alienation, the retention of traditional ecclesiastical structures, and slow church evolution toward modern values. Such variables reflect a cramped (or deprived) professional climate. Schoenherr and Greeley (1974), in several diagrammed routes to resignations, displayed the following influences on the decision to leave: inner-directedness, modern values, work dissatisfaction, and loneliness. These factors also imply deprivation of a satisfactory work or life climate.

Many threads of continuity exist among these three studies, including the one presented here, whether they are viewed from a psychological or a structural standpoint. They include a gap between lower clergy and hierarchy, professional autonomy (or inner-directedness), modernization (or progressivism or change-orientation), social support (or loneliness), and work satisfaction (or passivity or alienation). This constellation of deprivations can be considered one route to resignation.

Another second parallel in all three studies is the partial explanatory role of the common deprivation constellation. The other investigators placed heavy emphasis on an additional factor—desire to marry (Schoenherr and Greeley 1974) or a letdown by a significant other (Schallert and Kelley 1970). In this study, facilitating factors came strongly into play.

In addition, the results of this study converge with data on general job turnover. Leaving one's job has been associated with dissatisfaction, professionalism, and various work conditions, including centralization and lack of social integration. Job turnover also has been associated with the possession of transferable skills and opportunities to go elsewhere (Price 1977). These conditions correspond roughly to facilitating conditions as presented here.

Questions naturally are raised about important variables from other research that were not treated in the present study. For example, how are these findings related to the strong relationship between resignations and the desire to marry (Schoenherr and Greeley 1974)?

Because priestly marriage is not a local option, the desire to marry does not translate to a diocesan policy issue. Therefore, it is not a diocesan-level cause of resignations, and it does not fit the present model.

The very irrelevance of the celibacy issue at the diocesan level may help explain why facilitating factors were more salient than causative factors. If the desire to marry exercises a strong and independent pull toward resignations at the individual but not at the diocesan level, the analyst would expect causative diocesan influences to be weak.

The lazy monopoly concept may be complementary to the finding about the desire to marry. Lazy monopolies are insensitive to constructive criticism; according to this line of reasoning, the Catholic hierarchy will not have answered fully the criticism of liberals until the Vatican changes its celibacy rule.

Another open question regards the relationship between this study and cynical knowledge. Cynical knowledge, a basis for priest decommitment (Goldner et al. 1977), is said to have developed during recent decades when Catholics became aware that hierarchical decisions were dictated by political and organizational considerations rather than by pure altruism. How does this explanation relate to the findings presented here?

The cynical knowledge theory is distinctive in placing major explanatory emphasis on the manner in which lower-level participants perceive actions of officials. By contrast, the deprivation approach, including the causative element in the present research, underscores the effects of official actions—namely the conditions of work and life for lower-level participants.

Perhaps cynical knowledge and deprivation vary together on occasion. For example, cynical knowledge among diocesan clergy may emerge in those places where bishops are thought to resist modernization because of political or selfish considerations. On the other hand, perhaps disillusionment arises from deprivation or from cynical knowledge operating separately.

The cynical knowledge theory implies that church officials attempt to maximize personal or political gain. Yet the lazy monopoly theory suggests that the hierarchy, in its unwillingness to face such issues as celibacy, often may seek only an adequate, nonoptimum solution. In either case, priest commitment may be lessened.

Questions obviously remain for future research. Which influences are more important for clergy commitment: the perception of a political and selfish hierarchy, or the alienation, passivity, and loneliness resulting from hierarchical decisions and experienced by clergy? Do we need a multisource explanation, or does a single type of explanation suffice? Which kind of monopoly causes higher resignation rates, the profit-maximizing monopoly or the lazy monopoly?

Regarding monopolies, researchers may ask under what conditions do organizations tend toward monopolistic practices? In particular, when do they become lazy rather than tyrannizing or profit-maximizing?

Additional studies are needed to discover whether the lazy monopoly applies to church actions at other periods or only for this single moment in church history. Since 1971, structural innovations, such as diocesan pastoral councils, pastoral planning commissions, priests' senates, and personnel boards—but not optional celibacy—have been institutionalized widely in the United States. The church may have begun to perceive the competition from attractive nonreligious career patterns as gaining strength, thereby challenging the monopolistic hold of the church on priests' lives; lazy monopolies are operative only when the competition is weak (Hirschman 1970:57–61).

Chapter Ten

Disorientation of the Seventies
and Some Modest Achievements

The Catholic Church of the 1970s continued to experience anguish as it moved more deeply into the period of implementation. Emphasis on problems of change does not negate the positive accomplishments of this period. A number of significant achievements occurred. We call them modest achievements not because they were trivial, but because they were new and not operating everywhere to full satisfaction. They constituted solid beginning steps toward the revolutionary changes set in motion by Vatican II.

In general, we were interested in understanding the special difficulties of implementing relatively radical changes. We have already seen many of the major conflicts and struggles, but were there not additional dislocations, perhaps more subtle and less noticeable to the outside observer?

Our analysis focused on organizational adjustment. The Catholic Church is a normative organization; new divisions and battles waged over old and new norms. There was intense struggle over one of the basic thrusts of the Second Vatican Council—restructuring toward consultativeness. We saw how the Church was working toward, but had not yet fully embraced, a new paradigm for itself. Instead, it suffered confusion over many religious symbols that had once helped integrate the Catholic structure.

The issues could be summarized under categories representing kinds of disarticulation: cultural, structural, and symbolic. Beyond the more dramatic normative clashes, exploration centered on the subtle struggles arising from various sets of taken-for-granted beliefs and customs. What were some salient disarticulations in the Catholic cultural system? What were the problems of implementing new structures, as seen from the angle of those participating in them? What were some of the symbolic disarticulations as experienced by performers of key functions?

The progress that dioceses made toward realizing the directives and spirit of Vatican II was also of interest. As informants told of their diocesan struggles and goals, they also made known many of their successes.

In personal interviews conducted during the late 1970s, Seidler met with two persons in each of six selected dioceses: the director of Pastoral Planning and the president of the Priests' Senate. By reason of their official responsibilities, persons occupying these positions would be attuned to diocesan progress in the spirit of the council. Both would also understand the concrete difficulties of implementation.

At the same time, each represented a unique perspective developed largely in connection with the job. The director tended to be more of an insider or a close advisor to the bishop, whereas the president was usually an opposition leader. Sometimes their comments showed sharp differences.

The interview asked each informant how the diocese was progressing toward the goals of Vatican II and what special difficulties it was experiencing. Interviews usually lasted more than an hour, and there was a great degree of cooperation. These officials seemed eager to tell their stories.

Additional informants answered similar questions oriented more to the whole population of American dioceses. These informants included the president of the National Federation of Priests' Council (NFPC), a past president of the NFPC, and several priests and former priests who attended the 1977 Convention of the National Association of Pastoral Renewal.

Cultural (Normative)
Disorientations

By cultural disorientation, we mean any disarticulation of the system caused by a cultural item (such as a norm or a belief). Examples include a new structure that malfunctioned because of old beliefs (cultural lag), a new dominant norm that left certain participants disoriented (anomie), and sharp differences among participants in dominant beliefs or orientations (culture conflict).

Attempts to equalize the voices of various interest groups within the dioceses often met subtle resistance. Where new structures were created, old mentalities frustrated hopes of increased consultativeness. Informants complained that the priests' council, the pastoral council, or both, constituted mere window dressing. In one diocese, considered relatively progressive, the bishop used these councils to endorse his already-decided plans or his already-signed contracts. He and his staff made no effort to involve the council in real decision making, even though they regularly told the council that they wanted their input. In another diocese, the personnel board—in theory a body of elected representatives of the priests—had become instead an instrument of the archbishop. Again, the director of the board consulted with board members in appearance only.

As one informant said, "We in the Church have no tradition to equalize voices." Rather, "we still view all authority as vested in one person." Another informant explained the persisting endorsement by many of a top-down authority viewpoint. He said that many people want the bishop to be a strong leader because, they say, one needs "big models," such as a bishop who is "prophet-leader."

Normative traditionalism, or cultural lag, seemed to work against the adequate performance of new structures. The structures were now in place, but they were not fulfilling their potential.

A significant segment of priests apparently embraced a new model of professionalism. As the old clerical syndrome faded, this new professionalism emerged. It included a sense of competence based on maturity and good training, the ability to make independent judgments, strong dedication, a pastoral orientation, and increased attention to career-related reading and discussions.

System-wide manifestations of the new professionalism included various norms and structures, such as the principles of attractiveness and voluntarism in applying for diocesan positions (replacing simple appointment or seniority), and continuing education for priests such as sabbaticals, workshops, midlife career counseling, and special studies.

Byproducts of the new professionalism, at least in some places, included a rejection by many clergy of the rank of monsignor and the incorporation of new diocesan guidelines to equalize pay scales among priests.

Problems of disorientation resulted. Priests in the 45-to-50 age group felt anomie about their career advancement. The new requirements for job placement (expertise, specialization, competitive recruitment) sometimes left them dangling. Older priests, trained to be generalists who could do all things, could not compete with the younger ones, who had received specialized training.

The principle of competitive and voluntary recruitment had limitations. Some dioceses had to fill unwanted pastorships, perhaps located in the wilds. When no one applied for such positions, personnel committees had to rely on the old system of simple appointment.

The new professionalism undercut traditional clergy community as well as clergy culture. Younger and more professional priests apparently lessened their involvement in the many traditional forms of priest gatherings. For some, this change may have expressed some aspects of the new professionalism, such as their independence and maturity. For others who had developed an additional expertise, especially in a nontheistic science, it may have reflected the possession of added reference groups. Such professionally oriented priests had more outside points of contact, including secular mentors, professional organizations, and even libraries. The clergy culture was lost "to secularism and to relevance" in the wake of the new professionalism.

Younger priests often interpreted the new professionalism as suggesting a nine-to-five work day. Sadly gone, according to older informants, was the notion that priesthood was a profession one practiced and lived twenty-four hours a day. A sense of humor was also unfortunately missing in the younger men.

Dioceses reported varying gaps between those who held opposing viewpoints. In some places the differences could be described as liberalism versus traditionalism. In other dioceses some clergy were called freedom seekers, whereas others were rule seekers. Sometimes the division could be called a professional gap—clergy who were up-to-date professionally versus those who were not. At other times it was a psychological gap, separating change-oriented priests from those unable to change. Occasionally, the split put the bishop on one side of the fence and the priests on the other. In one diocese age seemed an important factor; priests under thirty-five were reported to be the innovators, and those over thirty-five were the conservatives.

These conflicts were reported as new; they were not the old progressive-traditional conflicts of the 1960s. Apparently, the mobilization fights of the 1960s had given way to the implementation battles of the 1970s. New issues arose in the wake of Vatican II—fights over new norms, such as freedom, professionalism, consultation, change, and other new clergy expectations. Often these issues originated in diocesan attempts to realize the spirit of the council.

Structural Disorientations

By structural disorientation we mean a lack of coordination or smooth functioning within a structure itself, or between structural (or aggregate) facts and other aspects of the social system. Several structural disorientations seemed to occur during the implementation period, as one might expect.

Implementing the structure of consultativeness involved an enormous struggle. To begin with, the new structures (personnel boards, priests' senate, pastoral council) all "demand lots of effort," as one priest said. Working from the grassroots upward was more difficult than simply waiting for top-down decisions.

In addition, "hierarchs win by default" at the grassroots (parish) level, one informant said. Apparently, those trying to follow consultative guidelines left openings that were filled by the hierarchs. Perhaps the hierarchs were better organized than the rest. Perhaps they knew the territory better. Perhaps they did not wait patiently to hear all voices. Perhaps they were simply better at taking action. In any case, old habits and structures did not coordinate well with the new structures.

Certain background conditions of many Catholics worked against consultative input. Many had learned more authoritarian ethnic structures and psychological structures from childhood. As adults, "they lapsed back to the social structures they grew up with."

More than one informant summarized the situation as follows: "We have the structures of democracy, but people are uncomfortable with them. It's an uneasy democracy." Apparently, the uneasiness derived from the lack of coordination between consultative structures and other behavioral, psychological, and organizational structures.

The new structures themselves—introduced for the sake of accountability, grassroots input, and subsidiarity—often increased diocesan bureaucracy. Of course, they were aspects of bureaucracy (Weber, in Gerth and Mills 1946), but they also introduced a new disarticulation. They created a bureaucratic problem.

One such problem flowed from the multiplication of intermediate boards and consultative groups. In one archdiocese, the following groups were either resurrected or newly created: consultors to the archbishop, twelve area pastors (consultors), priests' senate, personnel board, archdiocesan pastoral council, area councils, and parish councils. Confusion arose over the different groups' responsibilities. At times their duties seemed to overlap.

Solutions often emerged for this kind of problem. For example, the overlapping jurisdiction of the archbishop's consultors and the twelve area pastors was solved by specifying and narrowing the responsibilities of the area pastors. In the future, they were to inform the archbishop about the pastoral needs of their areas.

Another bureaucratic problem was the increased attention that pastors needed to give to all these boards, councils, and other groups. Even if not directly involved by membership in any of them, ordinary priests needed to petition or respond to these groups from time to time. We can call this problem one of increased energy or output—a first cousin to the well-known red-tape problem.

Finally, some dioceses suffered a simple coordination problem as bureaucratic departments and agencies increased in number. They needed information management systems.

Various dysfunctions followed the changes in structure. The turn toward collegiality and consultation unfortunately removed the bishop from important roles. In one archdiocese, the personnel board was quite active, independent, and controversial. Consequently, there were complaints that the archbishop was not sufficiently involved in personnel matters. Others said the personnel board was less personal [than the ordinary, in the old system]. Apparently, some individuals accepted the decisions of the board only with great difficulty.

An informant from another diocese, referring to the whole consultative movement, said that as a result of the intermediate and representative structures, "priests practice their trade largely, not in isolation from, but without a deep causal connection with the Ordinary." He mused about the bishop's role: "Bishops do matter, but priests will be effective on their own talents and decisions. It is sad: the bishop is supposed to matter, and it is sad that he doesn't —not as a kingmaker, but as a charismatic leader, a focal point of pastoral leadership."

Team ministry, the organization of a parish staff so that all members share the authority equally, affords another example of structural dysfunction. Many priests had become disillusioned about team ministry, despite its successes. There were several problems: The idea was not tested carefully enough and resulted in "too quick and wholesale a plunge." Many teams broke up as a result. In addition, the strong administrators were disillusioned, largely because they possessed no real responsibility.

At the same time, an independent research association reached a more positive conclusion. The Center for Applied Research in the Apostolate (CARA) analyzed questionnaires from seventy-nine (of all eighty-one) available active and former members of team ministry in Hartford, along with other related interviews and questionnaires (for example, from twenty-six parish councils). CARA concluded that team ministry had been generally successful and had improved ministerial effectiveness (CARA 1975). On a variety of measures—team effectiveness, value of pastoral involvement, work challenge, work satisfaction, commitment, and ministerial effectiveness—team priests scored high. In fact, they almost always scored higher than the comparison group: priests in the same diocese who were examined in the 1968 Yale study (Hall and Schneider 1973). Occasionally, they were compared with priests in general (NORC 1972).

Only rarely did the data hint of possible disillusionment. Since 1968 a small group of team priests has suffered a change for the worse in self-perception—the degree to which a priest saw himself positively as a supportive, involved, and intellectual person. This small group consisted of former pastors and specials (those engaged full-time in special nonparish jobs); their self-image declined substantially between 1968 and 1974. One can only speculate about the reasons for such a decline. CARA did not have the data to probe that question, but perhaps confusion over responsibility, or the simple lack of it, may have been difficult for a few former pastors and specials.

Team ministry apparently produced mixed results. Though mostly positive, a few outcomes—team breakups, disillusionment, and a worsening self-image—were negative. Although functional in general, team ministry was dysfunctional for a small subgroup.

Among other structural dysfunctions, two are worth mentioning. A new elitism had developed in some dioceses. Some priests were "in" with the bishop, plotting and leading the new structures and strategies. In the meantime, the rank and file felt unaffected by the "great ideas of the senate, chancery," and other elite bodies.

In addition, rising expectations that change would solve all problems led to disillusionment. Naturally, priests expected their new senate and other structures to promote their goals effectively; one informant said that the initial enthusiasm was followed by "cold water being thrown on a lot of things; if we wait long enough, it [change] will all go away." An informant in another diocese said that the clergy mood about change was dispirited and very fragile. Another informant said the new structures, such as parish councils, had lost credibility among the priests. According to another, even the militants had given up.

The new structures left many priests at sea. Such revolutionary changes undercut their old sacred roles and left them partially adrift. Consequently, a great search began for new priestly roles. Committees, councils, and teams tried to create new roles based on collegiality or on new notions of pastoral ministry. The major issues of conflict (authority, freedom, change, and social issues) suggested in part that priests were often attempting to work out new roles in these areas, though they were under attack.

In addition, the climate of uncertainty produced varying goals in this search. Associate pastors searched for what they could do better than pastors, such as the new pastoral ministry. Pastors searched for authority somewhere in the whirlwind of change.

In sum, the search for new roles represented functional and dysfunctional aspects of change. On the one hand, new roles actually came into being to fulfill the spirit of Vatican II. They included team ministry, new pastoral ministry, pastoral planning, and grassroots input. On the other hand, many priests were apparently at a loss as they tried to define their new roles.

Clergy shortages, of course, were a direct outcome of morale problems and disillusionment, as well as the result of rational thinking, desire to marry, alienation, and passivity. In any case, the shortages were observed in the combination of increasing priest resignations and dramatically increased seminary losses. They became a structural fact for most dioceses.

There were six disarticulations—dysfunctions that derived from priest shortages. The more creative priests were lost; that left dioceses with those of lesser imagination. Consequently, those dioceses suffered a loss of potential leadership.

The shortages resulted in increased clergy tension and stress. Because of the losses, many priests who remained were given extra responsibilities and were often rushed quickly into pastorships, leading to overwork and premature transition to leadership.

The shortages put limitations on the program of special education for priests. In a tight situation, dioceses could not afford to have many priests on sabbaticals or in special studies.

The shortages often led to a maintenance mentality, which was dominated by anti-intellectualism, an antichange orientation, the desire to keep a place in the old system, and social, political, and economic conservatism.

Such shortages also triggered changes in recruitment policies—changes that some considered unsuitable for the tasks at hand. To fill clergy vacancies, dioceses often imported highly conservative foreign priests or priests from religious orders. Frequently, these importations reduced priestly cohesion. Dioceses also recruited churchy types, often young conservative Catholics without interest in social issues. Such men were far different from the socially active priests who had labored during the 1960s and early 1970s.

In summarizing such solutions to the problems of recruitment and shortage, one informant said that his diocese was dominated by the old theology. It set policies based on practical necessities, given the old thinking. Instead of doing something imaginative and constructive, such as employing resigned priests, the diocese followed the maintenance mentality, putting a finger in the dike by stopgap policies.

The switch from recruiting boys in elementary and high school to targeting college students had disorienting repercussions. Pastors who formerly helped recruit seminarians from among altar boys in their parish schools were suddenly out of touch with the recruitment process. Consequently, they lost their former continuing connection, through these boys of the parish, with the seminary and with the larger diocesan system. The pastors felt a loss of identity.

Symbolic Disorientations

Symbolic disorientations are dislocations due to the loss, change, or creation of important symbols. Symbols play a decisive role in sustaining religious involvement (Greeley 1981). When a deficiency of symbol occurs, religious commitment may be endangered. Communication between parts of the social system also may be hampered, as one part may assume one set of dominant symbols and another part may assume a different set.

The disruption of symbolic rewards coincided with the disruption of basic Church symbols. In the post–Vatican II setting, with its emphasis on social leveling, consultativeness, new professionalism, declericalization, and openness to the world, many priests rejected the old reward system. Monsignorships were either phased out or rejected by potential recipients. They simply did not fit the new orientations.

One informant made the following statement in describing the old reward system, which had broken down because peer acceptance was down: "It used to be a set, well-known pattern. Advancement followed this mold: First, one became an assistant pastor. Next, you moved to a mountain or rural parish. Third, you got a city parish. And finally, you became a monsignor. This pattern had peer understanding and clarity."

In the new era, priest appointments guided by personnel boards did not have the same tone. Apparently, difficult assignments were not seen as stepping stones to higher rewards; instead they seemed to cause greater anguish. As one informant put it, "If an appointment is very difficult to accept—and sometimes you have to assign someone—the priest thinks the archbishop doesn't accept him."

What other rewards were available? This informant's diocese had experimented with some alternatives, including the establishment of think groups throughout the archdiocese and the encouragement of openness among the clergy. In addition, they tried to introduce new honors, such as a priest-of-the-year citation. According to an informant, "The priest of the year is honored at Holy Thursday Mass and at a lunch." Finally, "the archbishop goes to each parish once a year—at least he tries. He tries to honor priests by the visit. He personally thanks them." Yet, such rewards produced only a slight result. "It is still hard to find a good reward system. We're still searching. These things don't seem to be enough and are a bit artificial."

Most Catholics were probably familiar with additional symbolic disarticulations, especially the ones that most affected laity as well as clergy. There were liturgical disruptions of symbol. In place of rosary, genuflections, crucifixes, and silence came a host of new symbols, many of them reflecting the new emphasis on the congregation. They included increased congregational singing, vocal dialogue between priest and people, handshakes, clapping, the homily, and emphasis on the Bible. In the transition, many priests and laity seemed to experience a sense of homelessness and confusion because the symbols—and meaning—were disrupted.

Symbolic disruptions occurred in the theological realm. God's love and mercy, Jesus as Brother and Savior, and the positive side of salvation gradually overshadowed the earlier emphasis on Mary, Purgatory, sin, and a judgmental God. Many loved the new approach; but some complained that the Church was becoming soft. Others seemed determined to keep their anchor in the old symbols despite the new theological tide. Still others appeared to be lost and groping.

There were the symbolic disruptions in the realm of significant Church persons or key functions. We have already noted the desire of some priests for big models and strong prophet leaders. In the transition to a more open and consultative style, many priests and bishops attempted to become leaders who listened to many voices. Other alterations, as in the clothing, life-style, and social involvement of priests and women religious symbolized new roles of these key functions. Such transitions also affected Catholics variously; some clergy and laity seemed especially dismayed.

Such disruptions were more than mere psychological disorientations. They reflected a disarticulation between parts of the Catholic system. Confused and dismayed Catholics (whether clergy or laity) had difficulty relating to the new liturgy, the new theology, and their sacred models who had caught the new spirit. Conversely, new-mold Catholics communicated poorly with old-style liturgies, theologies, and key functions.

Modest Achievements

The informants also underscored the achievements of their dioceses, despite the main focus on problems of aggiornamento. They seemed to view these accomplishments as real and solid, though often enmeshed in difficulties. The following list suggests goals that at least some dioceses were able to accomplish.

There was a new professionalism among priests. Signs of the new professionalism included increased maturity and competence of younger clergy and new training in specialized areas, so young priests could move easily into the available clergy positions. It also included widespread attention to special education for priests in midcareer.

The move toward social leveling or destratification took various forms. Some dioceses rejected the practice of giving priests the elite, honorific title of monsignor. Team ministry was also an attempt to equalize the status of pastors and assistant pastors. Consultative structures, such as priests' senates and pastoral councils, spoke concretely of respect for priests and other Catholics. The spirit of collegiality seemed to work its way gradually toward teamwork rather than self-glorification.

Consultative structures included priests' senates, pastoral councils, parish councils, area consultors, think groups, and other mechanisms that encouraged wider consultation and grassroots input. They were clearly an attempt to implement Vatican II statements on collegiality, shared ministry, the priesthood of the laity, and so forth. As Fichter maintained (1977), consultative restructuring was the main outcome of Vatican II.

In many dioceses, one sensed a new form of professional respect for clergy and an attention to their rights. This existed apparently not only in a new atmosphere or clergy climate, but in real structures such as personnel boards, priests' senates, grievance procedures, and mechanisms for priests' special education, both during the seminary and in midcareer.

In some chancery offices, changes were obvious. There was a new administrative spirit. As one informant said, the chancery in his diocese "was now more pastorally oriented, with fewer people, and it's not a kingdom." In contrast with the old days, the chancery officials were not "ecclesiastical climbers, nor sycophants." They would not mind standing up to the bishop. In one diocese these administrators, called the "king's court," included a top church jurist and a graduate of the Harvard Business School. The rest of the clergy reportedly got along quite well with these administrators.

In addition, many dioceses created a new role—pastoral planner. The person occupying this office was responsible for diocesan planning so as to implement Vatican II more fully.

There was better seminary education. Besides the emphasis on specialized programs, informants often said that the theology itself was an improvement over the material of pre–Vatican II days.

Underlying the above accomplishments was the general acceptance of a number of council-inspired norms and values. These included collegiality, consultativeness, a new professionalism, the new theology, the spirit of Vatican II, the principle of attractiveness and personal choice in job placement, the authority of service, and destratification.

According to some informants, clergy were generally happy and the clergy climate was much improved in the 1970s. In addition, some dioceses reported that priests enjoyed a freer (and more positive) attitude of criticism. Finally, their spirit of dedication was strong.

Contested Implementation

During the implementation phase, many dioceses apparently realized major accomplishments in the spirit of the Second Vatican Council. At the same time, the struggle to implant the new norms, structures, and symbol systems took on gigantic proportions. Often there were side effects, such as the disorientation of segments of the diocesan social system. Often, too, the old culture or structure lingered, as in the widespread expectation of the strong leader. Finally, there were countless ways in which the new attempts at revitalization could run off the tracks.

We may note the two-faced nature of structure building. On the one hand, the drive to implant new structures and new forms of behavior resulted in immediate progress and often received good press. On the other hand, the forces of negation, including cultural lag, inertia, and ideological disagreement, often attacked in strength. Similarly, both positive and negative aspects surrounded the attempts to construct new norms and symbols.

Much of the problem could be attributed simply to the pains of building new structures, cultures, and symbol systems. The old beliefs, symbols, and structural references were not easily replaced.

The disarticulations also suggested a continuing conflict, but now, the contest occurred less between the forces of modernization and of traditionalism. Rather, it often pitted those committed to more radical change against those pushing for moderate change. This battle was quite clear in the different perspectives of those representing the priests' senate and those representing the central administration (pastoral planners). Pastoral planners were distinctly more sanguine about progress than were the presidents of priests' senates. By contrast, presidents strongly criticized the central administration or the bishop for lack of leadership in keeping with Vatican II.

During this era, then, contested accommodation took the form of a battle over implementation. Differing factions clashed, including those who hoped that aggiornamento would blow away and those who wanted the complete elimination of monocracy. Beneath the surface struggle to make the new norms and structures work lay a deeper conflict among the various ideological interest groups: traditionalists, mainstream updaters, and more radical reformers. We may label this period *contested implementation.*

Chapter Eleven

Movement Meets
Countertrends

We have seen strains and struggles as the Catholic Church in America moved through the momentous 1960s and 1970s. We noted early the radical and massive changes enacted by worldwide Catholicism at the Second Vatican Council and saw the evidence of change in the United States. Then we turned to research on the special difficulties and achievements of the mobilization and implementation periods of the post–Vatican II years in the United States.

The findings tended to flesh out the explanatory framework of contested accommodation by specifying issues of accommodation, parties in the various conflicts, and particular forms of conflict. In addition, the data supported the social movement stage theory by displaying different emphases (in issues, protagonists, and forms of conflict) in the 1960s and the 1970s. Finally, the Catholic Church experienced different forms of disarticulation during mobilization and implementation.

Major findings included the following:

- Basic and resistant issues dominated the conflict scene of both phases (mobilization and implementation). These issues included authority, freedom, and change, especially in liturgy.
- More during the 1960s than during the 1970s, conflicts revolved frequently around authority and clergy life-style. During the 1970s, there was a greater variety of conflict issues, and the conflicts extended to new organizational junctures and additional secondary issues. Also during the 1970s, more lay Catholics, organizations, and "other" hierarchy were involved in the conflicts.
- The birth control controversy in Washington, D.C., and in less dramatic form elsewhere in the American Church, was largely a vertical conflict.
- Protest by diocesan priests during the 1960s on a national scale was relatively tame and only sporadically organized. Yet by contrast with preceding decades of ecclesiastical calm, such dissent was worthy of special note.
- Progressive leadership, especially incorporating consultation and fostering cross-status friendships, was the effective model in preventing clergy rebellion.
- Episcopal reaction to clergy conflict was largely disciplinary in the short run, as bishops turned in response to more traditional leadership patterns. This response appeared to be a failure, because it apparently did not produce peace and unity.
- Priest resignation rates for dioceses during the 1960s were triggered most of-

ten by facilitators rather than by causes—namely, staffing by religious clergy, percentage of Catholic population, and regional dominance.

- At the diocesan level, priest resignation rates during the 1960s had no discernible impact on episcopal leadership policies.
- By the end of the mobilization phase (1971), clergy apparently developed an idealized norm: local bishops should jettison autocratic leadership and embrace the consultative style.
- During the implementation phase, dioceses experienced a variety of disarticulations. These included cultural disorientations (such as cultural lag, anomie, and culture conflict), structural disorientations (such as dysfunctions of structure, bureaucracy, and priest shortages), and symbolic disorientations (as in the reward system).
- Modest diocesan achievements of the 1970s included a new professional spirit among priests, partial destratification, the implantation of consultative structures, and increased respect for priests' rights.

As we have seen, much of the conflict and disorientation after Vatican II concerned authority structures and styles. Consultative/progressive leadership coped best with potential conflict; priests generally adopted an idealized norm of consultative leadership; attempts to build consultative structures engendered subtle and not-so-subtle resistance.

In the Church—and perhaps elsewhere—consultative leadership has several limitations. The very notion of popular rule, though supported by such Vatican doctrines as the priesthood of the laity, runs counter to the tradition of top-down authority. Many people who must cooperate to make consultative structures work will probably never change their basic stance toward authority. These are most likely to include those who still want the bishop to be a strong prophet-leader.

By the 1970s, when many bishops and chancery offices were moving toward more consultative structures, the stumbling blocks to complete achievement became clear. These included cultural lag, structural habit, and the sheer effort required to build consultative structures. A common complaint was that a bishop regarded the new structures as consultative only; thus he could, and often did, disregard proposals. In addition, hierarchs win by default, others slip back to the autocratic structures of their ethnic childhood, and still others simply do not make the effort to provide solid input.

Some of these difficulties seem to be inherent in the religious context. For example, beliefs in top-down authority and in the consultative nature of new structures are consistent with the belief in a God who speaks in a special way to pope and bishops. Such beliefs will probably persist among many Catholics, helping to link them with their traditional religious heritage.

Evidence from the 1970s suggested that at the diocesan level, the Church was operating less and less as a lazy monopoly. As dioceses attempted to introduce new forms of ministry, wider consultation, increased respect for priests' rights, and grassroots participation in decision making, they obviously were paying attention to former complaints. In addition, by the 1980s some dioceses helped to sponsor gatherings of former priests, and bishops listened to their concerns.[1] In such dioceses, leaders were clearly trying to mend fences and construct a humane setting for priestly work.

At the level of worldwide Catholicism, however, the 1980s seemed to duplicate the late 1960s. Under Pope John Paul II, priests were expected to follow traditional practices from religious garb to political noninvolvement. This pope began to reissue release papers for priests wishing to resign, after a period in which he had refused to give any such dispensations.

This two-level interpretation may help us understand why resignation rates remained relatively high. Though clergy conditions were sometimes improving at the diocesan level, they remained relatively constant at the international level. Therefore, clergy commitment to some dioceses probably remained high, even while it sank in regard to Vatican policies—that is, to worldwide Catholicism.

New social structures commonly appear on the agenda for action after the phases of mobilization and legitimation. During these periods, ideological battles seem to dominate the scene. Thus, when the implementation era arrives, many persons have already embraced the new norms; the new task is how to make them operative. As a result, we see the attention to structure building, to putting the new norms into operation.

Setting up the structures is far easier than making them work effectively. Without much trouble, one can issue an edict, a new organizational chart, or a game plan showing how the new structure will function. Yet, it is not so easy to induce the players to follow the spirit behind the structure.

The introduction of new structures may even be a ploy to give the appearance of organizational progress. Informants often said that structures were doomed by the attitudes of those setting them up. For example, bishops who set the agenda of priests' senates and later refused to follow any of their recommendations seemed to set up the structures only for window dressing.

We have noted that the Church in transition seemed to have dismantled its old paradigm without fully creating a new one. Yet the studies reported here present hints of a new paradigm, at least for the moderately progressive mainstream. Perhaps it is time to specify this paradigm.

The former paradigm might be called the sacred or divine Church, with its emphasis on mystery, austerity, and vertical authority. Images of the Latin Mass, Friday fish, the saints, and obedience to the pope and other superiors all fit this understanding.

What shall we call the new paradigm, after reflecting on the data presented here? One answer is the participatory Church, a church that emphasizes the human side without abandoning its link with the divine. In this new paradigm, people participate to the extent that they are treated with dignity and respect; their interests are represented properly.

Major struggles of the post–Vatican II phases focused heavily on the human side of religion. We noted, for example, that conflicts of both phases centered largely on accommodation. Yet that accommodation was frequently an acceptance of human rights, or humanly derived knowledge, or contemporary human structures, or the human condition; hence, the struggles over authority, consultation, freedom, and birth control. Liturgical change, too, which inspired frequent conflict, moved from the mysterious to the understandable, from sacred silence to increased human participation.

Disarticulations and achievements also reflected this thrust: priest resignations reflected a new, pragmatic approach to church authority and personal life. The struggles to build new reward systems, new structures, and new cultures involved massive attention to the human condition. Finally, achievements conveyed the same message. Dioceses seemed to incorporate such humanly created structures, norms, and values as consultation, professionalism, and human rights.

Tremendous energies were devoted during these years to building a new ecclesiastical setting that allowed for greater participation, which corresponded to the bottom-up theologies that dominated this period. As McBrien (1969) noted, existential theology became dominant. Similarly, the leading candidate for an emerging church paradigm was the human Catholic Church.

At the same time, in keeping with the new pluralism in the Church, competing paradigms will exist side by side in Catholicism. We would expect traditionalist and progressive (human) paradigms to continue.

The major concepts and theories outlined in our early chapters served to unify and guide the analysis. At this point, these concepts and theories may appear in new light. Contested accommodation was presented as a framework for understanding in what ways, why, and how Catholicism had changed at the national and international (Western) levels. Dioceses responded in different ways to the struggle. As one past president of the National Federation of Priests' Councils said, dioceses ranged from those in which there was no progress to those that had the reputation and gave the appearance of progress, with varying shades in between. In his view, some struggle existed in all dioceses.

One might categorize these dioceses, depending on the orientation of the bishop and other factions within the diocese, as cooperative modernization, modernization through cajoling, conflict, and collective resistance to modernization. In cooperative modernization, most Catholic factions embraced aggiornamento. In modernization through cajoling, a strong and progressive bishop led a diocese with a tradition of conservatism. In the case of conflict, most commonly a traditional bishop confronted a relatively progressive and outspoken Catholic faction. In the final category, all major diocesan factions resisted aggiornamento.

The interplay between movement and countermovement, a major feature in social movement outcomes (Mottl 1980), was important prior to Vatican II. By the 1980s, when Pope John Paul II embraced aspects of the traditionalist Catholic movement, the emergence of a countermovement phase was obvious.

Even in the late 1970s, informants frequently expressed their misgivings about the traditionalist influence on their diocese from new recruits, seminary training, or priests imported from foreign countries. Many of these comments came from diocesan leaders who clearly wanted to move ahead without conflict and foot-dragging.

Pope John Paul II, however, bestowed legitimacy on the traditionalist countermovement in a variety of ways. As the Church moved into the 1980s and beyond, one could ask, "Which will prevail in the long run—movement for aggiornamento or traditionalist countermovement"? That question may not seem altogether realistic, given the foothold of aggiornamento, but certainly the traditionalist movement will slow the progress of the social movement for change within the Church.

The historical information of chapter 4 suggests a pattern in movement development that has often been overlooked: the formation of content and goals as well as organizational ties (e.g., Freeman 1983). In this movement for change within Catholicism, the first phase saw the creation of minimovements (such as those for liturgical change and for the vernacular), which coalesced around the time of Vatican II.

From these minimovements came ideas and theologies—the underlying logic that eventually dominated the thrust for change. A process of generalization also occurred as the movement focused on aggiornamento, or change in general, or accommodation. Even so, the specific issues were worked out decades before the council in the minimovements that presented ready-made rationales to the framers of the Vatican II documents.

Countertrends

The 1980s have brought a variety of trends, both worldwide and local, to the Catholic Church. Unlike John XXIII and Paul VI, who guided the Vatican Council and promoted change, Pope John Paul II has attempted to slow the aggiornamento movement, and perhaps even wishes it to stop completely. As noted earlier, such an elite and powerful actor may affect strongly the direction and speed of the movement.

In the first eighteen months of his reign (late 1978 to early 1980), Pope John Paul II displayed a traditionalist stance in a number of actions (see Marton 1980 for most of the following information). He chose the archconservative head of Opus Dei as special friend and informal advisor (Kamm 1984). He reached an accommodation with traditionalist French Archbishop Marcel Lefebvre, allowing him to continue ordaining priests and deacons in Switzerland in defiance of an earlier Vatican ban. He proclaimed his negative views on the ordination of women. He banned Hans Küng, one of the most prominent Western liberal theologians, from teaching under Church auspices. He summoned the equally renowned theologian Edward Schillebeeckx to Rome for questioning. He reined in the Dutch Church in what was called a victory for traditional doctrine. Finally, he stopped issuing dispensations to priests who wished to be laicized, although he later allowed dispensations for reasons more narrowly defined than his predecessor, Paul VI.

These early acts prefigured accurately the long-term reign of a traditionally oriented pope. In the 1980s, he continued trying to curb the movement for change that, in his view, was going too far. His actions include the following:

- He restored the Tridentine Mass, allowing occasional celebrations under specified conditions (*Catholic Trends:* October 20, 1984; November 17, 1984).
- He called an extraordinary session of the Synod of Bishops for December 1985, to revive the extraordinary atmosphere of Vatican II and to clarify its subsequent trajectory (ibid.: February 9, 1985). He was apparently concerned that some had gone too far in following the spirit of Vatican II.
- He told all priests to get out of politics, especially urging the four priests in the Sandinista government of Nicaragua to resign their official posts (ibid.: September 22, 1984).
- He condemned liberation theology (ibid.: September 8, 1984), with special cautioning against the use of Marxist analysis. Likewise, he condemned the writings of Franciscan Father Leonardo Boff, a well-known liberation theologian of Brazil (ibid.: March 23, 1985), a stand he somewhat reversed later.
- He banned the use of altar girls (ibid.: November 3, 1984).
- He continued the tough stand on birth control in a long series of talks on married love (1979–1984) (ibid.: December 1, 1984).
- He abrogated the Jesuits' four-hundred-year tradition of passing on the top leadership by appointing interim caretakers of his own type and overlooking the leader chosen by the previous Jesuit General, Pedro Arrupe (*Time:* November 9, 1981). Clearly, he feared that the Jesuits were becoming too liberal.
- He also intervened in matters of the Discalced Carmelites, announcing that the Vatican would write a new constitution for the order's cloistered convents based on a sixteenth-century rule (*Catholic Trends:* March 9, 1985).

- He ordered women religious who signed a paid announcement on pluralism and abortion, which appeared in the *New York Times*, to retract their statement or risk expulsion from their orders (*Catholic Trends:* March 9, 1985).
- He curbed Father Charles Curran's teaching responsibilities as a faculty member at Catholic University (*NCR:* March 21, 1986; *WP:* March 13, 1987).
- He reiterated the Church's traditional teaching on homosexuality in a formal decree on the topic (*NCR:* November 7, 1986).
- He disciplined Archbishop Hunthausen of the Seattle diocese by removing many administrative duties from his purview and appointing a vice-administrator (Wehrle) to handle them. (*NCR:* September 19, 1986).
- He spoke against in vitro fertilization through the "Instruction on Respect for Human Life in its Origin and on the Dignity of Procreation" (ibid.: November 22, 1987).

Some may argue that the pope was merely diciplining excesses, but the evidence seems overwhelming that he went far beyond attacking what moderates would call excessive (Marton 1980; Whale et al. 1980). The issues he addressed went to the heart of the movement for change. They included what we have defined as primary issues of the movement: authority, freedom, liturgical change, new theology, and symbolic roles of priests, brothers and women religious. They also included many other important issues, such as women's concerns, marriage and sexual norms, social issues, married clergy, and experimentation in worship.

Some church leaders have publicly expressed concern about the pope's tactics to slow down the movement. Father Gerard Austin, chair of the theology department of The Catholic University of America in Washington, D.C., said that the reinstatement of the Tridentine Latin Mass was a terrible move, a ruling that would undermine the changes in the liturgy brought about by the Vatican Council (*Catholic Trends:* October 20, 1984). On the same issue, representatives of thirty-two bishops' conferences, including that of the United States, sharply criticized the Vatican decision. These representatives, who had gathered in Rome for a congress of leaders of National Liturgical Commissions (ibid.: November 3, 1984) expressed "concern, regret, and dismay." They said that allowing the Latin Tridentine Mass would undercut efforts to implement Vatican II. They added that the ruling was inconsiderate of Catholics who accepted the liturgical changes only with difficulty, and that it seemed to "violate the collegial sense of the worldwide episcopate."

The representatives at the liturgical congress also voiced other concerns, including the banning of women as acolytes and lectors—a move that, according to Bishop John Cummins, chair of the U.S. Bishops' Committee on the Liturgy, most American Catholics found difficult to understand, appreciate, or accept. Cummins noted, "Many American Catholics perceive [that] the prohibition symbolically exhibits a discriminatory dichotomy between lay men and lay women, rather than a theologically based discipline." The bishops' conferences of England, Scotland, Wales, and Ireland agreed, stating that the ban "preserves the unfortunate impression that the church regards women as second-class citizens." The New Zealand bishops decided not to use the liturgical rites for the installation of acolytes and readers "precisely because of the pastoral harm which would be caused by a discrimination which we are unable to defend theologically."

Some bishops' conferences thought that cultural adaptations in the liturgy were occurring too slowly. For example, the bishops of India complained that Vatican prohibitions on experimentation in the liturgy had hampered efforts toward merging liturgy and custom.

Bishops' conferences of Indonesia, Malaysia, and Singapore said, "It is necessary to rethink the possibility of ordaining married men and permitting lay ministers to administer certain sacraments, e.g., anointing of the sick." In these and other countries there was a grave shortage of priests, and lay persons commonly presided over weekly liturgical services.

A study of religious life in the United States, ordered by the Vatican, found tension between religious communities and the Vatican Congregation for Religious and Secular Institutes. In addition, many women religious felt that they had not participated in the life of the Church as much as they desired (ibid.: October 20, 1984).

Sister Theresa Kane, former president of the Leadership Conference of Women Religious, criticized the climate for discussion. Speaking to the National Assembly of Women Religious, she said that there was no atmosphere for dialogue in the church on questions of authority or of women's sexuality issues. She added that women should be "the primary authors of the documents, of the pronouncements, of any of the articulations of church that define women" (ibid.: August 25, 1984).

Finally, in a letter to Pope John Paul II, Spanish Father Felipe Sainz de Baranda, head of the world's Discalced Carmelites, expressed "disgust" at the "very hard tone and the polemical content" of the letter announcing that the Vatican would write the new constitution referred to above. Father Sainz de Baranda said that the Vatican had sided with the minority of the order's nuns who opposed post–Vatican II renewal. About 80 percent of the nuns wanted a constitution based on experimental declarations approved by Pope Paul VI; some 20 percent wanted a rule based on the 1581 rule of St. Teresa of Avila, according to the priest (ibid.: March 9, 1985).

Many Jesuits were also upset by the way in which the pope abrogated Jesuit procedures for interim management and election of a new Jesuit General (*Time:* November 9, 1981). As mentioned above, the pope disregarded the wish of the previous general, Father Pedro Arrupe, and appointed the conservative Father Dezza as interim manager of the Jesuit Order. Many considered this interference humiliating and unnecessary, although the more traditional Jesuits sided with the pope and hoped for a slowdown of the movement for change.[2]

Local traditionalists also expressed their views. When the American bishops developed their pastoral letter on Catholic Social Teaching and the U.S. Economy, prominent Catholic laity composed a more conservative opposite view, endorsing the free-market profit system as the most moral economic approach (*Catholic Trends:* November 17, 1984). The leaders of this lay commission were former U.S. Treasury Secretary William Simon and theologian Michael Novak.

Movement Momentum

Despite the shadows cast by Rome, the movement in the United States seemed destined to continue at least in intermittent sunlight. In the areas of social responsibility, shared decision making, new structures, and continuing the momentum for change, church leaders were still poised for progress.

Cardinal Joseph Bernardin of Chicago, in an interview with a German magazine, pointed proudly to a maturing American Church and cited recent bishops' statements. He said they had brought a moral dimension to American public policy (ibid.: December 29, 1984). These statements included the American Bishops' Pastoral Letter on War and Peace and the Pastoral Letter on Catholic Social Teaching and the U.S. Economy (ibid.: November 17, 1984). Each criticized some aspect of American public policy, such as nuclear buildup and certain aspects of capitalism.

The American bishops also addressed other social issues. Seventeen bishops condemned apartheid as an "evil system" and urged the Reagan administration to end its policy of "constructive engagement" with South Africa (ibid.: December 1, 1984). In a pastoral letter in 1983, the bishops committed themselves to enhance Hispanic ministry (ibid.: October 20, 1984).

To continue the momentum for change, American Catholics proposed a number of new structures. Father Donald Heintschel, associate general secretary of the National Conference of Catholic Bishops, suggested that each diocese have its own synod to continue aggiornamento (ibid.: December 29, 1984). Theologian Anthony Padovano (1985) spoke of the opportunity and need for building base Christian communities. Others suggested an ecumenical (nonterritorial) Catholic diocese, perhaps based in New York, appealing to alienated Catholics across the country (Baute 1984).

New roles were also discussed. Father Heintschel (*Catholic Trends:* December 29, 1984) mentioned several of these, some of which were already in practice. They included deacons or lay persons acting as administrators of parishes, priest circuit riders (celebrating Mass at several parishes), and team ministry. He also noted that the near future would bring serious discussion of the redistribution of priests and the roles of women, especially in liturgical celebration. Additional topics also promised to come up as the bishops began to prepare for the 1986 Synod of Bishops in Rome, whose theme was "The Mission of the Laity in the Church and in the World" (ibid.).

In addition, many people were talking about a married priesthood. In a survey sponsored jointly by the National Federation of Priests' Councils (NFPC) and the Corps of Reserve Priests United for Service (CORPUS), and conducted by the Gallup organization, American Catholics, by almost a two-to-one majority, favored permitting priests to marry and to continue to function as priests. Overall, 58 percent of Catholics favored married priests, 33 percent opposed them, and 9 percent did not express an opinion. The following groups supported the married priesthood at least two-to-one: women, persons 30 to 49 years old, high school graduates, those from upper-income homes, and persons living in households in which the chief wage earner was employed in business, the professions, or in a blue-collar job (*Emerging Trends:* September 1983).

Yet the continuation of the movement rested on more than the observations of elite Catholics. Having invested so much energy in the new Catholicism, the dioceses would not easily abandon aggiornamento.

Finally, even the pope was not a complete traditionalist, especially regarding social issues and international conflict. He often spoke out for justice, human rights, and liberation (*Catholic Trends:* September 22, 1984). His encyclical of 1981 ("On Human Work") found a rigid capitalism in error (ibid.: October 6, 1984). He almost lost his life for his public support of Solidarity, the unlawful Polish workers' union. He ordained two married Anglican priests into the Roman Catholic priesthood, thus intensifying the discussion about a married priesthood. He articulated a near reversal of his earlier position on liberation theology. In June 1988, he excommunicated Cardinal Lefebvre for elevating four clergy to the rank of bishop. The priests were connected with the traditionalist Society of St. Pius X, and selection of bishops is a papal prerogative. In some small ways, even this traditional pope has encouraged a movement forward.

A Survivor Church

The pages of this book have described a Church both shaken and fresh. It teetered and stumbled through a major revolution, enduring conflict at every point along the journey that has lasted almost six decades of the twentieth century. Conflicts and disarticulations touched the deepest foundations of the movement for change. They also struck basic chords in the religious beliefs of many Catholics. Truly, the Church—its sacred structure and its members—underwent a transformation that would have shaken the strongest giant.

At the same time, the Catholic Church gave evidence of new vitality. The tone of surveys and informants reflected optimism about many of the changes, and about what the Church could still become. This Church was not caught in an eternal mold, but was prepared to experiment; it stood ready to challllenge social injustice and conflict. It was prepared to try the new structures of shared responsibility, team ministry, personnel boards, and so forth. Though opposition and struggles ensued, one strong underlying theme was the willingness to try on the new look.

The Roman Catholic Church once again in its history survived, largely by incorporating features of contemporary life. Despite the Church's turn toward rigidity at the end of the nineteenth and the beginning of the twentieth centuries, it moved again toward flexibility and openness. Often led by members of exempt religious orders—a mechanism for change mentioned earlier—precursor minimovements started the long process of aggiornamento.

The Church also used many other mechanisms of change. The most dramatic, of course, was the ecumenical council (Vatican II), but there were other important stimulants. These included synods of bishops, a direct chain of reporting to Rome, extraordinary decrees from Rome, professional theologicans and toleration of diversity, especially in localized environmental niches.

Thus the Church, through modernization, seemed more fit for survival. It was still fashioning a new social niche, but the one it seemed likely to attain would give it a better chance of long-term survival. Members seemed more optimistic about their Church, and it could now articulate with the rest of society in a more satisfying way.

For all its changes, however, the Church maintained its fundamental identity. It retained twenty centuries of tradition, its long-standing Catholic scope, and its Christian beliefs. In addition, it retained the basic tripartite organizational structure: the Vatican, the diocese, and the parish. Yet, as in other times and places, this Church had transformed many of its prominent features, including language, the manner of self-presentation, decision-making structures, and attitude toward other religions. Thus, it demonstrated a feature of long-term viable organizations adapting to the times while remaining a distinct entity.

Appendix A

Methodological Information
for Chapter Six

Conflict incidents included all disputes in which at least one side took a specific action aimed at an antagonist who would most probably recognize the attack. These criteria excluded mere opinions expressed about controversial topics, editorial comments, general policies of authorities (even if broadly critical of segments of society) and beginnings of movements that had not yet focused on a target. Included were dramatic challenges to authority, unusual litigation, back-and-forth public accusations, personal confrontations, protests, and symbolic resignations from Church service—for example, where a dispute prompted an order of obedience to one who would not comply. Truly conflicting sides always engaged in at least quietly confrontative behavior. Very quiet disputes that were settled quickly probably escaped all media, including the *NCR*, but the *NCR* apparently covered almost every dramatic incident.

Internal conflicts were those in which all significant aspects of the conflict were inside the Church, including primary antagonists and matters of contention. External conflicts were those directed largely outside the Church. In these cases, a significant aspect of the battle—such as a mjaor antagonist or matter of contention—lay outside the Church.

Protagonists were all parties involved in the conflict. These included individuals, organizations, and communal or status groups (such as parishioners or priests of a certain category).

Issues were the matters of contention—the topics over which a fight occurred. These matters included a range of interpretations, symbols, norms, and assumptions about the Catholic Church, which were suggested rather directly by the *NCR*. Coding was developed to correspond to the data and then was applied to all the cases. Often more than one issue was involved in a single conflict incident, and conflicts were coded accordingly.

The most salient issue was the one about which the conflict seemed to revolve most centrally, as reflected in the *NCR* accounts.

Coding

To select conflict incidents, two research assistants with detailed guidelines read all pages of all issues of the *NCR* for the time periods under examination, picking out the conflict incidents and recording all pertinent information. This information was coded later into the categories for this research by three other persons, who were blind to hypotheses. Codes were developed from an initial reading of the synopses into pertinent subcategories: the content of issues, the type of protagonist, and whether the conflict was intra- or extraorganizational, or both.

To ensure the relative independence of each incident, coders combined material on initial and follow-up articles about the same dispute. This accumulated information was then synthesized for the final coding of a single conflict incident. In addition, when a complicated dispute involved more than one episode and different sets of protagonists (as when laity complained to a bishop after a public conflict between a reporter and an editor for the diocesan newspaper), the second conflict episode was appended to the first as an addendum, but not as a separate conflict incident. On the other hand, if two conflict incidents appeared to be more clearly independent, even though reflecting a long-standing feud, they were coded as separate.

Sample Reliability
and Bias

One hundred incidents in all were coded for the three years in the 1960s and 145 for the four years in the 1970s. Of these, 65 and 88 were purely internal conflicts for the 1960s and the 1970s, respectively.

This sample included not simply all conflict events, but newsworthy and known conflict events within Catholicism. To be printed, such conflicts must have been perceived as important. Though such selectivity may present problems for some research, in this case the perceived nature of the phenomenon corresponded to its importance, for conflict is salient only to the extent that it is perceived as such by the parties to the conflict and by the news reporters.

Several possible biasing factors were considered. Conflicts in remote areas, with little access to the media, may have been missed. Such omissions probably did not matter, however, because both decades would have been affected equivalently. Editors occasionally decided to summarize a set of similar conflicts in a single article. In such cases—rather rare—separate incidents were coded as such only if enough information was given about the specifics of each event. In one case, in a summary article about the unionization of Catholic school teachers, four of the five conflicts mentioned in that summary article had already been featured previously; thus, no information was lost. In the only other such case, the reporter referred to a single concrete example, which was reported as typical of such events around the country. In this case, conflict events were missed, but again, this factor seems to be of minor importance; both decades should have been treated similarly, and the summarizing treatments seemed rare.

Other possibly biasing factors, however, suggest a different treatment of the two decades; these include selectivity and changes in *NCR* staff or policy. Selectivity, always present, may have been determined by such factors as satiation, which makes the tenth or twentieth incident of a particular type less interesting than the first. If selectivity was at work, the 1970s automatically would have displayed fewer conflicts of the type common in the 1960s. Yet the data show no evidence of this, as the most common types of conflict of the 1960s were also reported in great numbers during the 1970s. In addition, the continuation of such conflicts seemed to hold a special fascination for reporters, perhaps because specific actors, coalitions, and situations were always somewhat new, and also perhaps because the Catholic Church was so unused to open conflict.

Finally, changes in the *NCR*'s staff and the lessened controversy about the newspaper might indicate a subtle shift of policy in the 1970s. The president of the board of directors quit in 1967 because in his view the paper had become too controversial "and did not present . . . the true Catholic Doctrines and teachings." Two popular columnists (Garry Wills and John Leo) also quit during the late 1960s, although not for the same reasons. During the 1960s, the paper also received complaints from Bishops Shannon and Helmsig for being one-sided or even anti-Catholic. It also received a barrage of criticism for publishing the leaked-out final report of Pope Paul's stand on birth control, again in the late 1960s. Such controversy was generally lacking during the 1970s—even the Jules Feiffer cartoons were gone—which may indicate a slight toning down in that period.

Yet in general, the reporting of the *NCR* was rather consistent over the two decades. Just as conflict in the wider society quieted during the 1970s, so did that within the Church; the lessened drama seems likely to reflect reality more than bias. In addition, as noted above, the *NCR* did not shrink from printing the same kinds of conflicts in the 1970s as in the 1960s. Finally, it did not avoid stories about controversy in general: according to these data, it reported an average of thirty-three incidents per year in the 1960s and thirty-six per year in the 1970s, and a good portion of these were covered in followup stories throughout the year. The *NCR*'s policy remained the same, and during those years it won several awards from the National Catholic Press Club.

Appendix B

Model of Rebellion for Chapter Eight and Operationalization of Variables for Chapters Eight and Nine

The Context of Rebellion

Understanding clergy dissent from the data was the challenge of this research. The extent of dissent could be seen directly from the data, and we expected it to be widespread. Other questions needed investigation within a larger framework which emphasized the interrelationships of a set of clergy factors. The effectiveness of ordinaries' styles of leadership required examination in context also. We considered the effectiveness in reducing conflict—though one could use many other operationalizations of effectiveness (see Coulter 1979).

Figure B-1 presents the general context for dissent. We expected leadership policies (X_1) and authority relations (X_2 through X_5) to most strongly influence priest rebellion (X_6) and its consequent solidarity (X_7). (See Appendix B for operational measures of all variables.) This prediction flowed from the nature of the Catholic organization and the specific conditions of those years. Bishops exercised great power and were highly important to the lives of priests. In addition, the changes initiated by Vatican II set the more progressive clergy against the more traditional bishops. Other studies have shown that the massive number of lower clergy (in contrast to bishops) supported progressive religious ideas during the late 1960s (NORC 1972; Fichter 1968). Also, clergy who followed the triumph of theological updating at the Vatican Council had increased expectations for change.

Environmental influences (Z_1 and Z_2), structural development, differentiation, and complexity (Z_3 through Z_9) should relate weakly to clergy rebellion. Both Catholicism in the late 1960s and a modified conflict perspective, which sees overt conflict as arising primarily from authority relations or from a conflict of interests (Coser 1957; Dahrendorf 1959), directed our expectations. Intraorganizational, vertical conflict arises more distantly from environmental forces and from structural development and complexity (Gouldner 1954). These forces initiate or intensify the strain within the authority relation.

As Figure B-1 shows, there should be less rebellion in dioceses where the bishop was progressive, where changes were adopted in the spirit of Vatican II, where power was decentralized, where the bishop's leadership style was modern, and where priests expressed greater professional autonomy and were allowed to do so by the bishop. In such dioceses, cross-status friendships among all classes of clergy were expected as well.

Greater conflict should be present where bishops exercised a disciplinarian approach to social control using negative sanctions and in dioceses where there was a more administratively inclined bishop and a more professionally oriented lower clergy.

Figure B-1 includes the bishops' reactions to priest rebellion too. Using the same reasoning as above, we expected strong conflict to further produce non-progressive leadership, more use of negative sanctions, and more ideological polarization.

Variables Z_1 through Z_9 were operationalized with data from Luzbetak 1967.

Z_1 Urban Concentration: proportion of parishes in towns or cities of greater than ten thousand population.

Z_2 Percent Catholic Population: percentage of Catholics in the population of the area.

Z_3 Diocesan Size (log): absolute number of Catholics in the diocese.

Z_4 Regional Dominance: status of diocese as province headquarters, that is, administrative center for several dioceses in a region (scored 1 or 0).

Z_5 Priests per Parish: average number of diocesan priests per parish run by diocesan clergy.

Z_6 Duration of Assistantship: average number of years a priest remains as assistant pastor before being promoted to pastor.

Z_7 Staffing by Religious Clergy: percentage of parishes run by religious clergy (those subject to superiors of religious orders, and not primarily under a bishop; instead under a jurisdiction whose area is much broader than a diocese).

Z_8 Teaching Corps (log): absolute number of priests engaged full-time in teaching. (We chose the absolute number rather than a percentage because we believed that a critical mass for unrest could be achieved by a sizable group of scrutinizing academics, whatever their percentage of membership.)

Z_9 Priests in Nonparish Work: percentage of diocesan clergy engaged full-time in nonparish work.

Variables X_1 through X_7 came from Seidler's survey of priest informants, 1971.

X_1 Consultative Leadership of Bishop: A four-item scale, including informant estimates of the following: willingness to hear grievances, encouraging the participation of all priests in decision-making processes of the diocese, desire for the diocese to serve all people both inside and outside the church, and overall leadership. Reliability (Ω) was .90; validity (P_{ts}) was .95. (For measures, see

Fig. B.1. Predicted model for clergy conflict

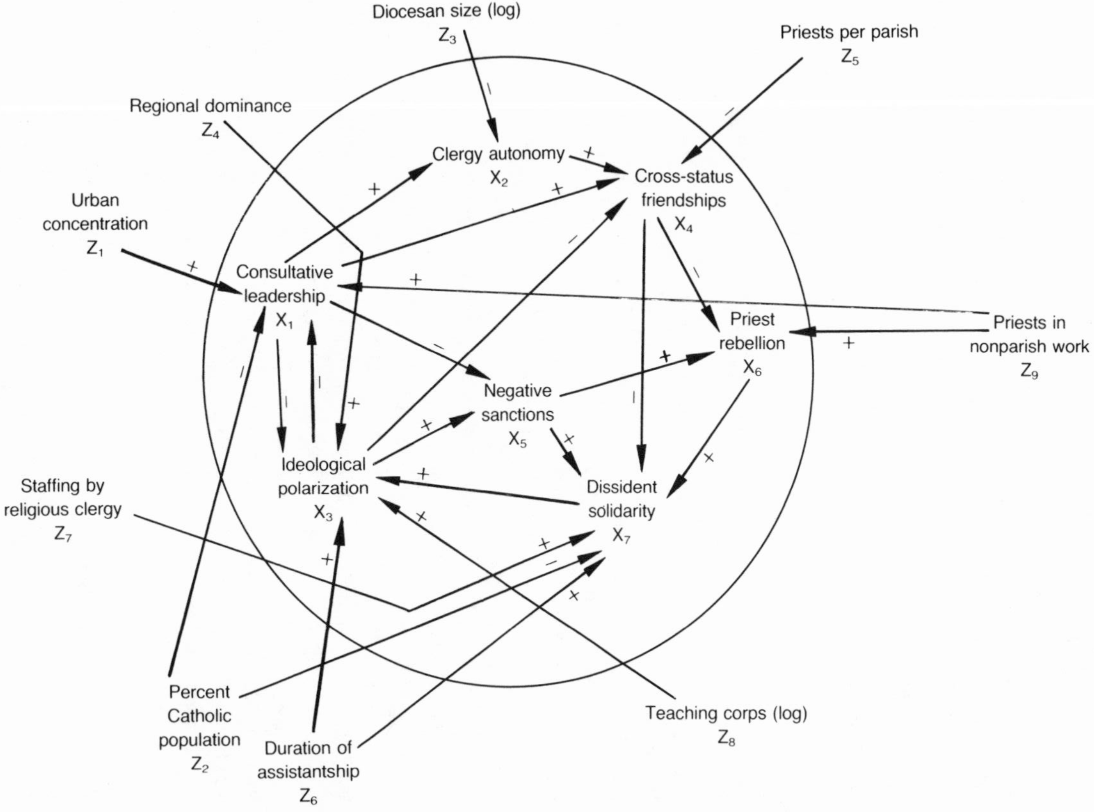

Heise and Bohrnstedt 1970.) In this model, consultative leadership (X_1) can be conceived of as representing, beside the items contained in that construct, a progressive episcopal attitude toward change and actual speed of adaptation to the new spirit of Vatican II. Progressivism and speed of adaptation (see following) were correlated so highly with consultative leadership that they were dropped from analysis.

Religious Progressivism of Bishop: estimated general attitude of the bishop regarding changes in the Church. Answers ranged from very progressive to very traditional.

Speed of Adaptation: a six-item scale in which informants estimated the relative speed at which their diocese had instituted renewal of the following kinds: liturgical renewal, ecumenical activity, new theological ideas, innovations in religious education, experimental life-styles for priests and religious, shared decision-making. Reliability (Ω) was .92; validity (P_{ts}) was .96.

X_2 Clergy Autonomy: estimated degree of autonomy enjoyed by diocesan priests.

X_3 Ideological Polarization: a three-item scale, giving an estimated percentage of diocesan clergy who disagreed with the bishop by thinking more progressively. The issues concerned the importance of guarding doctrine, enlarging church membership, and supporting humanitarian concerns. Reliability (Ω) was .84; validity (P_{ts}) was .92.

X_4 Cross-Status Friendships: a three-item scale, giving estimated degree of communication and friendship between pastors and head bishop, between assistant pastors and bishop, and between diocesan administrators and the rest of diocesan clergy. Reliability (Ω) was .88; validity (P_{ts}) was .94.

X_5 Negative Sanctions: estimated frequency with which the bishop punished his diocesan priests by undesirable transfers, calling on carpet, and other sanctions.

X_6 Priest Rebellion: estimated degree of dissent or opposition expressed by diocesan priests in reference to their chief bishop.

Two additional measures of priest rebellion were used. One was individual rebellion—the number of kinds of acts of individual rebellion which informants remembered as occurring in their diocese during the five-year period. The other was social rebellion—the number of kinds of acts of social rebellion which informants remembered as occurring in their diocese. The acts were the same for both individual and social rebellion, but for social rebellion they were committed by groups of priests rather than by individuals. For each measure a checklist of twelve kinds of rebellious acts was given to informants, who then checked them if they had occurred at least once during the period under investigation.

Correlations among these variables, priest rebellion (X_6), individual rebellion (X_{6a}), and social rebellion (X_{6b}) were as follows:

$$r_{x_6 x_{6a}} = .36, \ r_{x_6 x_{6b}} = .53, \ r_{x_{6a} x_{6b}} = .33.$$

X_7 Dissident Solidarity: estimated degree of camaraderie among diocesan priests who dissented with the chief bishop.

Appendix C

Additional Methodological Information
for Chapters Eight and Nine

Prelimin.. 'estigation. At first, about fifteen structural positions beside pastor and assistant pastor seemed plausible informant positions because they existed in most dioceses. It was likely, however, that they represented different branches of the information grapevine and varying biasing pressures. Thus, Seidler decided to investigate the degree of knowledge and bias to be expected from people occupying these positions by virtue of the structural slots themselves.

Seidler sent questionnaires to fifty-one Catholic sociologists, particularly those specializing in the study of Catholicism. The twenty-seven who completed questionnaires rated each position on expected bias and knowledge of clergy-bishop relations. Focusing on the reporting of tensions between bishop and lower-level clergy, they estimated extent and direction of expected bias, whether in favor of bishop or of lower-level clergy. From the summarized ratings ten positions were chosen according to the following guidelines:

1. Only those with moderate to high degrees of expected knowledge were chosen.
2. As many as possible from the middle range of expected bias were chosen —that is, those predicted to be relatively unbiased.
3. Positions expected to produce the greatest bias were eliminated. For example, chancellors, expected to be most biased in favor of the bishop, were eliminated.
4. A relatively balanced set of positions was established by selecting a few from each side of the bias continuum after including all positions judged to be relatively objective. Thus, the final set of ten ranged from those expected to be protective of the bishop (such as Dean or Vicar) to those expected to be critical of him (such as a member of priests' senate or council).

Weightings of the responses were not considered necessary because the biases were expected to balance. In addition, several control variables that represented possible sources of bias were used to screen out error during the analysis itself.

The positions chosen were not always occupied in every diocese, nor was every diocese sufficiently differentiated to have every position. Although ten positions were contacted in most dioceses, some dioceses received fewer than ten questionnaires. Even so, six positions or more were always contacted and an average of seven questionnaires was completed in each diocese.

Reliability and validity. To test agreement of informants within each diocese, the split-half reliability formula was adapted to these data. After dividing informants in half for each unit of analysis, the correlation between mean scores of each half in all dioceses for a particular item was obtained. This correlation formed the basis for computing the split-half reliability coefficient. Average reliability among informants across a subsample of eight questionnaire items was .8.

This was an imperfect adaptation of the split-half reliability formula; informant halves often were imbalanced in expected bias, especially in those dioceses where the return rate was higher on one side of the bias continuum. In addition, the mere splitting of a small sample (ten or fewer) increases the appearance of disagreement by creating two very small units that are likely to have different means. Hence, the overall reliability coefficient is probably a low and conservative estimate of informant agreement.

We examined concurrent validity (see Kerlinger 1965:447ff.) by comparing a few items with information obtained in other studies or reports. Where similar data were collected by Greeley and Schoenherr (NORC 1972), the findings coincided with theirs. A correlation of .91 was found between the two matched sets of fifty-five diocesan resignation scores for 1966–1970—one obtained by informants in this study and the other provided by official records in the Schoenherr-Greeley study (1974). In addition, total resignation percentages in the United States for those five years were similar, though computed differently. In these data, the total was a weighted average of diocesan scores; in the Schoenherr-Greeley data, we extrapolated to the five-year period by adding the average yearly increment that they discovered in the four-year period of observation. Results were 6.34 percent in Seidler's data and 6.1 percent in their data.

Conflict events between bishops and clergy were checked against newspaper accounts; in a selected handful of dioceses, the events reported in the press also were recalled and reported by informants.

Assigning diocesan scores. For each item, diocesan scores were created by averaging responses given to that question by priest informants of that diocese. Because these responses concerned diocesan conditions and climate, they were considered structural estimates from the beginning, without need of transformation from individual to organizational unit of analysis. In chapter 9, agreement within diocese on resignation rates was high, as measured by a reliability score of .97. Agreement was also high between these resignation scores and those obtained through official channels by Schoenherr and Greeley (1974). (The Pearsonian r, comparing the two data sets in 55 dioceses, was .91.)

Sample of dioceses. This survey sampled all 137 dioceses. It eliminated only eight dioceses, either because they contained fewer than ten diocesan priests or because their boundaries had changed during the period of observation. For practical purposes, then, the total population was sampled. In most of the analysis for this study, however, 131 dioceses (96 percent of the cases) in which there were no missing data for any variable were used.

In 1966 the average membership of the American diocese was 305,000 Catholics. Yet there was considerable variation, from the 2.3 million Catholics in Chicago to the 3.3 thousand Catholics of Juneau. In addition, most of the small dioceses were located in the south and the west, while the large ones were located in the east.

Similar variation appeared in the figures on diocesan clergy. They ranged from a high of 1431 in Boston to a low of 18 in Brownsville, Texas, with an average of 251 per diocese (see Table C-1).

Table C.1. Size of Diocese as Indicated by Number of Diocesan Clergy

Number of clergy in diocese	Absolute frequency
10–99	29
100–199	44
200–299	31
300–399	28
1,000 or more	5
Total	137

Notes: Absolute skewness is 2.50 for ungrouped data.
The formula (Croxton and Cowden 1942:254) is $TT_3 = \frac{\Sigma x^3}{N}$

There was also wide variation in the degree to which diocesan boundaries included urban areas. The percentage of parishes located in rural areas ranged from zero percent to 99.8 percent.

Patterns of organizational development and complexity appeared to match those of secular organizations. Seidler compared diocesan data to figures given by Blau (1970) on governmental agencies, and found strong parallels. For example, the correlation coefficient relating organizational size (here, size of diocese) to number of local offices (here, the number of parishes managed by diocesan clergy) was exactly the same: .94. We also noted, like Blau (1970:210), the pattern of economy of administrative overhead. As size of diocese increased, span of control (number of Catholics per parish) increased with a decreasing rate of increase. Other similarities also existed.

Assumptions of analysis. Regression was the primary mode of analysis so appropriate assumptions, including linearity, homoscedasticity, and skewness were examined. All were found to be within acceptable ranges, especially after two variables (diocesan size and teaching corps) were given a log transformation because of excessive skewness. All the exogenous variables (Z_1-Z_9) formed interval scales. The rest (X_1-X_7) were ordinal; they had been derived from items with five to seven fixed response categories, yet had the appearance of interval scales after the averaging operation. Interval statistics were employed.

Analysis. The strategy was to develop an hypothesized nonrecursive causal model, showing both the antecedents and the consequences of priest rebellion (X_6) in chapter 8 and resignations (X_9) in chapter 9, and then to test this model using two-stage least-squares (TSLS) procedures to estimate coefficients. In developing causal networks, we placed variables in sequence according to theoretical considerations, previous research, and personal judgment. Where feedback was incorporated, it was assumed to be a quick adjustment rather than a gradual or long-range effect, in keeping with the nature of cross-sectional data and the assumption of two-stage least-squares analysis.

Because the model included two-directional causal paths, we followed two-stage least-squares procedures to estimate coefficients. There were seven equations for each stage and all exactly identified or overidentified the structural equations, leaving out at least $k-1$ variables from each equation (where k = the number of endogenous variables).

To diminish multicollinearity problems, we ruled out any independent variable that was correlated with another at .85 (Althauser 1971:453). Although a degree of multicollinearity probably persisted, findings turned out to be consistent, whether basic models were run with or without several substantially correlated variables. The findings reported here apparently represent the sense of the data.

All equations employed special control variables to screen out possible effects of measurement error. Such control variables included summary diocesan scores for position bias, religion liberalism bias, the extent of intradiocesan informant disagreement, and others (see Seidler 1974).

Two-stage least-squares analysis. Two-stage least-squares (TSLS) is used to obtain regression coefficients for equations of a static but nonrecursive model, in which the usual flow cannot be assumed to be one-directional or in which quick feedback is assumed. Because ordinary least squares would yield biased and inconsistent estimates of coefficients in such situations, an alternative, such as TSLS, is required. The problem with ordinary least squares is that the error terms of individual equations cannot be considered independent of the endogenous variables that appear in the same equation as independent variables.

To solve this problem, we put equations in reduced form; only exogenous variables were used as independent variables. Thus the values of endogenous variables are predicted jointly by all (and only) exogenous variables (here, the control variables mentioned above, and Z_1-Z_9). Next, these predicted values are substituted for all endogenous variables when they are acting as independent variables. Then their predicted values, in addition to observed values of pertinent exogenous variables are used to compute a set of coefficients for each equation.

This procedure assures that the resultant error terms will be uncorrelated with the independent variables of each equation, as long as the exogenous variables are truly exogenous. This reasoning, of course, implies that the variables are uncorrelated with disturbances. Under the assumptions that each equation is identified and that there are no specification or measurement errors, two-stage least-squares techniques will produce consistent coefficients with negligible large-sample biases (see Christ 1966:432 ff.; Namboodiri et al. 1975:513–519).

Notes

Chapter One

1. Traditional Catholicism here signifies a Church system that reflects the long-standing mentality of the Counter-Reformation, the Council of Trent, and the First Vatican Council. The councils underscored uniformity among Catholics, Catholic versus Protestant beliefs, conformity to the pope's thinking, and established authority (see chapter three).

2. *Technology* refers to the body of knowledge available to a civilization (in this case an organization), used for extracting needed resources, fashioning implements, or practicing manual arts and skills (Morris 1969). It is practical knowledge, as the Greek root *tekhne* suggests. Technological innovation often raises the upper level of performance by raising the energy level applied to the actions mentioned above (see Lenski and Lenski 1987; White 1949). In the case of the Church, practical knowledge includes that used in religious education, liturgy, ritual, preaching, and even fund raising. Increased energy intensity may not be necessary, but rather the focusing of energy in a newly relevant way. Liturgical reform and biblical preaching imply this focusing to obtain the needed resources, such as members' allegiance and religiosity.

Chapter Two

1. Any manual of rituals for the clergy published in pre–Vatican II days will explain the exact height for the priest's arms when raised at Mass, the exact way the fingers should be held, and great detail about other bodily postures, genuflections, bows, and incense burning. Even after the council, this congregation tended to continue attending to such details. In the early 1970s, for example, priests in the United States, and perhaps elsewhere, received copies of a letter from the congregation complaining about those clergy who were not sufficiently careful in wiping the chalice after communion.

2. The psychological control exerted by a bishop on priests was impressive. This psychological effect seemed to go beyond the normal nervousness that many people feel in the presence of their superior. It is explained largely by the potentially arbitrary and definitive nature of episcopal commands in the days when there were no grievance mechanisms, no personnel boards, and no formal avenue for considering the personal desires of the subjects. A change of assignment might come at any moment, without warning or consultation.

3. Examples of scholarly organs following this safe approach include the American Catholic Sociological Association, founded in 1940, and its official journal, the *American Catholic Sociological Review*, first published in 1940. In the 1960s, however, the *ACSA* changed its name to the *Association for the Sociology of Religion* and the *ACSR* became *Sociological Analysis*. Another example is the Conference Internationale de Sociologie Religieuse and its official journal, *Social Compass*. One may glance through articles

published in these journals during pre–Vatican II years to understand what was meant by Catholic or religious sociology.

4. This point is supported by the experience of Catholics who were reared in pre–Vatican II years. The *Baltimore Catechism*, in its many abbreviated or summarized versions, formed the universal backbone of Catholic religious education. Its question-answer style, which engendered a memorization approach to learning, is probably the most memorable example of traditionalism in this area.

Chapter Three

1. Evidence for this statement comes from a number of interviews conducted with clergy throughout the country. Such limitations were corroborated at almost every turn, both by several past presidents of the National Federation of Priests Councils and by lower-level clergy from coast to coast.

2. The Hartford Appeal, as it was later known, was originally entitled "An Appeal for Theological Affirmation" (see Dulles 1977:191–195). Issued in January 1975 by an ecumenical group of theologians convened by Richard John Neuhaus and Peter L. Berger and meeting in Hartford, Connecticut, the appeal is basically a rejection of thirteen propositions, such as the following: "Modern thought is superior to all past forms of understanding reality, and is therefore normative for Christian faith and life"; "All religions are equally valid . . . "; "The sole purpose of worship is to promote individual self-realization and human community." The eighteen signers of this statement included five Roman Catholics, among whom were the well-known theologians Avery Dulles, Gerard Sloyan, George Tavard, and Bruce Vawter (Dulles 1977:194–195). They decried the loss of the sense of transcendence (Dulles 1977:71) and sought "to expose the massive problems posed to all the churches by the rampant immanentism, secularism, psychologism, and sociologism of our age" (Dulles 1977:73). Catholic writers who were attacked at least implicitly by this statement included Piet Schoonenberg, Gregory Baum, Malachi Martin, David Tracy, Gabriel Moran, and Rosemary Ruether (Dulles 1977:71–91). Dulles believes that the Hartford Appeal had special relevance for Catholicism, which was caught in the post-Vatican period of "extraordinary collapse of institutional self-confidence" (Dulles 1977:90). Catholics and non-Catholics responded to the appeal, and a storm of controversy broke. Harvey Cox called the statement an act of "ecclesiastical triumphalism" (Dulles 1977:89); Martin Marty, along with Cox and Gabriel Moran, said the appeal set up straw men (Dulles 1977:79, 88). Marty also thought is was untimely, attacking secularism in an age of the multiplication of transcendencies (Dulles 1977:87–88. Others thought it called for a retreat from the Church's involvement in issues to social justice (Dulles 1977:83 ff.). The *New York Times* printed letters to the editor about the controversy, and Dulles devoted a whole chapter to the battle and to his own defense of the appeal (Dulles 1977:61–91).

3. Teilhard, Küng, and Schillebeeckx all represent a progressive theology. Their thinking, admittedly innovative, suffered chronic attacks and sometimes strong sanctions from Rome.

Pierre Tielhard de Chardin, born in France in 1881, was a Jesuit priest and one of the world's most distinguished paleontologists, who played a leading part in the discovery of

Peking Man (Aller 1967:10). Though he published in purely scientific journals, he was forbidden to air his ideas on philosophy or theology (Cuenot 1965), largely because of his interest in the convergence of evolution and Christianity. Through the last several decades of his life, his Jesuit superiors, under the influence of the conservatives in the Vatican, forbade him to publish 90 percent of his writings (ibid.:205). In addition, he was not allowed to speak to public audiences, and he was not permitted to accept the distinguished professorship at the College de France, offered him in 1948 (ibid.:268–270). His best known work, *The Phenomenon of Man*, completed while he was interned in China during the Japanese War and circulated among friends and scientists in mimeograph form (Aller 1967:10), was repeatedly refused the imprimatur and was not published until after his death in 1955 (Aller 1967:10; Cuenot 1965:266–271). For posterity, Teilhard appointed an executor of his writings before he died, and his manuscripts did not fall into the hands of the Holy Office in Rome (Speaight 1967:301).

Hans Küng was called to Rome on more than one occasion during the 1960s and 1970s to answer charges of unorthodox teachings (heresy). Finally, in December 1979, the Vatican's Sacred Congregation for the Doctrine of the Faith (previously known as the Holy Office of the Inquisition) ruled that Küng could "no longer be considered a Catholic theologian" (*WP*.: December 21, 1979). This decision, apparently supported by Pope John Paul II, was greeted with protest from all around the world within hours of its promulgation. In the United States, seventy leading Catholic theologians signed a statement publicly opposing the Vatican's decision. "Hans Küng is indeed a Roman Catholic theologian," read the statement, "whether or not we agree with his ideas" (ibid.). In Germany there were street demonstrations against the Vatican's ruling. German priests threatened to refuse to preach at masses if Küng were removed from his post on the faculty of Tubingen University. In addition, a group of distinguished German scholars formed a Committee on Human and Christian Rights in the Church (ibid.). These reactions apparently achieved a temporary reprieve. A week later, the pope agreed to meet with German bishops and reconsider the decree against Küng (ibid.). When the discussions ended, however, the pope stood firm: Küng's theology chair was removed. Yet he continued to teach at Tubingen because the state-run university gave him another faculty position.

Edward Schillebeeckx, a Dutch theologian and a leading articulator of new sacramental theology, has written widely on new ways of understanding the Eucharist while placing the theory of transubstantiation in historical context—that is, as a limited way in which the Church interpreted the Eucharist at a particular time. At times Schillebeeckx's formulations come close to Protestant notions (see Schillebeeckx 1963), and that is what worries the Vatican. He, too, has been called to Rome to account for his ideas.

4. Robert McAfee Brown relates this exchange concerning the activities of the Holy Office, which was charged with examining heresy and suppressing wrong opinions. Brown calls the exchange "by far the most dramatic moment of the second session" and describes it as follows (Brown 1969:165):

> Cardinal Frings of Cologne stated in the course of one of the debates that the activities
> of the Holy Office were "a scandal to the world." This forthright statement brought
> applause from the bishops and an angry reply, later the same morning, from Cardinal
> Ottaviani, head of the Holy Office. The importance of the exchange was that it

brought out into the open the need for reform at the very heart of the church. Cardinal Frings said publicly what previously was only said privately, and from that moment the problem could not be overlooked.

Brown attributes the sweeping reform of the Holy Office, announced by Pope Paul VI just before the end of the council, to Cardinal Frings's "courageous utterance" (Brown 1969:166). The congregation is now known as the Sacred Congregation for the Doctrine of the Faith, and its official task is no longer to suppress theological investigation but to foster it.

5. Strictly speaking, traditionalist Catholicism is not a reconstruction as we have defined it—a coherent merger of contemporary and traditional religious elements. Traditionalist Catholicism incorporates no contemporary elements. Nevertheless, it seems legitimate to call its attempts to formulate a viable Catholicism for today a reconstruction, because present ambiguity gives almost any theology a new thrust.

Chapter Four

1. The term *council fathers* refers to all of those eligible to vote during the council. They numbered some twenty-three hundred, and included all bishops who ruled a diocese as well as heads of certain male religious congregations (see Fesquet 1967:17; Kaiser 1963: 84). A few lay Catholics and a number of Protestant theologians were invited to be "observers," whereas nonvoting "experts" (Latin *Periti*) participated by giving instructions to individual bishops and groups of bishops.

2. Curialists were those associated with the Roman Curia (the papal bureaucracy), which on the whole was extremely conservative and wished to embrace no new ideas. Many of the agencies or commissions of the curia were headed by Italian cardinals, who were voting members of the Vatican Council. They also had a dominant part in arranging the preliminary agenda and first drafts of the documents that were discussed. The majority of council fathers rejected almost all the preliminary work of the Curialists, including the agenda and the ordering of issues (see Rynne 1968).

3. When over 60 percent of council fathers voted to send the first draft of the document on Revelation back to the drawing board, Pope John intervened to order to a complete redrafting of this document. Technically, a two-thirds majority was required in that vote unless the pope intervened. Because of his intervention, the old two-source theory of Revelation, represented in the first draft, was soon replaced (Fesquet 1967; Rynne 1968). Another early and crucial event occurred when the slate of commission members for drafting various documents—dominated by Curialists and Conservatives—was presented to the council fathers. Cardinal Lienart of France rose and said in substance,

> We are not disposed to accept the list of candidates proposed to us until the Council meets again. We have had too little time to choose our own candidates, since the Council Fathers do not know one another well enough yet. We therefore ask for a further delay in order to get our bearings (cited in Fesquet 1967:21; see also Rynne 1968:53).

Cardinal Frings of Cologne seconded his colleague and also suggested that cardinals should be allowed to sit on such commissions. Both declarations were met with hearty applause and were unanimously approved (Fesquet 1967:22; Rynne 1968:53). Brown

(1969:161–162) mentions the success of the Lienart-Frings motion as an important early turning point of the council.

Chapter Five

1. Some priests, as well as religious brothers and women religious (sisters, nuns), belong to a variety of religious congregations and perform a range of specialized functions, including religious education, general teaching at all levels (usually in Catholic schools), missionary work, and health care.

2. The ordinary *(Ordinarius loci)* is the head bishop of a diocese.

3. Interdicts are ecclesiastical penalties against groups (such as parishes) whereby the offenders are prohibited from certain liturgical services or from administering or receiving certain sacraments. The interdict may also be rendered against a place, in which case people may not take part in the prohibited religious services in that place (Foy 1978:369).

4. We abbreviate the mobilization-implementation stage simply as the mobilization stage to emphasize the dominating feature of that period.

Chapter Six

1. At the time of these events, Seidler was living in North Carolina with direct access to the clergy grapevine. Interpretations derive from a number of sources, including the accounts of diocesan priests, newspaper reports, and personal observation of Bishop Waters's authority style over a five-year period.

2. These conclusions were derived from comments written on returned questionnaires, as well as from interviews, described in chapter 8 and appendix C.

3. More precisely, the years of each time period corresponded to issues of the *National Catholic Reporter*. For 1966, the year began on October 27, 1965 (the date of volume 2, issue 1) and ended on October 12, 1966 (the date of the last issue of volume 2).

4. For an overview of the four major American branches of the Catholic Traditionalist movement, which sprang up in reaction to the liberal thrust of Vatican II, see William Dinges (1983). They were as follows: (1) the Catholic Traditionalist Movement, Inc., launched in 1964 by Gommar De Pauw, a Maryland seminary professor, and later headquartered in Westbury, New York; (2) the Orthodox Roman Catholic Movement, established in 1973 by a Connecticut priest, Francis Fenton, and two lay Catholics; (3) the Traditional Catholics of America, a group centered in Colorado Springs, Colorado, that broke away from the Orthodox Roman Catholic movement; and (4) the Society of St. Pius X, founded by French Archbishop Marcel LeFebvre. Though headquartered in Europe, it had established a chain of about eighty chapels throughout the United States by 1980.

All these segments of the Traditionalist movement claimed to represent the remnant of faithful Catholics, but their schismatic tendencies were expressed in various ways. At one end of the spectrum stood the Society of St. Pius X, which split rather completely from Rome. At the other end were the priests who celebrated the Tridentine Mass regularly for an orthodox congregation, but did so quietly and still remained loyal to Rome (see Dinges 1983). Yet the position of the latter seemed precarious because Rome had forbidden such a celebration.

5. The sprecial air of drama comes across when one reads through the reports of these conflicts of the 1960s. The orientation of each side to the conflict—declaring that God was on their side—certainly added to the excitement and drama. Perhaps the 1960s were more dramatic simply because of the newness and the sudden realization of the massive gulf separating each sacred position. The drama was expressed in long declarations, in novel protest activities, and in episcopal reactions. These included such actions as Father William DuBay—the organizer of a priests' union—renewing his obedience to the bishop before a large number of fellow priest-retreatants. The birth control controversy also occasioned high drama, as when large numbers of Catholics walked out of church when Cardinal O'Boyle of Washington began to preach about the topic.

Chapter Seven

1. The number of Washington dissenters varied from report to report, the highest was around fifty-five. This variation appears to represent real shifts over time, as some dissenters recanted, and other priests later joined the ranks of dissenters.

2. This number (317) may include some already mentioned, as it is difficult to keep the newspaper accounts straight.

3. This independent quality was evident from a number of viewpoints, Diocesan histories persisted in continuing diocesan cultures. One could note large variations in empirical indicators from diocese to diocese (Seidler 1974). Individual bishops still imprinted their own style on the diocese.

Chapter Eight

1. A pretest of the study presented here confirmed the wide variation. Items of relational infrastructure, adaptive strategy, bureaucratic development, and many other features produced scores from one end of the continuum to the other. Apparently such major factors as diocesan size, episcopal independence, and the relationship between diocese and environment caused the immense differences discovered by researchers.

2. The demographic data presented here represent information collected by Louis Luzbetak and displayed in *Clergy Distribution, USA* (Luzbetak 1967). Ninety-four percent of this information came directly to Luzbetak from chancery offices in 1967; where chancery offices did not cooperate, the data were obtained from the *Official Catholic Directory* of 1967. The time of data collection for the latter source ranged between late 1966 and early 1967. We will assume that the demographic data refer to the period of early 1967, the beginning of the second year of Seidler's study.

3. Priests were relatively mobile within the diocese, however. Assistant pastors in particular rotated rather often from parish to parish.

Chapter Nine

1. That diocese made major modifications in the work structure of priests since the study and in answer to the problems pointed out in the study.

2. As mentioned above, exogenous variables were relatively stable variables, obtained from the demographic source and dating from 1966, the beginning of the period of observation. These variables were assumed to be only antecedents and not consequences.

3. In order to use identical variables, we had to drop two variables that were not theoretically appropriate for the analysis of conflict though they were used in Table 9.2 to study resignations: these were estimated clergy passivity and estimated degree of priest protest. As a result, explained variance figures reported in this textual paragraph differ somewhat from those given in the preceding paragraph.

4. Mean standard deviation of these variables was 1.61, high in comparison with all other variables. Standard deviations were standardized by dividing the possible range and multiplying by ten. An example of smaller variation occurred in the error or control variables, whose variation had been minimized consciously by the research design. They showed a mean standardized standard deviation of .68 (see Seidler 1974c:828).

5. This information came from informal sources—mainly from formerly active priests who went through the resignation process or from those who counseled priests desiring to leave, or from CORPUS, an organization of formerly active priests.

Chapter Eleven

1. In one diocese the bishop even invited the formerly active priests to enjoy a catered dinner in the undercroft (basement hall) of his cathedral. A large number of formerly active priests attended, along with their spouses, and the bishop gave a gracious welcoming speech, shortened, he said, by the fact that he was there not to preach but to listen.

2. We are grateful to Jesuit friends who have recounted the different Jesuit responses to the pope's actions.

References

Abbott, Walter M., ed.: 1966. *The documents of Vatican II*. New York: America Press.

Abel, Theodore. 1973. The pattern of a successful political movement. In *Social movements: A reader and source book*, edited by Robert R. Evans, 73–79. Chicago: Rand McNally.

Abell, Aron. 1960. *American Catholicism and social action*. Garden City, N.Y.: Doubleday.

Ahlstrom, Sydney E. 1975. *A religious history of the American people*. Vol. 2. Garden City, N.Y.: Doubleday (Image Book).

Albright, William Foxwell. 1949. *The archeology of Palestine*. Baltimore: Penguin Books.

———. 1966. *Archeology, historical analogy and early biblical tradition*. Baton Rouge: Louisiana State University Press.

Aller, Catherine. 1967. *The challenge of Pierre Teilhard de Chardin*. New York: Exposition Press.

Althauser, Robert P. 1971. Multicollinearity and non-addictive regression models. In *Causal models in the social sciences*, edited by H. M. Blalock. Chicago: Aldine-Atherton.

American Catholic Bishops. 1968. Human life in our day. *Catholic Standard* 18 (November 21).

Appleby, Scott. 1984. American Catholic modernism at the turn of the century. *American Catholic Studies Newsletter* 10 (Spring 1984):13–17.

Aubert, Roger. 1978. *The church in a secularized society*. Vol. 5, *The Christian centuries*. New York: Paulist Press.

Baciocchi, J. de. 1955. Le mystere eucharistique dans les perspectives de la Bible. *Nouvelle Revue Theologique* 77:561–580.

Bangert, William V. 1972. *A history of the society of Jesus*. St. Louis: Institute of Jesuit Sources.

Barnard, Chester I. 1946. Functions and pathologies of status systems in formal organizations. In *Industry and society*, edited by William Foote Whyte. New York: McGraw-Hill.

Baum, Gregory. 1962. *Progress and perspectives: The Catholic quest for Christian unity*. New York: Sheed & Ward.

———. 1964. *Ecumenical theology today*. Glen Rock, N.J.: Paulist Press.

Baute, Paschal. 1984. An ecumenical Catholic diocese: Why? *Diaspora* 16 (Fall):2.

Bedoyere, Michael de la. 1955. *The layman in the church*. Chicago: Henry Regency.

Bell, Daniel. 1973. *The coming of post-industrial society*. New York: Basic Books.

———. 1976. *The cultural contradictions of capitalism*. New York: Basic Books.

Bellah, Robert, Richard Madsen, William M. Sullivan, Ann Swidler, 1985. *Habits of the heart*. New York: Harper & Row.

Bendix, Reinhard. 1962. *Max Weber: An intellectual portrait*. Garden City, N.Y.: Doubleday Anchor.

Berger, Peter. 1963. A market model for the analysis of ecumenicity. *Social Research* 30(1):77–93.

———. 1967. *The sacred canopy*. Garden City, N.Y.: Doubleday.

Blalock, Hubert M. 1969. Comment on Coleman's paper. In *A design for sociology: Scope, objectives, and methods*, edited by Robert Bierstedt, 115–121. Philadelphia: American Academy of Political and Social Science.

Blau, Peter M. 1970. A formal theory of differentiation in organizations. *American Sociological Review* 35 (April):201–218.

Blau, Peter M., and Richard Scott. 1962. *Formal organizations: A comparative approach*. San Francisco: Chandler Publishing.

Blumer, Herbert. 1971. Social problems as collective behavior. *Social Problems* 18 (Winter):298–305.

———. 1974. Social movements. In *The sociology of dissent*, edited by S. Denisoff, 4–20. New York: Harcourt Brace Jovanovich.

Boyd, Malcolm. 1968. Ecclesia Christi. In *The underground church*, edited by Malcolm Boyd, 3–6. New York: Sheed & Ward.

Bright, John. 1959. *A history of Israel*. Philadelphia: Westminster Press.

Bromley, David G., and Anson D. Shupe, Jr. 1979. *"Moonies" in America: Cult, church, and crusade*. Beverly Hills: Sage Publications.

Brown, Robert McAfee. 1966. A response to the pastoral constitution on the church in the modern world. In *The documents of Vatican II*, edited by Walter M. Abbott, 309–316. New York: America Press.

———. 1969. *The ecumenical revolution*. Garden City, N.Y.: Anchor-Image.

———. 1978. Why Puebla Matters. *Christianity and Crisis* 38 (September 18):206–211.

Burns, Thomas, and G. M. Stalker. 1961. *The management of innovation*. London: Travistock.

Burstein, P. 1981. Social protest, public opinion and public policy. Paper presented at the American Sociological Association meeting, Toronto.

Cabrol, F. 1918. Religious orders (Christian). In *Encyclopedia of religion and ethics*, Vol. 10, edited by James Hastings, 693–713. New York: Charles Scribner & Sons.

Callahan, Daniel. 1963. *The mind of the Catholic layman*. New York: Charles Scribner & Sons.

———. 1968. How to get the papal monkey off the Catholic back. *National Catholic Reporter* 4 (October 9):5–6.

Callahan, Sidney Cornelia. 1968. *Beyond birth control: The Christian experience of sex*. New York: Sheed & Ward.

Center for Applied Research in the Apostolate. 1975. Team ministry: The Hartford model. *Origins* 5 (September 18):193–206.

Christ, Carl F. 1966. *Econometric models and methods*. New York: John Wiley & Sons.

Cogley, John. 1968. How they're making up their minds. *National Catholic Reporter* 4 (September 18):10.

———. 1973. *Catholic America*. New York: The Dial Press.

Coleman, James A. 1984. New directions in quantitative macro sociology. Talk given in Department of Sociology, Ohio State University, Columbus.

Congar, Yves. 1957. *Lay people in the church*. Westminster, Md.: Newman Press.

———. 1960. *The mystery of the church*. Baltimore: Helicon.

Coser, Lewis A. 1957. Social conflict and the theory of social change. *British Journal of Sociology* 8 (September):197–207.

Costello, Gerald M. 1984. *Without fear or favor: George Higgins on the record*. Mystic, Conn.: Twenty-Third Publications.

Coulter, Philip B. 1979. Organizational effectiveness in the public sector: The example of municipal fire protection. *Administrative Science Quarterly* 24 (1979):65–81.

Crowe, Frederick E. 1980. *The Lonergan enterprise*. Cambridge: Harvard University Press.

Cuenot, Claude. 1965. *Teilhard de Chardin: A biblographical study*. Baltimore: Helicon.

Cullman, Oscar. 1968. *Vatican Council II: The new direction*. New York: Harper & Row.

Cushing, Richard James, Cardinal. 1960. *The Christian and the community: Pastoral letter*. Boston: Daughters of St. Paul.

Cyrnes, Arthur G. 1970. Dogmatism of the Catholic clergy and ex-clergy: A study of ministerial role perseverance and open-mindedness. *Journal for the Scientific Study of Religion* 9:239–243.

Dahrendorf, Ralf. 1959. *Class and class conflict in industrial society*. Stanford, Calif.: Stanford University Press.

Dalton, Melville. 1964. "Conflict between staff and line managerial officers." In *Complex organizations*, edited by Amatai Etzioni, 212–221. New York: Holt, Rinehart & Winston.

Danielou, Jean. 1956. *The Bible and the liturgy*. Notre Dame, Ind.: University of Notre Dame Press.

Davis, Charles. 1967. *A question of conscience*. New York: Harper & Row.

Demerath, N. J., III, and Phillip E. Hammond. 1969. *Religion in social context*. New York: Random House.

Dillenberger, John, and Claude Welch. 1954. *Protestant Christianity*. New York: Charles Scribner's Sons.

Dinges, William D. 1983. Catholic traditionalist movement. In *Alternatives to American mainline churches*, edited by Joseph H. Fichter, 137–158. New York: Rose of Sharon Press.

Dolan, Jay P. 1981. American Catholicism and modernity. *Cross Currents* 31 (Summer):150–162.

Doty, Robert C. 1968. Pope and the pill: The debate deepens. *New York Times* (clipping undated):12E.

Douglas, Mary. 1982. The effects of modernization on religious change. *Daedalus* 3 (Winter):1–20.

Dulles, Avery. 1966. Introduction to the dogmatic constitution on the church. In *Documents of Vatican II*, edited by Walter M. Abbott, 9–13. New York: America Press.

———. 1970. "Loyalty and dissent: After Vatican II." *America* 122 (June 27):672–673.

———. 1974. *Models of the church*. Garden City, N.Y.: Doubleday.

———. 1977. *The resilient church: The necessity and limits of adaptation*. Garden City, N.Y.: Doubleday.

Durkheim, Emile. 1951. *Suicide*. New York: Free Press.

Dwyer, Lynn E. 1983. Structure and strategy in the antinuclear movement. In *Social movements of the sixties and seventies*, edited by Jo Freeman, 148–161. New York: Longman.

Eisenstadt, S. N. 1964. Social change, differentiation, and evolution. *American Sociological Review* 29 (June):375–86.

Eisenstadt, S. N., ed. 1968. *Max Weber: On charisma and institution building*. Chicago: University of Chicago Press.

Ellis, John Tracy. 1963. *Perspectives in American Catholicism*. Baltimore: Helicon Press.

———. 1969. *American Catholicism*. Chicago: University of Chicago Press.

———. 1972. The formation of the American priest: An historical perspective. In *The Catholic priest in the United States: Historical investigations*, edited by John Tracy Ellis, 3–110. Collegeville, Minn.: St. John's University Press.

———. 1979. American Catholicism, 1953–1979: A notable change. *Thought* 54:113–131.

Emerging Trends. 1983. Reagan, the pope most admired. Vol. 5, no. 3 (March):6.

———. 1983. "Americans want to hold the line." Vol. 5, no. 4 (April):4.

Etzioni, Amitai. 1961. *A comparative analysis of complex organizations*. New York: Free Press.

Etzioni, Amitai, ed. 1964. *Complex organizations*. New York: Holt, Rinehart & Winston.

Fesquet, Henri. 1967. *The drama of Vatican II: The Ecumenical Council, June 1962–December 1965*. New York: Random House.

Fichter, Joseph H. 1968. *America's forgotten priests: What they are saying*. New York: Harper & Row.

———. 1974. *Organization man in the church*. Cambridge, Mass.: Schenkman.

———. 1975. *The Catholic cult of the Paraclete*. New York: Sheed & Ward.

———. 1977. Restructuring Catholicism. *Sociological Analysis* 38 (Summer):154–166.

Foy, Felician A., ed. 1978. *1979 Catholic almanac*. Huntington, Ind.: Our Sunday Visitor.

Francis, E. K. 1951. *Minority groups: A revision of concepts*. London: Routledge & Kegan Paul.

———. 1964. Toward a typology of religious orders. In *Religion, culture and society: A reader in the sociology of religion*, edited by Louis Schneider, 517–531. New York: John Wiley & Sons.

Freeman, Jo. 1975. *The politics of women's liberation*. New York: Longman.

———. 1983. On the origins of social movements. In *Social movements*, edited by Freeman, 8–33. New York: Longman.

Gallup, George, Jr., and David Poling. 1980. *The search for America's faith*. Nashville: Abingdon.

Gamson, William. 1975. *The strategy of social protest*. Homewood, Ill.: Dorsey.

Gannon, Michael. 1971. Before and after modernism: The intellectual isolation of the American priest. In *The Catholic priest in the United States: Historical investigations*, edited by John T. Ellis. Collegeville, Minn.: St. John's University Press.

Gerlach, Luther, and Virginia Hine. 1970. *People, power, change: Movements of social transformation*. New York: Bobbs-Merrill.

Gilkey, Langdon. 1975. *Catholicism confronts modernity: A Protestant view*. New York: Seabury Press.

Gleason, Philip. 1972. Catholicism and cultural change in the 60's. *Review of Politics* 33:91–107.

Glock, Charles Y., and Rodney Stark. 1966. *Christian beliefs and anti-Semitism*. New York: Harper & Row.

Goldner, Fred H., R. Richard Ritti, and Thomas P. Ference. 1977. The production of cynical knowledge in organizations. *American Sociological Review* 42:539–551.

Goldstone, J. A. 1980. The weakness of organization. *American Journal of Sociology* 85:1017–1042.

Gouldner, Alvin W. 1954. *Pattern of industrial bureaucracy*. Glencoe, Ill.: Free Press.

Greeley, Andrew M. 1967. *The Catholic experience: An interpretation of the history of American Catholicism*. Garden City, N.Y.: Doubleday.

———. 1972. *The denominational society: A sociological approach to religion in America*. Glenview, Ill.: Scott, Foresman.

———. 1973. *The new agenda*. Garden City, N.Y.: Doubleday.

———. 1977. *The American Catholic: A social portrait*. New York: Basic Books.

———. 1979. *Crisis in the church*. Thomas More.

———. 1981. The failures of Vatican II after twenty years. *America* 146 (February 6):86–89.

Greeley, Andrew M., William C. McCready, and Kathleen McCourt. 1976. *Catholic schools in a declining church*. Kansas City: Sheed & Ward.

Greinacher, Norbert, and Alois Muller, eds. 1979. *Evangelization in the world today*. New York: Seabury Press.

Gusfield, Joseph. 1968. The study of social movements. In *International encyclopedia of the social sciences*, 14:445–450. New York: Macmillan.

Hadden, Jeffrey K. 1969. *The gathering storm in the churches*. New York: Doubleday.

Hage, Jerald. 1980. *Theories of organizations*. New York: John Wiley & Sons.

Hall, Douglas T., and Benjamin Schneider. 1973. *Organizational climates and careers: The work lives of priests*. New York: Seminar Press.

Handlin, Oscar. 1951. *The Uprooted*. New York: Grosset & Dunlap.

Hannan, Michael, and John R. Freeman. 1978. The population ecology of organizations. In *Organizations and Environments*, edited by Marshall W. Meyer, 131–171. San Francisco: Jossey-Bass.

Harney, Martin P. 1941. *The Jesuits in history*. New York: America Press.

Harrison, Michael I., and John K. Maniha. 1978. Dynamics of dissenting movements within established organizations: Two cases and a theoretical interpretation. *Journal for the Scientific Study of Religion* 17 (September):207–224.

Hasler, August Bernhard. 1981. *How the pope became infallible: Pius XI and the politics of persuasion*. Garden City, N.Y.: Doubleday.

Hastings, James, ed. 1918. *Encyclopedia of religion and ethics*. New York: Charles Scribner's Sons.

Haughey, John C. 1968. Conscience and the bishops. *America* 119 (October 12):322–324.

———. 1971. Priest-bishop relations: American perspective. *America* 124 (May 15): 518–520.

Haughton, Rosemary. 1979. *The Catholic thing*. Springfield, Ill.: Templegate Publishers.

Hawley, Amos. 1968. Human ecology. In *International encyclopedia of the social sciences*, 4:328–337. New York: Macmillan.

Hebblethwaite, Peter. 1968. *"Inside" the synod: Rome 1967*. New York: Paulist Press.

———. 1975. *The runaway church: Post-Conciliar growth or decline*. New York: Seabury.

———. 1980. *The new inquisition: The case of Edward Schillebeeckx and Hans Küng*. San Francisco: Harper & Row.

Heidel, Alexander. 1949. *The Gilgamesh epic and Old Testament parallels*. Chicago: University of Chicago Press.

Heise, David R., and George W. Bohrnstedt. 1970. Validity, invalidity, and reliability. In *Sociological methodology 1970*, edited by Edgar F. Borgatta and George W. Bohrnstedt, 104–129. San Francisco: Jossey-Bass.

Hennesey, James. 1981. *American Catholics: A History of the Roman Catholic community in the United States*. New York: Oxford University Press.

———. 1982. American Catholic bibliography. Working Paper Series, Charles and Margaret Hall Cushwa Center for the Study of American Catholicism, University of Notre Dame, Series 12, no. 1 (Fall):41 pp.

Hill, Richard et al. 1968. The response to 'Human life.' *America* 119 (September 7): 162–164.

Himmelfarb, Harold S. 1975. Measuring religious involvement. *Social Forces* 53 (June): 606–617.

Hirschman, Albert O. 1970. *Exit, voice, and loyalty: Responses to decline in firms, organizations, and states*. Cambridge: Harvard University Press.

Hitchcock, James. 1979. *Catholicism and modernity: Confrontation or capitulation?* N.Y.: Seabury.

Hoefnagels, Harry. 1969. *Demokratisierung der kirchlichen Autoritat*. Vienna: Herder.

Hoge, Dean R., and Jeffrey L. Faue. 1973. Sources of conflict over priorities of the protestant church. *Social Forces* 52 (December):178–194.

Hoge, Dean R., and Jackson W. Carroll. 1975. Christian beliefs, nonreligious factors, and anti-Semitism. *Social Forces* 53 (June):581–594.

Hopper, Rex D. 1978. The revolutionary process: A frame of reference for the study of revolutionary movements. In *Collective behavior and social movements*, edited by Louis E. Genevie, 118–128. Itasca, Ill.: F. E. Peacock.

Houtart, F. 1969. Conflicts of authority in the Roman Catholic church. *Social Compass* 16:309–325.

Hoyt, Robert G. 1968. D. C. priests. *National Catholic Reporter* 4 (October 2):3.

Hughes, Philip. 1961. *The church in crisis: A history of the general councils, 325–1870*. Garden City, N.Y.: Hanover House (Doubleday).

Jackson, Samuel Macauley. 1950. *The new Schaff-Herzog encyclopedia of religious knowledge*. Grand Rapids: Baker Book House.

Janowitz, Morris. 1978. *The last half-century*. Chicago: University of Chicago Press.

Jenkins, J. Craig. 1981. Sociopolitical movements. *Handbook of political behavior*, 4:81–153. New York: Plenum.

———. 1982. The transformation of a constituency into a movement. In *Social movements*, edited by Freeman, 57–70. New York: Longmans.

———. 1983. Resource mobilization theory and the study of social movements. *Annual Review of Sociology* 9:527–553.

———. 1984. *The politics of insurgency*. New York: Columbia University Press.

Jenkins, J. Craig, and Charles Perrow. 1977. Insurgency of the powerlessness. *American Sociological Review* 42:249–268.

Jones, Alexander, ed. 1966. Introduction to the Pentateuch. In *The Jerusalem Bible*, 5–14. Garden City, N.Y.: Doubleday.

Jonsen, Albert R. 1970. Loyalty and dissent: Theology and the university. *America* 122 (June 27):676–678.

Kaiser, Robert Blair. 1963. *Pope, council and world: The story of Vatican II*. New York: Macmillan.

Kamm, Henry. 1984. The secret world of Opus Dei. *New York Times Magazine* (January 8):38–41, 75–86.

Kelly, George A. 1979. *The battle for the American church*. Garden City, N.Y.: Doubleday.

Kelly, James R., and Donald R. Campion. 1970. Loyalty and dissent: Reflections of two sociologists. *America* 122 (June 27):676–680.

Kerlinger, Fred N. 1965. *Foundations of behavioral research: Educational and psychological inquiry*. New York: Holt, Rinehart & Winston.

Kiely, Pat. 1968. A cry for black nun power. *Commonweal* 88 (September 27):650.

Killian, Lewis M. 1973. Social movements: A review of the field. In *Social movements: A reader and source book*, edited by Robert R. Evans, 9–53. Chicago: Rand McNally.

Kim, Gertrude. 1980. Roman Catholic organization since Vatican II. In *American denominational organization: A sociological view*, edited by Ross P. Scherer, 84–129. Pasadena, Calif.: William Carey Library.

Koval, John P., Richard Bell, and Edgar W. Mills. 1970. Role stress among U.S. clergy, Catholic and Protestant. Presentation at the symposium sponsored by the Society for the Scientific Study of Religion at the American Association for the Advancement of Science annual meeting, Chicago.

Kuhn, Thomas S. 1962. *The structure of scientific revolutions*. Chicago: University of Chicago Press.

Küng, Hans. 1961. *The council, reform and reunion*. New York: Sheed & Ward.

———. 1968. *Truthfulness: The future of the church*. New York: Sheed & Ward.

———. 1976. *On being a Christian*. Garden City, N.Y.: Doubleday.

Kurtz, Lester. 1986. *The politics of heresy: The modernist crisis in Roman Catholicism*. Los Angeles: University of California Press.

Lally, Francis P. 1962. *The Catholic Church in a changing America*. Boston: Little, Brown.

Lang, Kurt, and Gladys Engel Lang. 1978. The dynamics of social movements. In *Collective behavior*, edited by Genevie, 96–108. Itasca, Ill.: F. E. Peacock.

Langlois, Edward. 1983. Isaac Hecker's political thought. In *Hecker studies: Essays of the thought of Isaac Hecker*, edited by John Farina. New York: Paulist Press.

Lasch, Christopher. 1979. *The culture of narcissism*. New York: Warner Books.

Lawson, Ronald. 1983. A decentralized but moving pyramid: The evolution and consequences of the structure of the tenant movement. In *Social movements*, edited by Freeman, 119–137. New York: Longman.

Lenski, Gerhard E. 1966. Power and privilege. New York: McGraw-Hill.

———. 1971. The religious factor in Detroit: Revisited. *American Sociological Review* 36 (February):48–50.

Lenski, Gerhard, and Jean Lenski. 1987. *Human societies*. 5th ed. New York: McGraw-Hill.

Lonergan, Bernard J. F. 1957. *Insight: A study of human understanding*. New York: Philosophical Library.

———. 1972. *Method in theology*. New York: Herder & Herder.

Luzbetak, Louis J. 1967. *Clergy distribution, U.S.A.* Washington D.C.: Center for Applied Research in the Apostolate.

MacKenzie, R. A. F. 1966. Introduction to the dogmatic constitution on Divine Revelation. In *Documents of Vatican II*, edited by Abbott, 107–110. New York: America Press (An Angelus Book).

Martin, David. 1978. *A general theory of secularization*. New York: Harper & Row.

Marx, Karl. 1964. *Selected writings in sociology and social philosophy*. Translated by T. B. Bottomore. London: McGraw-Hill.

McAvoy, Thomas T. 1969. *A history of the Catholic Church in America*. Notre Dame, Ind.: University of Notre Dame Press.

McBrien, Richard P. 1969. *Do we need the church?* New York: Harper & Row.

———. 1973. *The remaking of the church*. New York: Harper & Row.

———. 1981. *Catholicism*. Minneapolis: Winston.

———. 1982. Roman Catholicism: E pluribis unum. *Daedelus* 3 (Winter):73–83.

McCarthy, John D., and Mayer N. Zald. 1973. *The trend of social movements in America*. Morristown, N.J.: General Learning Press.

———. 1977. Resource mobilization and social movements: A partial theory. *American Journal of Sociology* 82:1212–1241.

McClorey, Robert. 1978. Priest crisis not coming; it's here. *National Catholic Reporter* 14 (May 5):1, 4–5, 20.

McCormick, Richard A. 1970. Loyalty and dissent: The magisterium—a new model. *America* 122 (June 27):674–676.

McKenna, Megan. 1983. Grassroots Catholicism. Paper presented at The Ohio State University Catholic Student Center (February 20), Columbus.

McKenzie, John L. 1956. *The two-edged sword: An interpretation of the Old Testament*. Milwaukee: Bruce Publishing.

———. 1966. *Authority in the Catholic Church*. New York: Sheed & Ward.

———. 1971. *The Roman Catholic Church*. Garden City, N.Y.: Doubleday (An Image Book).

———. 1979. *The Old Testament without illusions*. Chicago: Thomas More Press.

McNamara, Patrick H. 1977. What happened to Catholicism? Paper presented at the annual meetings of the Society for the Scientific Study of Religion, Chicago, Ill.

McNaspy, C. J. 1966. Introduction to the Constitution on the Sacred Liturgy. In *Documents of Vatican II*, edited by Abbott, 13–16. New York: America Press.

McPhail, Clark. 1971. Civil disorder participation: A critical examination of recent research. *American Sociological Review* 36 (December):1058–1073.

McSorley, Harry J. 1969. *Luther: Right or wrong?* Glen Rock, N.J.: Newman Press.

McSweeney, William. 1980. *Roman Catholicism: The search for relevance*. New York: St. Martin's.

Meissner, William W. 1970. Loyalty and dissent: A psychiatrist's report. *America* 122 (June 27):681–682.

Merton, Robert K. 1968. *Social theory and social structure*. New York: Free Press.

Merton, Thomas. 1967. *Mystics and Zen masters*. New York: Farrar, Strauss & Giroux.

Meyer, Katherine, and John Seidler. 1978. The structure of gatherings. *Sociology and Social Research* 63 (October):131–153.

Meyer, Katherine, and Charles Albright, CSP. 1987. *Review of the politics of heresy by Lester Kurtz, Social Forces* 66 (June):577–579.

Morgan, Gareth. 1986. *Images of organization*. Beverly Hills: Sage Publications.

Morris, William, ed. 1969.*The American heritage dictionary of the English language*. New York: American Heritage Publishing.

Mottl, Tahi L. 1980. The analysis of countermovements. *Social Problems* 27 (June): 620–635.

Murnion, Philip J. 1978. *The Catholic priest and the changing structure of pastoral ministry, New York, 1920–1970*. New York: Arno Press.

Murphy, Francis X. 1981. *The papacy today*. New York: Macmillan.

Murray, John Courtney. 1960. *We hold these truths: Catholic reflections on the American proposition*. New York: Sheed & Ward.

———. 1965. *The problem of religious freedom*. Westminster, Md.: Newman Press.

Namboodiri, N. Krishnan, Lewis F. Carter, and Hubert M. Blalock, Jr. 1975. *Applied multivariate analysis and experimental designs*. New York: McGraw-Hill.

National Catholic Reporter. 1966. Survey 3000 U.S. priests. *National Catholic Reporter* 3 (December 14). Reprint.

National Conference of Catholic Bishops. 1971. *Study on priestly life and ministry*. Washington, D.C.: United States Catholic Conference.

National Opinion Research Center. 1972. *The Catholic priest in the United States: Sociological investigations*. Andrew M. Greeley and Richard A. Schoenherr, co-investigators. Washington, D.C.: U.S. Catholic Conference.

National Register. 1970. "Carolina confrontation polarizing Catholics." *National Register* (May 10):7.

Neal, Marie Augusta. 1965. *Values and interests in social change*. Englewood Cliffs, N.J.: Prentice-Hall.

———. 1970–1971. The relationship between religious belief and structural change in religious orders. *Review of Religious Research* 12:1–16, 153–164.

New York Times. 1983a. Pope set to issue new church laws easing strictures. (January 23):1.

———. 1983b. Historic revision of Catholic laws signed by pontiff. (January 26):1.

Newman, John Henry. 1960. *An essay on the development of Christian doctrine*. Garden City, N.Y.: Doubleday.

Nichols, Peter. 1981. *The pope's divisions*. New York: Holt, Rinehart & Winston.

Niebuhr, H. Richard. 1929. *The social sources of denominationalism*. New York: Henry Holt.

Noonan, John T. 1965. *Contraception*. Cambridge: Harvard University Press.

Norris, Frank B. 1962. *God's own people*. Baltimore: Helicon.

Nottingham, Elizabeth K. 1971. *Religion: A sociological view*. New York: Random House.

Novak, Michael. 1964. *The open church*. New York: Macmillan.

———. 1967. *A time to build*. New York: Macmillan.

Oberschall, Anthony. 1973. *Social conflict and social movements*. Englewood Cliffs, N.J.: Prentice-Hall.

———. 1978. Theories of social conflict. *Annual Review of Sociology* 4:291–315.

Official Catholic Directory. 1969. Wilmette, Ill.: P. J. Kennedy & Sons.

O'Brien, David. 1973. Hecker and the Paulists. *Paulists* 83:32–35.

———. 1981–1982. Toward an American church. *Cross Currents* 31:457–473.

O'Brien, David J. 1968. *American Catholics and social reform: The New Deal years*. New York: Oxford University Press.

O'Connor, John. 1968. Should the pope retire? *Look* 32 (December 10):31–35.

O'Dea, Thomas. 1969. *The Catholic crisis*. Boston: Beacon Press.

Olsen, Marvin E. 1978. *The process of social organization*. New York: Holt, Rinehart & Winston.

O'Malley, John W. 1983. Developments, reforms, and two great reformations: Towards a historical assessment of Vatican II. *Theological Studies* 44:373–406.

Ong, Walter J. 1957. *Frontiers in American Catholicism: Essays in ideology and culture*. New York: Macmillan.

Osborne, William A. 1968. Religious and ecclesiastical reform: The contemporary Catholic experience in the United States. *Journal for the Scientific Study of Religion* 7 (Spring):78–86.

Padovano, Anthony. 1985. The ministerial crisis in today's church: Problem or opportunity? *Diaspora* 16 (Winter):1, 6–7.

Pareto, Vilfredo. 1935. *The mind and society*. New York: Harcourt Brace Jovanovich.

Park, Robert Ezra. 1952. *Human communities*. New York: Free Press.

Parsons, Talcott. 1951. *The social system*. Glencoe, Ill.: Free Press.

———. 1966. *Societies: Evolutionary and comparative perspectives*. Englewood Cliffs, N.J.: Prentice-Hill.

Pelikan, Jaroslav. 1966. A response to the constitution on the sacred liturgy. In *Documents of Vatican II*, edited by Abbott, 179–182. New York: America Press.

———. 1983. The enduring relevance of Martin Luther 500 years after his birth. *New York Times Magazine* (September 18):43–45, 99–104.

Perrow, Charles. 1979. The Sixties Observed. In *The dynamics of social movements*, edited by Mayer Zald and John McCarthy, 192–210. Cambridge, Mass.: Winthrop Publishers.

Perry, Joseph B., Jr., and M. D. Pugh. 1978. *Collective behavior: Response to social stress*. St. Paul, Minn.: West Publishing.

Phillips, Gerard. 1956. *The role of the laity in the church*. Chicago: Fides Publishers Association.

Piven, F., and R. Cloward. 1977. *Poor people's movements*. New York: Pantheon.

Pondy, Louis R. 1967. Organizational conflicts: Concepts and models. *Administrative Science Quarterly* 12 (September):296–320.

Poulat, E. 1969a. *Integrisme et Catholicisme integral*. Paris: Casterman.

———. 1969b. 'Modernisme' et 'integrisme': Du concept polemique a l'irenisme critique. *Archives de sociologie des religions* 27:3–28.

———. 1977. *Catholicisme, democratie et socialisme: Mgr. Benigni*. Paris: Casterman.

Powers, Joseph M. 1967. *Eucharistic theology*. New York: Herder & Herder.

Price, James L. 1977. *The study of turnover*. Ames: Iowa University Press.

Pritchard, James Bennett. 1958. *Archeology and the Old Testament*. Princeton: Princeton University Press.

———. 1962. *Gibeon, where the sun stood still: The discovery of the biblical city*. Princeton: Princeton University Press.

Rahner, Karl. 1961. *Theological investigations*. Baltimore: Helicon Press.

———. 1969. *Grace in freedom*. New York: Herder & Herder.

Reese, Thomas J. 1983. A survey of the American bishops. *America* 149 (November 12):285–288.

Reichley, A. James. 1986. *Religion in American public life*. Washington, D.C.: Brookings Institution.

Roof, W. Clark. 1974. Religious orthodoxy and minority prejudice: Causal relationship or reflection of localistic view. *American Journal of Sociology* 80:643–664.

———. 1978. Alienation and apostasy. *Society* 15 (May–June):41–45.

Roof, Wade Clark, and William McKinney. 1987. *American mainline religion: Its changing shape and future*. New Brunswick, N.J.: Rutgers University Press.

Roof, Wade Clark, and Christopher Kirk Hadaway. 1977. Shifts in religious preference—the mid seventies. *Journal for the Scientific Study of Religion* 16:409–412.

Rose, Arnold. 1967. *The power structure*. New York: Oxford University Press.

Ruether, Rosemary R. 1975. *New woman, new earth*. New York: Seabury.

———. 1977. *Mary, the feminine face of the church*. Philadelphia: Westminster Press.

Rynne, Xavier. 1963. *Letters from Vatican City*. New York: Farrar Strauss.

———. 1967. *Vatican Council II*. New York: Farrar Strauss & Giroux.

———. 1968. *Vatican Council II*. New York: Farrar Strauss & Giroux.

Sacred Congregation on Clergy. 1970. Priests' councils: Circular letter of the sacred congregation for the clergy to the presidents of episcopal conferences. *The Pope Speaks: The Church Documents Quarterly* 15 (Summer):157–162.

Schaff, David Schley. 1950. Trent, Council of. In *The new encyclopedia of religious knowledge*, edited by Samuel M. Jackson, 10:1–3. Grand Rapids: Baker Book House.

Schallert, Eugene J., and Jacqueline M. Kelley. 1970. Some factors associated with voluntary withdrawal from the Catholic priesthood. *Lumen Vitae* 25:425–460.

Schellebeeckx, E. 1963. *Christ the Sacrament of the encounter with God*. New York: Sheed & Ward.

———. 1967. *The real achievement of Vatican II*. New York: Herder & Herder.

Schneider, Louis, and Louis Zurcher. 1970. Toward understanding the Catholic crisis:

Observations on dissident priests in Texas. *Journal for the Scientific Study of Religion* 9 (Fall):197–207.

Schoenherr, Richard A., and Andrew M. Greeley. 1974. Role commitment processes and the American Catholic priesthood. *American Sociological Review* 39:407–426.

Schoenherr, Richard A., and Annemette Sorensen. 1976. Organizational structure and changing size in U.S. Catholic dioceses. Paper presented at the annual meeting of the American Sociological Association, New York.

———. 1982. Social change in religious organizations: Consequences of clergy decline in the U.S. Catholic Church. *Sociological Analysis* 43 (Spring):23–52.

———. 1987. Power and authority in organized religion: Disaggregating the phenomenological core. *Sociological Analysis* 47:52–71.

Schultenover, David G. 1981. *George Tyrrell: In search of Catholicism*. Shepherdstown, W. Va.: Patmos Press.

Scott, Joseph W., and Mohammed El-Assal. 1969. Multiversity, university size, university quality and student protest. *American Sociological Review* 34:702–709.

Seidler, John. 1972. Rebellion and retreatism among the American Catholic Clergy. Ph.D. diss., University of North Carolina, Chapel Hill.

———. 1974a. Priest protest in the human Catholic church. *National Catholic Reporter* 10 (May 3):7, 14.

———. 1974b. Priest resignations, relocations, and passivity. *National Catholic Reporter* 10 (May 10):7, 14.

———. 1974c. On using informants: A technique for collecting quantitative data and controlling measurement error in organization analysis. *American Sociological Review* 39:816–31.

———. 1979a. Priest resignations in a lazy monopoly. *American Sociological Review* 44:763–783.

———. 1979b. Toward a middle range explanation of changing Catholicism. Paper presented at the annual meetings of the Society of the Scientific Study of Religion, San Antonio, October.

———. 1981. Changing issues within Catholicism. Paper presented at the annual meetings of the Association for the Sociology of Religion, Toronto, Canada.

———. 1986. Contested accommodation: The Catholic Church as a special case of social change. *Social Forces* 64 (June):4.

Seidler, John, Katherine Meyer, and Lois MacGillivray. 1977. Collecting data on crowds and rallies: A new method of stationary sampling. *Social Forces* 55 (March):507–518.

Shiner, Larry. 1967. The concept of secularization in empirical research. *Journal for the Scientific Study of Religion* 6 (Fall):207–220.

Simpson, Richard L. 1969. Lateral conflicts among managers: Toward a political model of organizations. Unpublished manuscript.

Smelser, Neil J. 1962. *Theory of collective behavior*. New York: Free Press.

———. 1963. *Theory of collective behavior*. Glencoe, Ill.: Free Press.

Snyder, D., and W. R. Kelly. 1976. Industrial violence in Italy, 1878–1903. *American Sociological Review* 82:131–162.

Snyder, David, and Charles Tilly. 1972. Hardship and collective violence in France, 1830–1960. *American Sociological Review* 37:520–522.

Speaight, Robert. 1967. *The life of Teilhard de Chardin*. New York: Harper & Row.

Spector, Malcolm, and John I. Kitsuse. 1973. Social problems: A re-formulation. *Social Problems* 21:145–159.

Spencer, A. E. C. W. 1966. The structure and organization of the Catholic Church in England. In *Uses of Sociology*, edited by J. D. Halloran and Joan Brothers, 91–125. London and Melbourne: Sheed & Ward.

Spilerman, Seymour. 1970. The causes of racial disturbances: A comparison of alternative explanations. *American Sociological Review* 35:627–649.

Steeman, Theodore M. 1969. The underground church. In *The religious situation: 1969*, edited by Donald R. Cutter, 713–722. Boston: Beacon Press.

Stewart, James H. 1978. *American Catholic leadership: A decade of turmoil*. The Hague: Mouton.

Struzzo, John. 1970. Professionalism and the resolution of authority conflicts among the Catholic clergy. *Sociological Analysis* 31 (Summer):92–106.

Suenens, Leon Joseph. 1968. *Coresponsibility in the church*. New York: Herder & Herder.

Suenens, Leon Joseph, Cardinal. 1965. *The church in dialogue*. Notre Dame, Ind.: Fides.

Suhard, Emmanuel Cellestin, Cardinal. 1948. *Growth or decline? The church today*. South Bend, Ind.: Fides.

Szafran, Robert F. 1977. The occurrence of structural innovation within religious organizations. Ph.D. diss., University of Wisconsin-Madison.

Tana de Zulueta. 1980. *The man who leads the church: An assessment of Pope John Paul II*. San Francisco: Harper & Row.

Teilhard de Chardin, Pierre. 1960. *The divine milieu*. New York: Harper & Row.

———. 1965. *The phenomenon of man*. New York: Harper & Row.

The Official Catholic Directory. 1969, 1970. New York: P. J. Kenedy.

Tilly, Charles. 1978. *From mobilization to revolution*. Reading, Mass.: Addison-Wesley.

Time. 1979. Collision course. (July 16):70.

———. 1981. John Paul takes on the Jesuits. (November 9):59.

Tracy, David. 1975. *Blessed rage for order*. New York: Seabury.

———. 1981. *The analogical imagination*. New York: Crossroad.

Tracy, David, Hans Küng, and Johann B. Metz, eds. 1978. *Towards Vatican III: The work that needs to be done*. New York: Crossroad.

Tracy, David, Hans Küng, and Johann B. Metz, eds. 1978. *Toward Vatican III: The work that needs to be done*. New York: Seabury.

Troeltsch, Ernst. 1931. *The social teaching of the christian churches*. New York: Macmillan.

Turner, Ralph H., and Lewis M. Killian. 1972. *Collective behavior*. Englewood Cliffs, N.J.: Prentice-Hall.

U.S. Lutheran-Roman Catholic Dialogue Group. 1983. Justification by faith. National Catholic *Documentary Service* 13 (October 6):277–299.

Vaillancourt, Jean-Guy. 1980. *Papal power*. Berkeley: University of California Press.

Vallier, Ivan. 1969. Comparative studies of Roman Catholicism: Dioceses as strategic units. *Social Compass* 16:147–184.

van den Berghe, Pierre. 1963. Dialectic and functionalism: Toward a theoretical synthesis. *American Sociological Review* 28:695-705.

VanderZanden, James W. 1960. The klan revival. *American Journal of Sociology* 65: 456–462.

Vawter, Bruce. 1956. *A path through Genesis*. New York: Sheed & Ward.

———. 1959. *The Bible in the church*. New York: Sheed & Ward.

Veblen, Thorstein. 1934. *The theory of the leisure class*. New York: Modern Library.

———. 1948. *The portable Veblen*. Edited by Max Lerner. New York: Viking Press.

Vera, Hernan. 1982. *Professionalization and professionalism of Catholic priests*. Gainesville: University Presses of Florida.

Wallace, Anthony F. C. 1956. Revitalization movements. *American Anthropologist* 58 (April):264–281.

Ward, Leo. 1959. *Catholic life, U.S.A.: Contemporary lay movements*. Saint Louis: Herder & Herder.

Washington Post. 1972. 6 priests punished by Buffalo diocese. (July).

———. 1979. Vatican suspends order against Hans Kung; Pope to meet German bishops. (December 23, 1979):A17.

Weber, Max. 1947. *The theory of social and economic organization*. New York: Oxford University Press.

———. 1954. *Max Weber on law in economy and society*. Cambridge: Harvard University Press.

———. 1958. *The Protestant ethic and the spirit of capitalism*. New York: Scribner's.

Wedel, Mrs. Theodore O. 1966. A response to the decree on the apostolate of the laity. In *Documents of Vatican II*, edited by Abbott, 522–525. New York: America Press.

Wegmann, Robert G. 1969. The Catholic clergy and change: An analysis. *Cross Currents* (Spring):178–197.

Weigel, Gustave. 1960. Forward. In *An essay of the development of Christian doctrine*, edited by John Henry Cardinal Newman, 7–20. Garden City, N.Y.: Doubleday.

Weigart, Andrew J., and Darwin L. Thomas. 1969. Religiosity in 5-d: A critical note. *Social Forces* 48 (December):260–263.

Weil, Martin. 1968. 200 walk out on cardinal at Masses. *Washington Post* 91 (September 23):A1, A23.

West, G. 1981. *The national welfare rights movement*. New York: Praeger.

Whale, John, ed. 1980. *The man who leads the church: An assessment of Pope John Paul II*. San Francisco: Harper & Row.

White, Leslie. 1949. *The science of culture*. New York: Grove Press.

Wilensky, Harold L. 1964. The professionalization of everyone? *American Journal of Sociology* 70:137–158.

Wilson, John. 1973. *Introduction to social movements*. New York: Basic Books.

Winter, Gibson. 1968. *Religious identity: A study of religious organization*. New York: Macmillan.

Wood, James R. 1981. *Leadership in voluntary organizations: The controversey over social action in the Protestant churches*. New Brunswick, N.J.: Rutgers University Press.

Woodward, Kenneth L. 1968. The papacy in crisis. *Newsweek* (August 26):90–91.

Wright, George Ernest. 1961. *The Bible and the ancient near east: Essays in honor of William Foxwell Albright*. Garden City, N.Y.: Doubleday.

Yankelovich, Daniel. 1981. *New rules: Searching for self-fulfillment in a world turned upside down*. New York: Bantam.

Yinger, J. Milton. 1970. *The scientific study of religion*. New York: Macmillan.

Zalba, Marcellinus. *Theologiae moralis compendium*. Madrid: Biblioteca de Autores Cristianos.

Index

abortion, 79, 85, 87, 92

accountability (within the Church), 9

aggiornamento (updating): background for, 37–42; clergy rebellion and, 107, 117–118; countermovement and, 162–166; defining, 25–27; delegitimation of authority, 27–28; implementation of, 36, 61, 63, 64, 82, 87, 89, 146–157, 158, 159, 160; laying the foundation for, 35; legitimation of, 36, 50–54, 61, 62, 63, 68; mobilization and, 35–36, 54–60, 61, 63–64, 71, 72–73, 74, 82, 87, 88–89, 91, 109, 117, 128–130, 158, 159; movement in U.S. and, 166–167; precursor movements and, 42–50; pre–Vatican II, 10–12; as a process, 28–34; stages of, 35–37, 61–62; structural and organizational, 24–28. *See also* modernization

Ahlstrom, S. E., 40, 42

American Canon Law Society, 104

Americanism, *see* Catholic Church in America

apostasy rates, 2, 9

archaeological investigation, biblical interpretation and, 19, 30, 31

Arrup, Pedro, 163, 166

Association of Catholic Trade Unionists, 45

authority: birth control issue and, 96–97, 98, 99, 100–104; changing Church and, 106; the Chruch in U.S. and, 18, 38–40; conflict and, 75–76, 82, 83, 85, 86, 87, 90; delegitimation of, 27–28; implementation of change and, 147; modernization and, 68; papal (Vatican II), 52; resignations and, 132, 135; staff-line problems and, 100–102; Vatican I and, 38. *See also* diocesan authority conflict (U.S. church)

autonomy professional), 100, 121, 127, 135

Bea, Cardinal, 59

belief system (shared international Catholic), 8

Bernardin, Cardinal Joseph, 103, 166

Berrigan, Daniel, 33, 74–75, 77

Bible: archaeological investigations and, 19, 30, 31; hierarchy and, 46; movement, 46–47; new emphasis on, 154; translation of, 66

bill of rights (Christian community), 100

birth control: John Paul II and, 163; Paul VI and, 2, 92, 93–94, 95, 99, 100–101, 103; as vertical conflict, 158

birth control conflict (U.S. church), 79, 85, 86; historical background on, 92–95; ideological and organizational aspects of, 95–103; modernization and changes in attitude toward, 104–108; resolution of, 103–104

bishops: authority and, 100–102, 108; diocesan authority conflict and, 111–113, 121–123, 126–127; diocesan councils and, 147; implementation and, 66, 67; major findings concerning, 158, 159, 166–167; new structural arrangements and, 150–151; parish

O'Dea, Thomas, 3
Olsen, M. E., 24
ordination of women, *see* women re-
    ligious
ordinations (rate of), 128
organization of Catholic Church
    (worldwide), 8–10
organizational diversity of the Church
    (from hermits to social activists),
    15–16
Origin of Species (Darwin), 39
O'Shaughnessy, Michael, 45
Ottaviani, Cardinal, 58, 59

Pacem in Terris (John XXIII, 1963),
    13, 60
Padavano, Anthony, 166
papal infallibility, 17, 37, 38–39
parish councils, 155
Parsch, Pius, 47
participatory church concept, 161
Pastor Aeternus, 38
pastoral council, 147, 155
pastoral ministries, 152
pastoral planner, 155
patriarchal mentality (of the Church),
    10
Paul VI, 13, 25, 27, 52, 55, 59, 61,
    66, 81, 125–126, 162, 163, 165;
    birth control and, 2, 81, 92, 93–94,
    95, 99, 100–101, 103
Peace on Earth (John XXIII, 1963),
    13, 60
personalist revolution, 21
personnel board, 147, 150, 153
Phenomenon of Man, The (Teilhard
    de Chardin), 13, 49
Pius X, 33, 34, 40, 42
Pius XI, 13
Pius XII, 25, 31, 47
political action conflicts, 77
political Catholicism, 33
political protests, 2
political regimes, 16

politics, John Paul II and, 163
priest appointments, 153
priest rebellion. *See* diocesan author-
    ity conflict
priest resignations, 70; Church as
    lazy monopoly and, 139–145;
    Church structure and, 130–139;
    consequences of, 129, 131, 134–
    139; investigation of causes of (by
    bishops), 130–131; leadership and,
    138; major findings concerning,
    158–159, 160; marriage and, 2–
    3; in mobilization phase, 128–
    130; rate of, 128
priests: bishops and, 65; career ad-
    vancement and, 148; John XXIII
    and, 51; mailed survey to, 6; mar-
    riage and, 2–3, 77–78, 79, 82, 83,
    165, 167; modernization and, 65;
    personal interviews and, 6–7; pro-
    fessionalism and, 21–22, 148, 155,
    159; protest and, 116; recruit-
    ment of, 148, 153; shortage of,
    152–153; worker, 52. *See also*
    diocesan authority conflict (U.S.
    church)
priests' senates, 160
professionalism (clergy), 21–22, 148,
    155, 159
protest: political, 2; ways of priestly,
    116
Providentissimus Deus (Leo XIII,
    1893), 46

Quadragesimo Anno (Pius XI, 1931),
    13, 44

racial equality, 45–46
Rahner, Hugo, 56
Rahner, Karl, 56, 98
Reagan administration, 166
religious erosion, 30, 31
religious orders, hierarchy and, 15
Rerum Novarum (Leo XIII, 1891),
    11, 13, 32